READY-TO-USE
ACTIVITIES AND MATERIALS ON
WOODLANDS INDIANS

A Complete Sourcebook
for Teachers K-8

READY-TO-USE
ACTIVITIES AND MATERIALS ON
WOODLANDS
INDIANS

A Complete Sourcebook
for Teachers K-8

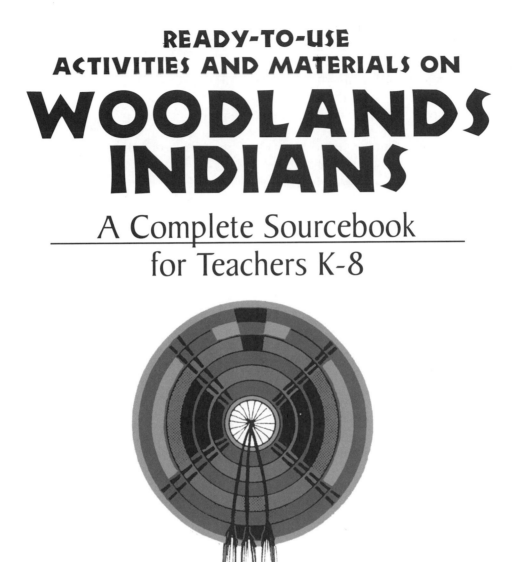

DANA NEWMANN

NATIVE AMERICANS RESOURCE LIBRARY

PRENTICE HALL
Paramus, New Jersey 07652

97-190

Library of Congress Cataloging-in-Publication Data

Newmann, Dana.
    Ready-to-use activities and materials on Woodlands Indians : a complete
sourcebook for teachers K-8 / Dana Newmann.
       p.   cm.—(Native Americans resource library : unit 4)
    ISBN 0-87628-610-4 (pbk.)
    1. Woodland Indians—Study and teaching (Elementary) 2. Woodland
Indians—Study and teaching—Activity programs. 3. Indian crafts.
I. Title. II. Series: Newmann, Dana. Native American resource library : v. 4.
E76.6.N48 1997 vol. 4
[E78.E2]
978'.00497 s—dc21   97-25946
[372.89]   CIP

Production Editor: Zsuzsa Neff

© 1997 by The Center for Applied Research in Education

Printed in the United States of America

10 9 8 7 6 5 4 3 2 1

ISBN 0-87628-610-4

**THE CENTER FOR APPLIED RESEARCH
IN EDUCATION**
West Nyack, NY 10994
A Simon & Schuster Company

On the World Wide Web at http://www.phdirect.com

Prentice Hall International (UK) Limited, *London*
Prentice Hall of Australia Pty. Limited, *Sydney*
Prentice Hall Canada, Inc., *Toronto*
Prentice Hall Hispanoamericana, S.A., *Mexico*
Prentice Hall of India Private Limited, *New Delhi*
Prentice Hall of Japan, Inc., *Tokyo*
Simon & Schuster Asia Pte. Ltd., *Singapore*
Editora Prentice Hall do Brasil, Ltda., *Rio de Janeiro*

This book, _The Woodlands Indians_, is the fourth and last volume of _The Native Americans Resource Library_. These books have been — literally — years in the making. During this time I've been so lucky to have the constant encouragement and help of my editor, Susan Kolwicz, as well as the fine support of Editors Zsuzsa Neff, and Diane Turso.

I have appreciated the efforts of the desktop publisher, Audrey Kopciak, our "silent partner."

Many thanks to the Native American reviewers of these books: Abby Moquino and Ella Jones of New Mexico, Margaret Adams of California, Eunice Larabee of Wyoming and Cindy Davenport of Massachusetts. Their suggestions and ideas were, in every case, invaluable to me!

I am indebted to my friend, anthropologist and author Peter Nabokov for loaning me personal photographs and hundreds of reference books. Living as I do in northeastern New Mexico, I could never have obtained such fascinating resource materials without his generous help!

My thanks also go to Robert Easton, co-author of _Native American Architecture_ (Oxford University Press), for kindly loaning me many of the historic photographs from his book.

Alba, you kept my spirits up whenever they began to fail — and Gene, it's been a LONG journey, this project, which wouldn't have been completed without your care, perseverance — AND your computer — I gotta admit.

So: although only one name appears on the spines of these books, they have, as you can see, been realized through the efforts of MANY. I do hope you will find reading — and using — these volumes _rewarding_!

All my best to you,
Dana

ABOUT THE AUTHOR

A graduate of Mills College in Oakland, California, Dana Newmann has been an elementary teacher for more than 15 years. She has taught in California and New Mexico and for the U.S. Army Dependants Group in Hanau, Germany.

Mrs. Newmann has authored a variety of practical aids for teachers, including *The New Teacher's Almanack* (The Center, 1980), *The Early Childhood Teacher's Almanack* (The Center, 1984), and *The Complete Teacher's Almanack* (The Center, 1991).

She presently lives in Santa Fe, New Mexico, where for the past eleven years she has worked for Project Crossroads, a nonprofit educational resource organization. Mrs. Newmann heads the elementary school program, telling folktales in the schools, and conducts workshops for teachers throughout the state and the Southwest.

ABOUT THE NATIVE AMERICAN REVIEWER
OF THIS BOOK

Cindy Davenport is a Creek-Cherokee descendant. Her primary work has been in cross-cultural youth programs. She was the Native American Scholar of HANA (Hispanic, Asian, Native American Association), 1985-87. Her personal interests include hiking, live music, reading Southern literature, and going to Native American pow-wows. Cindy lives in Amherst, MA, where she is the Program Director of the Amherst Writers and Artists Institute.

A FEW WORDS ABOUT
THE NATIVE AMERICANS RESOURCE LIBRARY

The *Native Americans Resource Library* is a four-book series that introduces you and your students in grades K-8 to the lives of the peoples who have inhabited North America for thousands of years. The four books in this Resource Library are:

- Ready-to-Use Activities and Materials on *Desert Indians (Unit I)*
- Ready-to-Use Activities and Materials on *Plains Indians (Unit II)*
- Ready-to-Use Activities and Materials on *Coastal Indians (Unit III)*
- Ready-to-Use Activities and Materials on *Woodland Indians (Unit IV)*

Each unit in the series is divided into the following sections:

- "Their History and Their Culture"—Here you'll find information about the historical background of the particular region...food...clothing...shelter...tools...language...arts and crafts...children and play...religion and beliefs...trade...social groups and government...when the Europeans came...the native peoples today...Historic Native Americans of the particular region.
- "Activities for the Classroom"—Dozens of meaningful activities are described to involve your students in creating and exploring with common classroom materials: native shelters, tools, jewelry, looms; also included are directions for making and playing traditional Native American games; foods of the particular region...and much more!
- "Ready-to-Use Reproducible Activities"—These are 41 full-page worksheets and activity sheets that can be duplicated for your students as many times as needed. The reproducible activities reinforce in playful and engaging ways the information your students have learned about a particular region.
- "Teacher's Resource Guide"—You'll find lists of catalogs, activity guides, professional books, and children's books covering the specific region you're studying.

Throughout each book in the series are hundreds of line drawings to help illustrate the information. A special feature of each book are the many historic photographs that will help "bring to life" the Native American tribes as they were in the 19th and early 20th centuries!

The *Native Americans Resource Library* is designed to acquaint you and your students with this important and complex subject in a direct and entertaining way, encouraging understanding and respect for those people who are the *first* Americans.

CONTENTS

THE WOODLANDS INDIANS:
THEIR HISTORY AND THEIR CULTURE
1

THE WOODLANDS INDIANS: ACTIVITIES FOR THE CLASSROOM
181

THE WOODLANDS INDIANS: READY-TO-USE REPRODUCIBLE ACTIVITIES
211

THE WOODLANDS INDIANS:
TEACHER'S RESOURCE GUIDE
257

A NOTE FROM THE AUTHOR
ABOUT THIS BOOK

The first settlers of this continent have been known traditionally as American Indians. In recent years many people have come to think this term is inaccurate, based as it is on Christopher Columbus's mistaken idea that he had arrived at islands off of India. Today some descendants of those original settlers still use the term American Indian, while others prefer to define themselves as Native Americans, or First Americans. Furthermore, the Eskimo-Aleut peoples of the Arctic region—whose ancestors crossed over the Bering Strait thousands of years after the original migrations—are often referred to separately as Native Alaskans.

In the pages that follow we look at the lives of those early Americans who settled the present-day states of the Northeast and Southeast: how they may have arrived there, and how they organized their lives during the centuries since then. Next we will consider the effects on these peoples of the arrival of the Europeans and, last, we will look at the contemporary life of those who today live in this large and diverse area.

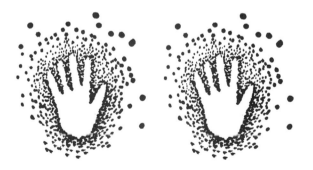

Today it is essential that students realize that their way of life is not solely the creation of the twentieth-century people. Much that is beautiful and that enriches our museums, our libraries and—potentially—our lives, has been given to us by the first inhabitants of the Northeastern and Southeastern states. Our children should understand this; this book will show you and your students the specific gifts we have received from these early Americans.

Native American cultures teach each person to have respect for all living things, emphasizing what it means to live in harmony with one's surroundings; they show that every action in the natural world has consequences. These are essential lessons for each of us to understand—and to teach—as we enter the twenty-first century.

It has been my intent to write clearly and simply, so that even young chidren may understand a very complex subject; these pages offer only a first glimpse into a vastly fertile and unique area of study. It is my hope that this book will be just the beginning for you and your students in your explorations into Native American studies—together!

Dana Newmann

THE
WOODLANDS
INDIANS

Their History
and Their Culture

PREHISTORY

Between a million and half a million years ago there were at least four times when large areas of the earth were covered with ice.

Sometime toward the end of the last glaciers—some 25,000 years ago—Mongolian people began to move across the Bering Strait, which was then a land bridge. They walked the 55 miles from Siberia to Alaska—and became the very first North Americans![1]

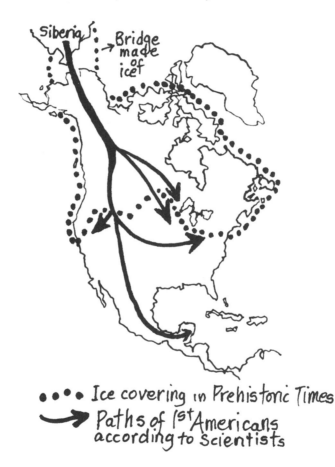

Over the next centuries the descendants of these people would continue moving southward until they populated the continents of both North America and South America—all the way from Alaska to Tierra del Fuego.

When we speak of the Northeast and Southeastern region, the Woodlands, we mean roughly the area of the United States to the East of the Missouri and Mississippi rivers all the way to the Atlantic Ocean. Included are some 29 present-day states.[2]

Except for the rivers and lakes, all of Northeastern America from the snow banks of the North to the swamps of the South were covered by a lush forest. Majestic trees of birch, maple, basswood, cedar, pine, spruce, elm, and oak grew from the sandy Eastern beaches to the edge of the great midwestern plains. So dense was this forest that its scent could be noticed miles out to sea!

3

"We then smelt so sweet and so strong a smell, as if we had been in the midst of some delicate garden."

—noted by Sir Walter Raleigh's first expedition
as it was sailing toward the coast of the Carolinas, 1585

Along the Southeastern coast stood sand dunes, salt water marshes, and some grasslands. Cypress trees grew there. To the west, a thousand-mile long plateau backed up against the Appalachian Mountains and, south of these mountains—stretching to the Mississippi River—was an area of rich black fertile soil.

In the North, the Great Lakes were bordered by rocky beaches, and forests covered those lands.

In the South, swamps, marshes, and tropical vegetation were homes for alligators and crocodiles.

PREHISTORIC WOODLAND PEOPLES

From about 25,000 B.C. to around 5000 B.C. the early people in other parts of North America were big-game hunters. They made stone-headed tools and would work in groups to stampede wild animals off cliffs or into swamps.[3]

The early Woodland people, however, hunted smaller game animals—squirrels, deer, turkey, and opossum. They used flint and chert points when they hunted.[4] The dense forests and woods also gave these people wild berries, fruits, and nuts.

It was between six and seven thousand years ago that an extraordinary discovery was made by the early people who were living in present-day Wisconsin. On the southern shores of Lake Superior they found odd nuggets that had probably been left behind by the Ice Age glaciers.

At first the people chipped and flaked the soft lumps off these nuggets and pounded the lumps into projectile points ("arrowheads") and blades. Then they saw that these rocks would give much more of the soft material if they heated the stones and next dropped them into cold water. The change of temperature cracked the stones and left out in the open the soft copper—for that's what this material was! Any stone that might be left behind on the copper was chipped off by the workers. In this way, they collected the copper until they had enough to hammer into projectile points, knives, spear heads and other tools, and ornaments including rings, necklaces, breast plates and bracelets.[5]

The copper tools were given extra strength by gently heating them after they were formed.

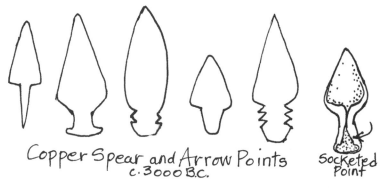

Copper Spear and Arrow Points
c. 3000 B.C.

Socketed Point

These early people may have been the world's first metal workers. They definitely were the first people to work metal in the Americas!

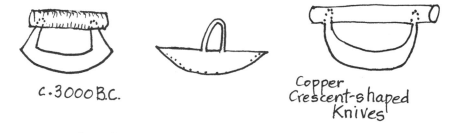

c. 3000 B.C.

Copper Crescent-shaped Knives

The Wisconsin metal-working was extraordinary and it was also temporary. By about 1500 B.C. (3,500 years ago) it had disappeared. This is probably how that happened: The weather changed; the days were warmer. This made the deer, caribou, beaver, and other game move north (into Canada). The early copper-workers moved north also, following the game until at last they had left all the copper-filled rocks behind. With no copper at hand, the people stopped working the metal. A thousand years would pass before large groups of people in North America would again make copper tools and ornaments!

Early Southeast Copper Pendant

Time passed. Some of these Eastern peoples began to live together in big towns. For example, at Indian Knoll, Kentucky, more than 1,000 human skeletons dating back to 3000 B.C. have been dug up; grave offerings and ornaments were buried with many of these skeletons. Also found were 55,000 artifacts: tools, jewelry, utensils—some of which were made from seashells and thin sheets of copper, both of which were probably traded from people from far-off areas. Prepared clay floors, with fire markings (hearths) and vertical post slabs (windbreaks), are evidence of this early settlement.

Other such early town sites have been found in Illinois, Alabama, Florida, and Massachusetts.[6]

By 1500 B.C. pottery-making was known in many parts of the east. Did it come from Northeast Asia as some scientists say? Or had it been brought by Scandinavians from Iceland and Greenland? Some archaeologists see strong Mexican influences in the Woodlands' pottery—is this how it arrived? Whatever its roots, pottery-making was widespread in the Woodlands by 1000 B.C.

Eastern
Woodlands Cooking Pots
(Prehistoric)   Missouri   Fish form
Handles

THE MOUND BUILDERS

There are more than 100,000 mounds in present-day United States, some dating back to 1000 B.C. These huge earthworks were monuments, some high narrow banks of soil in the shapes of birds, deer, alligators or bear, and others huge domed or conical mounds on which other (wooden) structures once stood. Often, but not always, burials are found inside such mounds. The majority of these earthworks are found in the valleys of the Missouri and Mississippi rivers, but some were built as far south as the Gulf of Mexico.[7]

Some mounds are still much as they were when they were made by these early people. However, highways, golf courses, and farms have flattened many mounds.

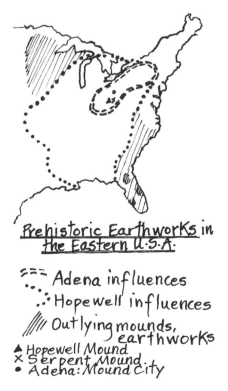

Prehistoric Earthworks in
the Eastern U.S.A.

‡‡‡ Adena influences
·.· Hopewell influences
/// Outlying mounds,
          earthworks
▲ Hopewell Mound
✕ Serpent Mound
● Adena: Mound City

The Adena (c. 1000 B.C.—c. A.D. 400)

The first Mound Builders were the Adenas who lived mainly in the Ohio Valley. The name *Adena* comes from the Adena Estate in Ohio where the signs of their life were first found in modern times.

The Adenas were a settled people, well organized, with a strong sense of religion. They were tall—many of the women were over six feet and the men nearly seven feet in height. Their skeletons show that they were a strong powerful people with large foreheads, big brow ridges, and round heads.[8] They lived in small villages of round vertical houses with thatched roofs. They ate deer, raccoon, shellfish, snails, raspberries, walnuts, chestnuts, and papaw fruit. The later Adenas may have raised sunflowers, squash, and pumpkin.

Like many early peoples, they went to great lengths to honor their dead. At first, this meant building low mounds over their burial pits.

The body was placed in the burial pit and then painted with red ocher clay. Next, they dressed it with copper jewelry, a headdress (if this had been an important person), and laid carved clay pipes by its side. Thirty-five to forty men each went to some nearby place, scooped up soil, and brought it back to the burial pit where they used it to cover the body. Their work continued until a small mound had formed over the body and the leader then said the mound was finished.

Adena Carved Stone Tablet
100 B.C.-100 A.D.
from the Adena Mound, Ohio
The notches at the bottom may be calendar-like; the topmost 'faces' may be the sun & moon.

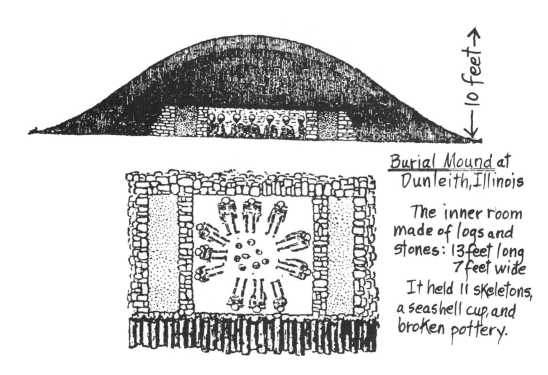

←10 feet→

Burial Mound at Dunleith, Illinois

The inner room made of logs and stones: 13 feet long 7 feet wide
It held 11 skeletons, a seashell cup, and broken pottery.

Sometimes mounds had several layers and held many bodies and artifacts. The Great Serpent Mound built by the Adenas near Cincinnati, Ohio is 1/4 of a mile long, 30 feet wide, and 5 feet high. It is shaped like an uncoiling serpent. Four hundred feet away is a cone-shaped burial mound. We do not know the actual meaning of the Adena effigy mounds—just as we cannot be certain what at last became of these people. We do know that with time they left Ohio and moved on to present-day Alabama and New York.

1,000-Year-old Adena Effigy Mound
The GREAT SERPENT Mound
It is ¼ of a mile long, 30 feet wide, and
5 feet high. Other Adena effigy
mounds are made in the shapes of
bears, birds, alligators. These are
not burial mounds, but may have
been part of burial ceremonies.

The Hopewell (c. A.D. 400 - 500)

About 2,400 years ago another group of early people—the Hopewells, named for the owner of an Ohio farm where many of their artifacts were first found[9]—came into the south central Scioto Valley. (See Photo 1.)

Photo 1. Aerial photo taken in 1934 of Hopewell site (Newark, Ohio) which was in use by A.D. 200. The circle is 1,200 feet in diameter. *Courtesy Smithsonian Institution.*

We don't know if the Adenas and the Hopewells ever actually fought each other, but we can tell that soon after their arrival, the Hopewells became ever more powerful while the Adena began to weaken. Perhaps the two groups began intermarrying and the Hopewells started to take over the Adenas' land and ways. We can't be sure. Eventually the Hopewells were left with the land much to themselves.

For a thousand years the Hopewells were the strongest group of people in the Midwest. They were remarkable artists and crafts people. They made jewelry of copper, shell, bone, pearls, and mica. They wove fine mats, decorated their pottery, and carved wood, metal and bone figures. They were fine metalworkers, too, making a wide variety of tools and ornaments out of copper and sometimes out of silver and gold!

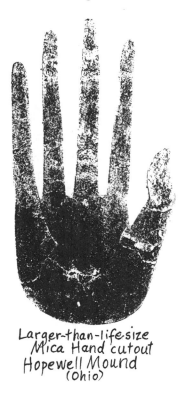

Larger-than-life-size
Mica Hand cutout
Hopewell Mound
(Ohio)

These people were food gatherers, hunters, farmers, and great traders. They traded their pipestone, flint, and pearls for luxury goods (copper, obsidian, grizzly teeth) which, in part, would be used to fill the tombs in their mounds.

The Hopewells were well organized and got their leaders from their upper class. Theirs was a loose grouping, or confederation of tribes, and at its strongest it covered the area from Kansas to the Atlantic and from the Great Lakes to the Gulf of Mexico.

The Hopewell earthwork itself, in present-day Newark, Ohio, was a large collection of burial mounds, a vast effigy of an eagle and a 2-1/2-mile long hallway to the banks of the Licking River. The Hopewell complex covered 4-1/2 square miles: It had avenues, plazas and circles.

"In entering the ancient avenue for the first time the visitor does not fail to experience a sensation of awe, such as he might feel in passing the portals of an Egyptian temple."

—written by Ephrain Squier, a 19th-century archaeologist

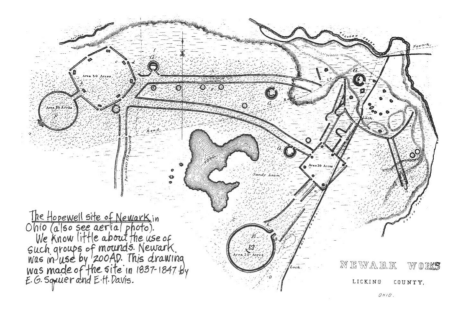

The Hopewell site of Newark in
Ohio (also see aerial photo).
We know little about the use of
such groups of mounds. Newark
was in use by 200AD. This drawing
was made of the site in 1837-1847 by
E.G. Squier and E.H. Davis.

NEWARK WORKS
LICKING COUNTY.
OHIO.

We have learned by digging up the Hopewell mounds how the Hopewell people built them. First, the place for the earth mound was chosen. Then the trees were cut down and the top soil was taken off. Next, the area was plastered, a little below ground level, with clay. Sand or gravel was sprinkled over this and a big wooden building[10] was made on top to hold the bodies of the dead.[11]

Talon: Mica cut-out, 6½"X11"
100 B.C.- A.D. 100
Hopewell Mound, Ohio

Other things besides bodies were put in these grave houses: Rocky Mountain grizzly claws and teeth; copper from Lake Superior; mica from South Carolina; shells, shark teeth and alligator teeth from the Gulf of Mexico. Some burials held thousands of river pearls.

Finally, the entire death house was covered with earth to make a mound.

19th-Century Excavation of a Southeastern Burial Mound.

We do not know what became of the Hopewell people. They were no longer living in their mound cities when the Europeans arrived in the 18th century. These powerful people had vanished, leaving their mighty earthworks as memorials.

From about A.D. 700 to 1700 other peoples in North America built mounds, many of which were much larger than those at Hopewell. These were farther south, from St. Louis to the Gulf of Mexico. These earthworks were flat-topped pyramids and each had a wooden temple built on top. Some of these mounds were made in layers—as many as 12—and we know they were used for worshipping, not burial, as graveyards have been found close by the mounds themselves.

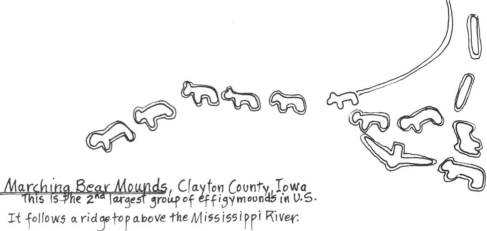

, Clayton County, Iowa
This is the 2ⁿᵈ largest group of effigy mounds in U.S.
It follows a ridge top above the Mississippi River.

Many low earthen platforms in the shapes of birds, animals, and people began appearing in the Wisconsin and Iowa areas about A.D. 500 just as the (Ohio) Hopewell were disappearing. Were these earthworks directly descended from the Ohio effigy mounds such as the Great Serpent? We do not know, but they continued to be made for centuries—even into modern times.

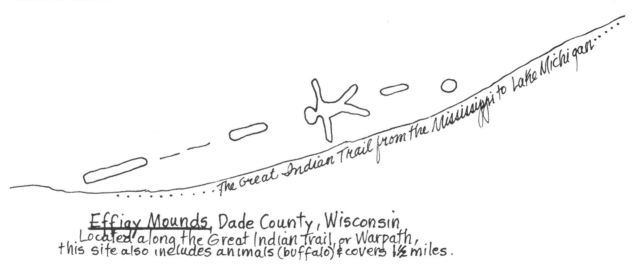

Effigy Mounds, Dade County, Wisconsin
Located along the Great Indian Trail, or Warpath,
this site also includes animals (buffalo) & covers 1½ miles.

Cahokia

Between A.D. 700 and 1400 there was, in present-day Illinois, the most advanced prehistoric Indian settlement north of Mexico. Today it is known as Cahokia Mounds.[12] The city, at its height, covered 6 square miles and had 20,000 citizens. Their houses lined straight streets or faced large plazas. A 15-foot-high stockade wall surrounded the inner city.[13]

Archaeologists have found many thousands of artifacts at Cahokia. After years of studying these, they have learned that: Large farms lay outside the city itself. There the Cahokian farmers raised corn, squash, sunflowers, lambs quarter, May grass, and little barley. Combined with hunting, fishing, and gathering wild food plants, this still didn't provide enough food to feed the thousands of Cahokians, so farmers from outlying villages had to also help with the food supplies.

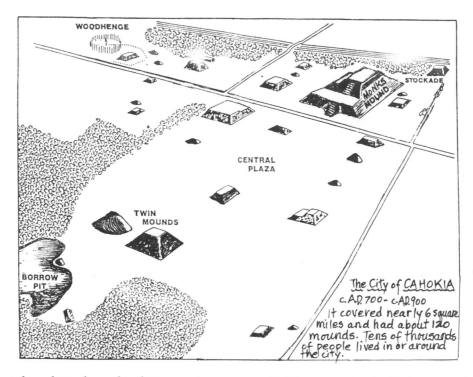

Their social, political, and religious views were highly organized. Rich powerful chiefs ruled over Cahokia and the smaller villages. A living god was their main ruler and he lived atop the huge mound on the main plaza.

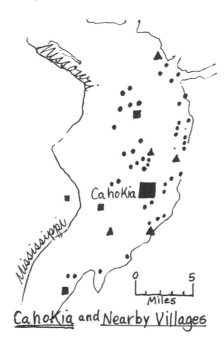

When the city was at its strongest (A.D. 1100-1200) it had over 120 mounds.[14] These were made completely of soil which the people had carried in baskets on their backs to the places of construction. The soil that they dug up left deep holes called borrow pits—which can still be seen today!

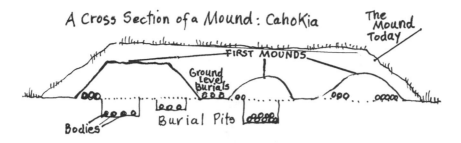

Three kinds of mounds were made in Cahokia:

1. The platform mound with its flat top on which religious buildings, or houses for the very rich, stood.
2. The ridge-topped mound was built to mark a very important location.
3. The cone-shaped (conical) mound may have also marked an important place or it could have held the body of a very powerful man.

Most Cahokians were buried in cemeteries and their mounds were mainly used for religious ceremonies, not burials.

MONKS MOUND   The largest mound in Cahokia—the largest prehistoric earthen construction in the New World—is Monks Mound. This great platform mound built over several centuries (A.D. 900-1200) was named for the Trappist monks who lived near it in the early 19th century.

Monks Mound's base covers over 14 acres and it rises in 4 terraces to over 100 feet in height. A huge building—50 feet high—stood on top of it. Here the chief ruler of Cahokia lived, and *from* here he led religious ceremonies and ruled the city!

The mound itself is almost 200,000 square feet at its base.[15] It would have taken more than 20,000 truck loads of dirt to build such a mound and yet the only tools those early builders had were baskets, skin bags, and their human hands!

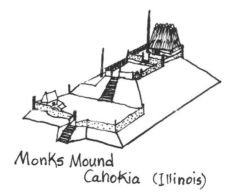

Monks Mound
Cahokia (Illinois)

It is a puzzle why the city of Cahokia ended. Maybe a change in weather after A.D. 1200 made farming and hunting difficult. Perhaps war, disease, or a weakening of political power were to blame. We do know that around A.D. 1200, the city began to grow smaller. By the 1400s Cahokia had been abandoned.

This little Birdman was found engraved on a sandstone tablet which was excavated on the east side of Monks Mound.

It may be that the man is wearing a bird mask.

Natchez

As late as the 18th century one great mound-builder people lived on. These were the Natchez who lived near present-day Natchez, Mississippi. In the 17th century French explorers found these people and described them at length in journals and diaries.

Like the Cahokians, they were ruled by a living god, the Great Sun,[16] who lived on the highest pyramidal mound in the main village. When he died, his house was burned down and the mound on which it had stood was covered over with earth. This enlarged the mound, and made it so that a new building for the new god might be built on the very same spot.

Across an open plaza from the Great Sun's Mound was the Temple Mound. This was some 20 feet in height with steps to the top. There stood the cypress log temple (30 feet square and

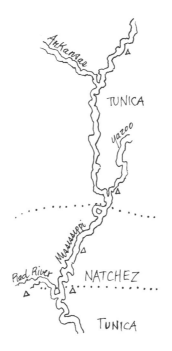

10 feet tall). It had two rooms. In the first was a fire forever kept burning as a symbol of the sun itself. In a cane coffin nearby lay the body of the last, the former, Sun God. In the second room was a stone statue of the Great Sun who had come long ago among the Natchez as a messenger from the Great Spirit. It was he who gave them their laws and customs and when after many years he grew old, he turned himself, they say, into this stone statue to be honored by the Natchez ever after.

Death was very important to the Natchez. Much of their art—their designs on their jewelry and pottery, their sculpture—is about human sacrifices, beheadings, and death.

When the Great Sun—or any Natchez nobleman—died, it was the custom that those close to him—wives, pipe-bearer, doctor, servants of all kinds—would offer themselves to be killed so they might be buried with their master and go with him into the next world where they would find "all kinds of exquisite (foods)...and their delightful and tranquil days will flow on in the midst of festivals, dances, and women." From the journal of Matwun LePetit, 17th-century French missionary, describing the expected afterlife of the Natchez.

In 1729 the French governor of the area ordered the Natchez to leave their main village and its mounds so that he could build a plantation there. The Natchez said they would not leave and, in a surprise attack, killed 200 of the Frenchmen and beat the governor to death.

The French, with troops from New Orleans and the help of some Choctaw Indians, struck back at the Natchez. Finally the Great Sun and a large group of Natchez were made to surrender. The French burned some of them at the stake and shipped the rest off to slavery on the plantations of Santo Domingo in the Caribbean. So it was that the Mound Builders of North America at last came to their end.

Notes for "Prehistory":

1. This is the common understanding of anthropologists but is not accepted by many Native Americans, who rely on their creation legends to explain their presence on this continent. Even scientists disagree about the time of the first appearance of people in America. Some would date it as far back as 50,000 years ago and others as recently as 12,000 years ago.

2. These states include: Wisconsin, Illinois, Missouri, Arkansas, Louisiana, Michigan, Indiana, Kentucky, Tennessee, Mississippi, Alabama, Ohio, West Virginia, Virginia, North Carolina, South Carolina, Georgia, Florida, Pennsylvania, New York, Vermont, Maine, New Hampshire, Massachusetts, Connecticut, Rhode Island, New Jersey, Delaware, Maryland, and parts of Minnesota, Iowa, Kansas, Oklahoma, and Texas (as well as southern parts of Ontario, Quebec, and New Brunswick)!

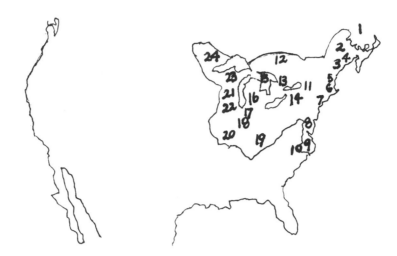

The Northeast Culture Area
and the Native Peoples who lived there*

1. Micmac
2. Malecite
3. Penobscot
4. Passamaquoddy
5. Abnaki
6. Massachuset
7. Narraganset
8. Lenni Lenape (Delaware)
9. Nanticoke
10. Powhatan
11. Tuscarora
12. Algonquin
13. Huron
14. Iroquois tribes
15. Ottawa
16. Potawatomi
17. Kickapoo
18. Miami
19. Shawnee
20. Illinois
21. Sauk-Fox
22. Winnebago
23. Menominee
24. Ojibwa (Chippewa)

*These are only a few of the many many groups of early people who lived in the Northeast Culture Area.

3. Plainview, in northern Texas, is the earliest discovered site—9000 B.C.—of huge bison cliff drives.

4. In Meadowcroft Rockshelter, Pennsylvania, layers of rock chips and flakes and bones have been found that date from 4000 B.C. to historic times showing that this spot has had people living in it longer than in any other known place in North America!

The Southeast Culture Area
and the Native Peoples who lived there*

1. Tutelo
2. Catawba
3. Timucua
4. Miccosukee
5. Seminole
6. Apalachee
7. Creek
8. Cherokee
9. Yuchi
10. Chickasaw
11. Tuskegee

12. Alabamu
13. Mobile
14. Pensacola
15. Biloxi
16. Choctaw
17. Natchez
18. Chitimacha
19. Atakapa
20. Caddo
21. Tunica
22. Hasinai

* This is just a few of the many many groups of early people who lived in this Southeast Culture Area.

5. Copper bracelets, blades, and points eventually became trade items and have been found as far as the Great Plains, the Gulf of Mexico, and the Atlantic coast!

6. In about 2000 B.C. a settlement of early people (in present-day Boston) built a huge fish trap, or weir, of 65,000 sharpened sticks driven vertically into a clay bed near the river. Here schools of fish would become trapped and the men could wade in and spear thousands at a time. Today pieces of this prehistoric trap—The Boylston Street Weir—are still able to be seen.

Meadowcroft Rockshelter, Pa.
Layers of stonechips, shells,
bones dating from 4000 B.C. to
historic times show this is site of
longest human habitation in North
America

Shoop, Pa.
Objects made of non-local
materials show there was much
trading with other groups even
as early as 9000 B.C.

Plenge, N.J., Williamson and
Flint Run, Va.
Many hunting, quarry &
campsites dating from 9000 B.C.

Levi, Texas
Rock shelter and hundreds
of tools found in a forest here.

7. Mounds are found in present-day Arkansas, Mississippi, Indiana, Wisconsin, Iowa, Kentucky, Missouri, Ohio, Illinois, Georgia, Alabama, Tennessee, Oklahoma, and South Carolina.

8. This set the Adena people apart from the majority of the other early Woodland people who were usually slender in build with long narrow skulls.

9. In the 19th century a Captain Hopewell owned land in Ross County, Ohio. On it were found more than 30 mounds, so this place and its people came to be called Hopewell.

10. If this building was too large to hold a roof, smaller buildings to house burials were built inside the four walls.

11. The flesh was taken off the bodies of common people and sometimes the bones were burned and the ashes were put in log boxes up on platforms. The bodies of important people were laid out in log tombs on low clay platforms. Grave bowls were put all around these bodies and each bowl had a hole broken in it so that its spirit could go on with the dead to the afterlife.

12. Cahokia is named for a subgroup of Illinois Indians who were living in the area when the French arrived there in the late 1600s.

13. This 2-mile long wall was built not only for safety purposes but it also kept the common people out of the religious part of Cahokia—where the richest people lived!

14. A small ridgetop mound—Mound 72—was found to hold 300 ceremonial burials, mostly of young women in mass graves. The main burial was of a 45-year-old ruler who was laid on a blanket of 20,000 round seashell beads! Near him were many grave offerings and the bodies of those who were killed and burned to serve him in his next life: the skeletons of four men with their heads and hands cut off were found near the biggest burial pit which held the skeletons of 53 young women.

15. This is larger than the Great Pyramid (Cheops) in Egypt!

16. The Great Sun was the over-all god of the Natchez but he was helped by his mother (White Woman), his brothers (Suns), and female relatives (Women Suns). Together these were the highest class of the Natchez people. Under them came the nobles, then the honored men, and last the commoners (who were called by their superiors: the Stinkards!). It was, of course, the Stinkards who did all the work—they grew the food, hunted the game, and built all the mounds. Their main work was the growing of corn: they cleared the fields of cane, planted two types of corn, beans, pumpkins, tobacco, and eventually harvested the corn which they then could prepare into 42 distinctly different dishes!

FOOD

All people, in all cultures, have the same basic needs: food to nurture their bodies, and clothing and shelter to protect them from extreme heat, cold, and rain. This was true of the early Woodland peoples also.

MEAT

The people of the far North—the Algonquins, the Penobscot, and the Abnaki—could not raise corn because of the climate, so they lived a wandering life in search of game. Deer, bear, ducks, and fish were their foods—with moose as the most important part of their diet.

Moose

This huge animal had to be hunted one by one as they do not travel in herds like the buffalo. To trap moose early hunters set overhead snares that were triggered by the weight of the animal, or they used birch bark moose calls in the fall to produce the sound made by a mating moose: this would draw the large animal close enough for a hunter to shoot it with his bow and arrow. It was easier to bring down this huge creature in winter when the hunters, wearing snow shoes, could chase the animal into snow banks, and then surround and kill it.

Beaver

Beavers were a source of food—and valuable fur pelts! Traps were set along beaver trails and in the water near beaver dams. Often hunters would break up a dam and then club the animals to death as they came up out of the water.

Porcupines and Dogs

Both porcupines and dogs were sometimes eaten by the early Northern Woodland people.

Fish and Shellfish

Fish and shellfish were plentiful. Once in a while a seal might also be caught and cooked. Many of the Great Lakes tribes went fishing in canoes at night by torchlight. The fish were drawn to the surface of the water by the bright lights, and men, standing in the canoes, then speared the fish. Woven nets and weirs (underwater woven branch "fences") were also used to catch fish.

Ducks, Geese, and Partridge

These were some of the birds the people ate. These birds (as well as fish) were often smoked for later use.

Buffalo

These huge animals were hunted each summer and fall by the Miami (whose lands stretched from southern Lake Michigan into present-day Illinois and Indiana); the Winnebago, Sauk, and Fox also made these yearly hunting trips, leaving in their villages only enough people to care for the old and disabled—and to prepare the welcoming feast for the returning hunters!

Early Natchez men in the South hunted bear, buffalo, and deer.

In Florida alligators were killed in this way: three or four Timucuas rammed a 10-foot pole down the throat of the animal—several other men flipped the 'gater onto its back and it was shot with arrows and beaten with clubs until dead.

(from an old print)

Often the Timucuas smoked their game for use in the winter months. Fish, turkeys, wild cats, lizards, brown bear, deer, and alligator were smoked. These animals were gutted, but their skins, scales, and heads were left on before being placed on high racks above smoldering fires.

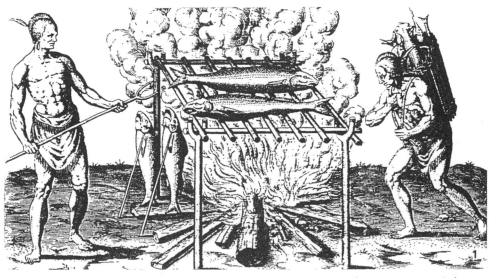

(from an old print)

Shellfish were also a favorite food of the early people in Florida. Clams, oysters, crabs, and crayfish were eaten. Fish were speared from dugout canoes or trapped in underwater weirs.

(from an old print)

WILD PLANTS

The Woodlands of the North and East gave the people many wild foods: grapes, cherries, raspberries, cranberries, blueberries, and gooseberries. There were beech, hickory, hazel, and butternuts as well as wild potatoes and onions.

In the South and Southeast the early people could gather wild nuts, fruits, and berries. These included cherries, grapes, persimmons, plums, and mulberries, and hickory nuts[1], chestnuts, pecans, walnuts, and acorns (which they probably leached to take out the bitterness).

Wild Rice

Wild rice grew—as it still does today—along thousands of lakes, streams, and ponds to the west and south of Lake Michigan. The Menominees[2], Ojibwas, and Potawatomis harvested this delicious grain using canoes: Usually a man poled the boat while two women bent the stalks alongside the boat and beat the stalks with paddles[3] to collect about half of the kernels while the other seeds fell to the bottom of the lake—replanting the wild rice crop for the following season!

Then the rice was dried in the sun or on a platform over a slow fire. The husks were beaten loose and winnowed away in a birch bark tray (on a windy day). The rice was boiled with maple syrup and used as the base of a stew.

(from an old print)

Maple Syrup

The Algonquins were called The Tree Eaters because maple sap was so important to them. They believed that Manabozo, their hero-god, purposely made maple syrup very difficult to make in order to remind the Algonquins of how precious this sweet is.

Maple syrup was made by tapping maple trees each spring—right after the families had returned from their winter hunts. Among the Menominees, each family had its own stand of maple trees to tap. A gash was cut in each tree trunk 1 to 3 feet above the ground and a cedar spout was inserted into the slit. A steady trickle of sap would run out of the spout and then flow into the birch bark containers below. Hot rocks were dropped into each "bucket" to bring the sap to a boil. First, the sap became a syrup and finally it turned to a sugar. It took 40 cups of sap ("sweet water") to make 1 cup of maple syrup!

Once each family had a year's supply of maple sugar, the band would break camp and return to its permanent campgrounds.

A bit of the sugar was then taken to the ancestral graves "to feed their spirits." A ceremonial feast was later held at which maple sugar was eaten in honor of Manitou, the Great Spirit.

PLANTS GROWN BY THE PEOPLE

The Iroquois believed that Sky Woman was their very early ancestress. Her daughter married a vine spirit and had two sons: Elder One and Warty One. Her first-born son, also called Good Mind, was sweet and kind to his mother, while the younger boy was often mean and cruel. Eventually one day Warty One hit his mother and killed her!

So it was that Good Mind dug a grave for her and with the help of his grandmother, Sky Woman, he buried her body. Sky Woman then called out: "Be ready, Good Mind, to soon greet many beings from below!" and with this his grandmother disappeared.

For weeks and weeks Good Mind stayed beside the grave, sprinkling it daily with water. Then, the Senecas say, one day he found an extraordinary thing had happened! The tobacco plant was growing from his mother's head, corn from her chest, squash and pumpkins from her stomach, bean plants from her hands, and wild potatoes from her feet! Good Mind rejoiced in the gifts that his mother had given to him and to all living people!

Corn[4]

Along the shores of the Great Lakes Huron and Michigan some of the early people—including the Ottawas, Potawatomis, Hurons, Sauk and Fox—planted and raised corn. In the spring the early people in the South also started to plant their corn crops. In the Southeast corn was the main food grown. The women were able to plant two different types of seed: one that ripened in just two months and was eaten in the summer, and another kind that took longer to ripen and gave bigger ears, the kernels of which were dried and stored for use throughout the winter.[5] These dried kernels were then made into a thin cereal, baked into cakes on a hot rock by the fire, and fried in bear grease, *or* wrapped in husks and boiled for eating. (Our first corn-husk wrapped tamales?!)

During the planting of crops a man turned over the soil, followed by a woman who made holes with a digging stick into which a second woman placed the seeds. Squash and beans were often planted between the corn stalks.

Crows and blackbirds were a threat to these planted crops, so the Indian people would build platforms in their fields from which special "scarecrow women" would yell, wave cloths, and make banging sounds to frighten off the birds. Sometimes the people also made bird-houses nearby for purple martins, which are natural enemies of blackbirds and crows.

In addition to the ways mentioned above, corn was also steamed in pits, boiled, roasted, parched, and made into flour. The Eastern Choctaws had a special way of handling corn. They bruised dried kernels in a mortar, removing the hulls and the bigger kernels. In the words of an early European settler, "They lett boyle...three or foure howres and thereof make a straung thick pottage" which today we call "hominy grits"!

From New England down to present-day Virginia, the early people planted their crops and then moved on to river camps or the seashore, where they spent the summer fishing. In

The earliest Known drawing by a European of an ear of corn.

the fall they returned to their villages to harvest the crops, pick berries and wild fruits, and hunt game—"very fatt in the Fall of the Leafe" as an early European put it.

Sunflowers

John White, an early colonist (end of the 16th century), described the heretofore unknown sunflower as: "a great hearbe in the forme of a Marigolde, about six foot in height."

Many of the Southeastern peoples raised sunflowers, the seeds of which they dried for later use. The coastal Algonquins ground the sunflower seeds and made them the basis of bread or soups. (These people also collected amaranth, a wild plant; the leaves are a salad green, and the ashes of a burnt dried plant become a salt!)

Beans[6]

Beans were grown by many of the Southeastern peoples. There, when the corn sprouted, beans were often planted on the same mounds with the two crops growing together, the corn's stalk becoming a bean pole for the climbing bean plants.

The Bean Plant   The Squash

Squash and Pumpkins

These vegetables were raised by many of the early farming people of the South and Southeast. They were eaten fresh or sliced and dried for use during the winter months.

In the far South tropical foods could be raised. For example, the Seminoles of Florida lived in little camps dotting the swamps. They were hunters and also had gardens of corn, sweet potatoes, sugar cane, bananas, and rice.

Even in the far South not everyone farmed. Take the Calusas, who lived in the westernmost part of present-day Florida. They had so much seafood at hand that they did not bother to plant crops. They have left behind huge piles of shells (middens). One such heap covers 70 acres to a depth of 15 feet—and other such refuse piles dot this whole area!

Notes for "Food":

1. In Florida the Creeks and Seminoles "pounded the hickory nuts into pieces, then cast them into boiling water, which, after passing through fine strainers preserves the most oily part of the liquid: They call this hickory milk; it is as sweet and rich as fresh cream and is an ingredient in most of their cookery, especially hominy and corn cakes."

   —William Bartram, English naturalist (early 17th century)

   It should be noted here that the English named a group of Muscogee people "Creek," as they found their villages lining the banks of creeks.

2. Their full name, Menominiwok, means "Wild Rice Men."

3. The Menominees tied the tops of nearly ripe rice stalks into bunches. Two or three weeks later the now-ripened stalks of rice were bent over the canoes' sides and beaten so that the wild rice fell to the floor of the boats.

4. The Creeks told of a woman who served a delicious unknown food. When asked where it came from, the woman refused to say.

   One night spies watched as she took off her clothes and then began rubbing her arms, legs, and body: hundreds of little grains fell from her and she caught these and put them in a cooking pot. The spies believed they were watching a witch and so they took the woman prisoner and she was to be put to death. She was given the right to choose how she would die.

   She asked to be put in a four-sided bin with the door locked and with no one being allowed to open it for seven days.

   All week long it thundered and lightning flashed. When, at last, the men opened the door to the crib, the woman was no longer there. In her place they found a huge pile of fresh ears of corn.

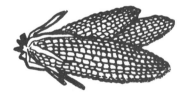

To the Choctaw corn was a god. They told how two hunters saw a pretty girl walking in the moonlight. They ran after her but she vanished, saying, "Come back in two months and see what I have given you." After two months they returned to the spot and found tall corn stalks growing right where she had last stood.

The Algonquins believe corn was given to them by Manabozo, the creator of the world and all of life. One day He sent his helper Mondanin, dressed in green and yellow, to wrestle with Hiawatha. They wrestled for three days. At last Hiawatha won and Mondanin said, "Take off my clothing and bury me in the earth." They did this and in time the first corn grew from Mondanin's grave.

5. The early people of the Southeast had many ceremonies to mark the passing of time, but the most important was the Green Corn Ceremony, or the Busk. It was celebrated at the end of the summer when the second corn ripened (see **Religion**).

6. The Iroquois honored the three sisters: Corn Maiden, Bean Maiden, and Squash Maiden. They celebrated the ripening bean plants at their Green Bean Festival when they thanked the Bean Maiden for helping their crop to grow—for making possible the renewal of life.

   Both the Chippewa and the Seneca gave thanks to spirits for the gift of beans. Because the Seneca thought beans had magic powers, this vegetable was always served to those who took part in the secret ceremonies of the Medicine Society—a very special group that had powers over all the "tribal doings."

CLOTHING

NORTHEAST CLOTHING

During the short Eastern and Northeastern summers, many early women and men wore skin breech cloths, light deerskin tops, and moccasins. In warm weather the children wore nothing.

Most of their clothing was decorated with quillwork, shells or feathers, and all of the grown-ups wore shell and shell bead jewelry. Wrist guards, earrings, and hair ornaments might also be worn!

The Menominees also wore jingling copper body ornaments.

The people of the far Northern woodlands had long winters. During this time everyone dressed warmly, wearing deerskin leggings and moccasins as well as fur cloaks and robes.

Belts

Belts held up breechcloths and leggings. They also gave a man a place to hang or hold his pouch or knife. Such belts were often made of leather, but among the Menominees and Seneca they were finger-woven by the women out of natural fibers such as nettles, buffalo hair, or basswood.

Breechcloths

This piece of clothing (also spelled breech clout) was worn by both men and some women. It was a piece of soft buckskin, about 12 inches by 72 inches, that was worn by passing it up between the legs and tucking each end, front and back, under the belt. These ends hung down like small aprons and were often beautifully decorated.

The Delaware men in summer often wore just a loin cloth and moccasins, while most of the men in the Northeast combined their breechcloths with shirts and/or leg coverings.

Shirts

Moose was a main source of leather for the Northern people. When the animal was skinned, a cut was made on the belly and up to and including the front two legs—in this way giving the people a "ready made" sleeved garment, requiring very little sewing.

During the short summers, light deerskin shirts were worn by both women and men of the Northeast.

Menominee women, of the Lake Michigan area, wore deerskin tunics over woven nettle-fluff shirts.

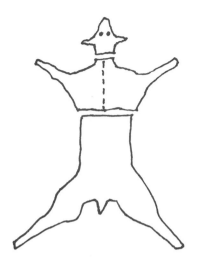

Skirts

Delaware women, as well as other Woodland women, wore knee-length skirts. The Senecas wore caribou kilts.

Leggings and Garters

These protective coverings were often made of buckskin and worn by both men and women; semi-tight leggings were common among the Woodland people. Mohawk men's leggings went from the upper thighs to the top of the feet. Garters held the leg coverings in place. Menominee women wore buckskin leggings that covered the ankle to the knee.

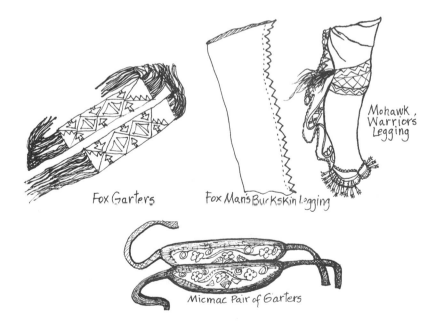

Fox Garters   Fox Man's Buckskin Legging   Mohawk Warriors Legging

Micmac Pair of Garters

Cloaks and Robes

During the long fierce winters, fur cloaks and robes woven of waterproof turkey feathers were worn. The Senecas used over-robes in winter.

Feather Robe

SOUTHEAST CLOTHING

It is not clear exactly what kind of clothing the early Southern people wore. We probably know less about these peoples, before the arrival of the Europeans, than we do about any other native people in North America.[1]

It was the custom each fall for the men of the Southern tribes (Nanticore, Powhatan, Secotan, Tuscarora, Shawnee) to go off to hunt, leaving the women behind in the village where they tanned hides and sewed clothing for winter.

Creeks or Muscogee women wore fanned leather wrap-around skirts, simple leather foot coverings, and shell necklaces. The Muscogee men wore loin cloths, foot coverings, and, occasionally, wide headbands made of tanned leather.

Seminole
Puckered-Top
Moccasin

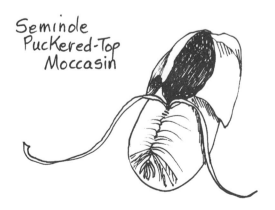

The Seminole[2] men wore deerskin breechcloths and buckskin leggings with fringed garters attached. They wore puckered-top deerskin moccasins. The women had tanned this leather with a mixture of dried deer brain, plant roots, and fibers.

Natchez women of present-day Louisiana blackened their teeth by chewing charcoal. Each woman wore a piece of animal skin to cover her chest and loins. Like the Timuacas, they wore skin robes and feather cloaks when it grew cold. Natchez men wore simple leather loin cloths and foot coverings.

Feather Robe
Cahokia

The Timuaca[3] women wore dresses made of Spanish moss. Each dress covered one shoulder and one side of the chest and then fell to the knees. In winter a woman might wear a feather or skin cloak over her dress. Each man wrapped a snuggly fitted loin cloth around his middle. Ceremonial hats were worn as well as gorgets[4], and metal cymbals were tied above the elbows and below the knees as musical decorations.

MOCCASINS

This lightweight footwear was worn throughout the Woodlands in the North, East, Southeast, and even in the far South!

Northwoods Puckered-Toe Moccasins (Cree and Chippewa)

This foot covering had a puckered-toe section. It was made in this way.

Step 1: The foot was outlined on a larger piece of leather sewn side by side with a smaller piece (which was often fully beaded with a floral design).

Step 2: Next, the gathering, or puckering, was done by taking stitches twice as large on the big piece of leather as on the smaller piece.

Step 3: Once the smaller piece was sewn on, a smooth stone was put inside the moccasin, under the gathered ridges, and a hammer was used to pound down the ridges on the outside of the shoe.

Step 4: Then the person put on the moccasin and held the sides up so the heel line could be marked and any excess leather was then trimmed off. Finally, the three pieces were neatly stitched together.

Step 5: Slits were cut along the ankle covering. Long laces, that could wrap around the ankle three or four times, were added.

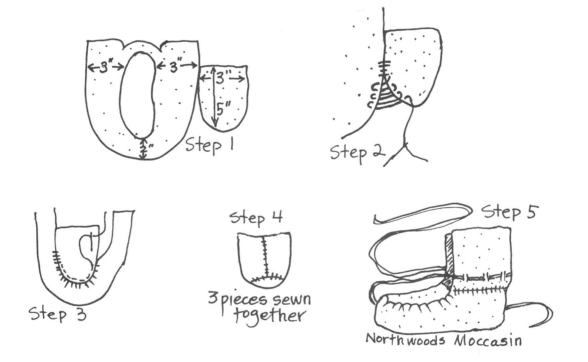

Top-Seamed Moccasins (Iroquois, Ojibwa, Shawnee)

This shoe has the main seam running up its front center beginning at the toe.

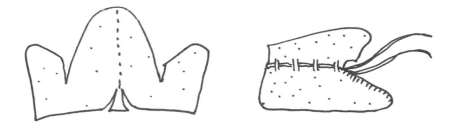

Southern Moccasins (Cherokee, Muskogee, Seminole)

Two rectangular pieces of leather (each 12" x 20") were cut in this way to make a pair of moccasins.

The laces were cut in a circle strip out of the upper corners of the leather. (See illustration 1.) Holes were punched along the edge of the longest side of the leather and one lace was run in and out of the holes from the middle of the leather to about one inch up on either side. (See illustration 2.)

Once this lace was pulled tight, a puckered heel was formed.

The remaining back of each moccasin was made tight by going in and out with the lace, which was finally tied in a knot at the top, the end of the lace being left to hang free. (See illustration 3.)

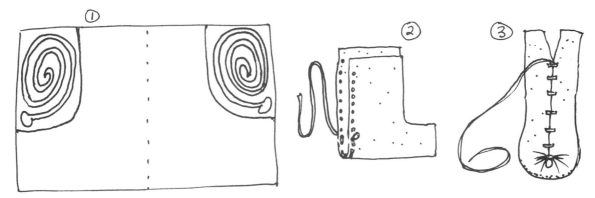

The second lace was inserted at the bottom front of the moccasin and used to sew up the front, making a zigzag pattern. Then the lace was pulled tight to form the toe and top of the shoe. (See illustration 4.)

Finally, the lace was tied and cut and the moccasin was completed. The free lace was wrapped around the leather-covered ankle to hold the moccasin in place. (See illustration 5.)

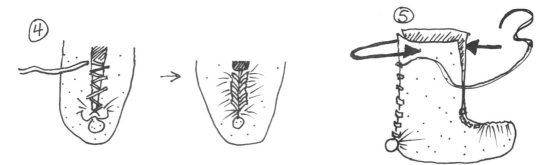

The Chippewa (Ojibwa) made snowshoes that they wore while hunting in the deep snow-drifts of winter.

Chippewa Snowshoe

HEAD GEAR

Fur hats

The Winnebago men wore distinctive fur hats that seemed to have "one wing." These hats were decorated with (bead or) quillwork and trophy feathers.

Winnebago

The Chippewa or Ojibwa man might wear a fur headband decorated with feathers.

The Micmac, of the very far North, had several styles of fur hats. The men wore a hat of moose skin made from the long hair of the animal's throat; a decorated panel was sewn at the back of this hat. Micmac babies wore little skull caps and the women wore a peaked cap that was decorated with handwork.

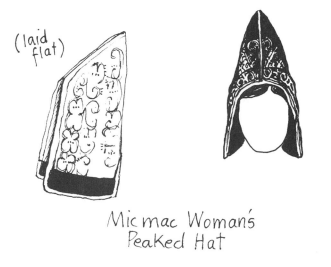

(laid flat)

Micmac Woman's
Peaked Hat

High-ranking men of the Fox and Sauk tribes along Lake Huron wore fur turbans that had deertail ornamentation.

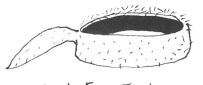

Man's Fur Turban
(Fox-Sauk)

Headdresses

The Eastern Indians are believed to have been the first to create the feather headdress long before it came into use on the Great Plains. The Algonquins and other peoples from Virginia to the St. Lawrence River wore a headdress of upright tail and wing feathers.

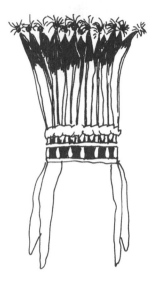

Seminole men of Florida wore turban-like hats with egret plumes.

Seminole
Headdress

BODY DECORATION

Each group had its own way of decorating its clothing and moccasins. Hair styles, tattoos, and body paint also were signs of a particular tribe.

Body Paint

When the Europeans called the Algonquins—and especially the Delaware—"redskins," they may not have been referring to the color of the native people's skin, but rather to their very common use of bright red face paint. This makeup was made by combining fat with red berry juice and ground minerals.

Women carefully rouged their eyelids, ear rims, and cheeks. The men would streak their faces and bodies with bloodroot and red ocher as well as white and yellow ocher clays. This was done after having plucked their heads bare using mussel shell tweezers, leaving only a crest of hair down the center.

Many other tribes—including the Fox, Secotan, and Ottawas—used body and face paints.

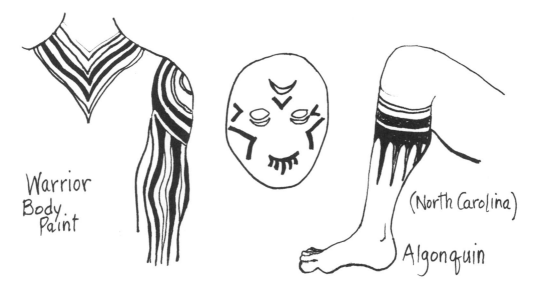

Warrior Body Paint

(North Carolina) Algonquin

Tattoos

John White, governor of the Raleigh colony in the late 16th century, painted the life of the Algonquins in the Northeast. He wrote "their legs, hands, breasts and faces were cunningly embroidered with diverse works."

Mohawk warriors tattooed their forearms and shoulders.

Muscogee (Creek) men had tattoos on the upper arms and shoulders and bands of tattoos at the middle of their thighs and calves.

The Natchez men tattooed their bodies, and plucked out their beard hairs using mussel shell tweezers.

The Timuacas covered their bodies from head to ankles with tattoos that were made by pricking the skin with a needle dipped in lamp black or in cinnabar. The designs announced each person's place in the tribe.[5]

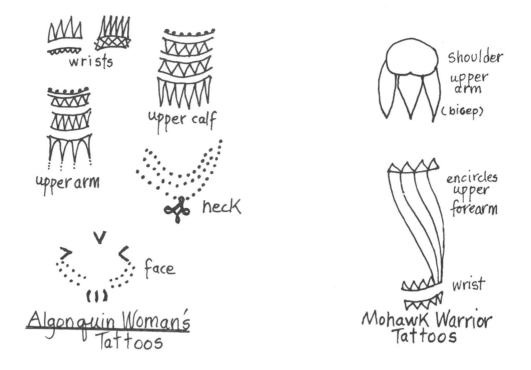

wrists

upper calf

upper arm

neck

face

Algonquin Woman's Tattoos

shoulder
upper arm (bicep)

encircles upper forearm

wrist

Mohawk Warrior Tattoos

Notes on "Clothing":

1. The first Europeans came into the South in the mid 16th century. Two hundred years passed before there were good written descriptions of these Southeastern peoples. By then—the end of the 18th century—their lives had been greatly changed by the European presence in their lands. We need to keep this in mind as we learn about the first people in the Southeast.

2. The Seminole tribe was formed in the 18th century when Muscogees and others of the Creek confederacy moved into Florida.

3. The last few Timuacas left Florida when the Spanish withdrew, in 1763.

4. A gorget (GOR-jit) was a large round shell ornament with two holes in the edge (so that it might be worn as a pendant). Gorgets were usually incised with designs. Many such

Etched Marine Shell Gorget
A.D. 100-300
(Missouri)

pendants have been found in prehistoric burials in the south. (See **Arts and Crafts**: "Jewelry.")

5. If a warrior should tattoo himself with designs to which he was not actually entitled, he would be forced to take off those tattoos—which was very painful to do!

SHELTER

NORTHEAST

Woodland Wigwam

In the mid 1700s Sam Hopkins described an Algonquin shelter:

"A Wigwam is an Indian House, in building of which they take small flexible Poles and stick them into the Ground, round such a space as they intend for the Bigness of their House, whether greater or less: those Poles they bend from each side and fasten them together, making an Arch overhead...After which they cover the whole with Bark of Trees, leaving a Hole in the Top for Smoak to go out."

A wigwam is a one- or two-family house of round or oblong floor plan built by Woodland Indians. Its bent-over sapling frame was lashed together with horizontal "stringers" tied in tiers to support the outer covering of reed or grass mats,[1] or sheets of birch, elm, or chestnut bark.[2] (See Photos 2, 3, and 4.)

Photo 2. Bark covering being unrolled and tied to frame this Chippewa wigwam. *Courtesy National Anthropology Archives, Smithsonian Institution.*

Photo 3. Chippewa house covered with birch-bark scrolls sewn together with spruce root. *Photo by E. D. Becker. Courtesy Minnesota Historical Society/Field Museum of Natural History.*

Photo 4. Ojibwa grass wigwam from September 1922. *Courtesy Nebraska State Historical Society.*

A hide or blanket covered the door opening. In the winter a double door-hanging was used.

Large wigwams had several hearths. Drying fish and strips of meat hung from cross-bars or stakes. All around each hearth would be bark buckets, polished wood or clay bowls, or a wooden mortar and pestle. Beds made of furs and skins (on top of mats or on foot-high "bed-steads") were also found around each fireplace. (See Photo 5.)

Photo 5. Door flap thrown back to show interior of Chippewa wigwam. *Photo by E. D. Becker. Courtesy Minnesota Historical Society/Field Museum of Natural History.*

What was it like living in a wigwam? It depends on whom you asked. Daniel Gooking of Massachusetts wrote in the early 1700s:

"I have lodged in their wigwams and have found them as warm as the best English houses."

Father Paul le Juene in 1633 wrote:

"This prison, in addition to the uncomfortable position one must occupy upon a bed of earth has four other great discomforts: cold, heat, smoke and dogs."

—To which other early journalists add: "fleas, bad smells, and the lack of privacy. . ."

The Cone-shaped Wigwam

The conical wigwam, covered with yellow birch bark, was the main shelter for northern (Atlantic coast) hunting tribes. The Chippewa of Minnesota and the Penobscot of Maine lived in such structures.

This was a strong single shelter. Straight cedar, fur, or spruce poles made the frame, and birch bark rolls sewn together became the cover. More poles were leaned against these bark sheets and bound together at the top, clamping down the bark cover. (See Photo 6.)

Photo 6. Algonquin conical wigwam, circa 1866. *Photo by W. H. Illingworth. Courtesy Minnesota Historical Society.*

Inside, the women laid interlaced sweet-smelling pine boughs, curved sides up, to form springy mattresses.

Extended Lodges (Chippewa)

A domed birch bark-covered wigwam could be lengthened quite easily—just as a single family bark and mat conical wigwam might be lengthened—by adding a ridgepole and so becoming a long lodge. (See Photo 7.)

Photo 7. Chippewa wigwam (long lodge) on the St. Croix. *Photo by S. C. Sargent, Taylor Falls, Minnesota. Courtesy Minnesota Historical Society.*

Great Lakes Summer House

This vertical walled house was gable-roofed, high ceilinged, and covered with bark. Often a ramada or arbor stood in front; this gave shade and offered a space for drying corn and meat. (See Photo 8.)

Photo 8. Summer house (covered with elm bark) of Sauk-Fox tribe, 1885. *Photo by W. S. Prettyman. Courtesy National Anthropology Archives, Smithsonian Institution.*

Sacred Buildings

THE MIDEWIWIN CEREMONIAL LODGE   The Midewiwin ceremonial lodge, largest structure built by the Great Lakes people, was an important ritual setting. The long frame was made of bowed saplings often covered with brush (or, later, with cloth) and could reach 100 feet or more in length. In the old days they were lined waist high with bark, boughs, or mats. Sacred cedar poles, "the trees of Life," stood up from the earthen floor, which was called "Mother Earth" or even "Lake Superior."

In this lodge religious ceremonies were held and here, too, were housed the sacred bark scrolls that recorded the different parts of the tribe's ceremonies. They are said also to be records of the tribe's history. (For bark scrolls, see **Activities for the Classroom**.)

Sacred Birch bark Scroll symbols

THE SHAKING TENT   This was the smallest structure built by the Great Lakes peoples. It had a bent sapling frame the size of a phone booth. Once the shaman went inside, he was believed to be at the center of the world, where he could make contact between humans and mythical beings. The booth was then covered with bark (or, later, canvas). (See Photo 9.) Those outside would soon begin to hear unusual sounds and cries coming from inside the tent, which would be swaying wildly![3]

Photo 9. Chippewa shaman and frame of shaking tent, 1934. *Courtesy Manitoba Provincial Archives, Milwaukee Public Museum of Milwaukee, Wisconsin.*

The Longhouse

For the Iroquois and Huron who lived in present-day upper New York state, the center of their daily life was the longhouse. Several of these buildings were grouped together to make large stockaded communities. It was the Iroquois creation myth that introduced this building to the people and explained how the longhouse should be organized.

Longhouse

   The Iroquois tradition says that in the beginning there was only a sky world lighted by the blossoms of a Great Tree. In this world lived "elder brothers"—those who came before the people and the animals were put here on Earth. They lived in long, bark-covered houses that each stood with one end door facing east and the other door facing west. The elder brothers living in a house were related to each other as clan kinfolk through the women's side of the family. There was a central aisle down the length of each house. Families slept along either wall of the house and cooking fires were shared by families opposite to one another.

   In the early 1700s the Iroquois longhouse was from 40 to 400 feet long and 10 to 30 feet wide.[4] (See Photo 10.) Its framing was made by poles each bent over in an arc. These were attached to the vertical standing poles that formed the wall supports.

Photo 10. Iroquois prehistoric post mold site at Howlett Hill, New York. *Photo by J. Tuck, 1967.*

   Although the Algonquins used birch bark to cover their wigwams, the Iroquois preferred elm for covering their longhouses. This elm bark was six feet long and one foot wide and the strips were overlapped and held in place by poles that were propped against the elm cover.

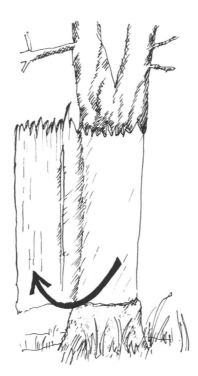

Cooking fires were vented through smoke holes that also provided light. The ceiling was blackened by smoke. A long central aisle divided the floor area. Every 20 feet or so there was a hearth with a smoke hole, shared by two families. The living areas were across the way from one another. On each side, tiers of low bunks about 6 feet wide were lashed to the wall posts. Under the platform—which had mats, furs, and stiff bark sheets—was a storage space. Above the bed was shelving that held baskets, weapons, cornhusk mats, herbs, and dried tobacco. The uppermost loft held larger items; in summer, it could become a lookout platform by simply pushing aside a shingle or two.

Longhouse Village   From an old print

There was always a simmering kettle of meat or corn going in each longhouse, no matter the time of day or night, and this was available for all. The inner walls were beautifully hung with braided ears of drying corn or fish. At the other end of the building was a flat-roofed area where firewood was kept in winter and where young children slept in summer. Tall poles leaned against the storage racks and were used for closing the smoke holes when it rained.

On the front and back doorways were shown the clan's totemic animal.

Every time a new couple was married, the longhouse would be lengthened to give the newlyweds a living space.

SOUTHEAST

Thatched House (Choctaw)

Palmetto leaves were used to cover the Choctaw pole frame house in Louisiana. (See Photo 11.)

Photo 11. Choctaw thatched house of palmetto leaves covering pole frame, circa 1881 in Louisiana. *Photograph not recorded. Courtesy National Anthropology Archives, Smithsonian Institution.*

Wattle and Daub House

This was a thatched-leaf pitched roof house with a front porch made from an extended front roof. The wattle and daub (stick and mud) walls had thatching on the upper third of the house walls.

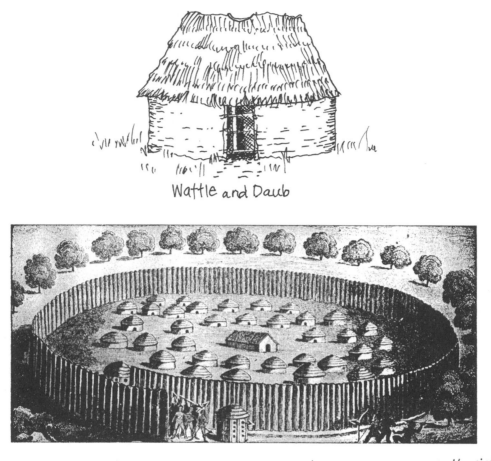

Wattle and Daub

Stockaded Village of Daub-Wattle Shelters   an old print

Chickee

Pole and thatch shelters (16 x 9 feet) called chickees were used by Seminole and Miccosukee Indians in southern Florida forests and swamps. They were arranged in camps where single or extended families (related through the women) lived.

Chickee

The sleeping and working chickee had a raised platform that gave the family dry seating or sleeping space when, as often happened, the ground was under water! These platforms also protected the people from swamp snakes, insects, and alligators. (See Photos 12, 13, and 14.)

Photo 12. Miccosukee roofer begins thatching a chickee with palmetto leaves by folding back the spines on the first layer. *Photo by Peter Nabokov.*

Photo 13. Seminole chickee builders in Florida. *Photo by W. C. Sturtevant, 1959.*

Photo 14. Chickee outer members extend from the main roof frame to support the extended eave.
Photo by W. C. Sturtevant and J. M. Goggin.

Among the group of chickees there would always be a cooking house with a star-fire (in place of a platform). This fire was fed by moving the logs inward as they burned.

A guest house chickee had several sleeping platforms, an extended hip roof, and diagonal braces at the four corners. (See Photo 15.)

Photo 15. Seminole chickee (guest) house with sleeping platforms, extended hip roof, and diagonal corner braces in Big Cypress, Florida, 1910. *Photo by A. B. Skinner. Courtesy Peabody Museum, Harvard University, 11 Divinity Avenue, Cambridge, Massachusetts 02138.*

Notes for "Shelter":

1. The Chippewas furnished their summer wigwams with bulrush wall and floor mats; they sewed cattails into outer roofing mats four feet wide and eight to ten feet long. These mats were pliable, lightweight, and good insulators. They could be taken down, rolled around household items, and be ready to head off toward a new campsite in a very short time.

2. Bark sheets were heavier than mats and more difficult to move, so whenever possible they were used for the winter wigwams.

3. Traditionally the medicine man would send out a supernatural helper (often a turtle) who would go to distant lands from which he could send back answers to questions asked by the people standing around the shaking tent. These questions usually were concerned with health, game, and well-being. The cries, bird calls, and quaking continued for a long while—sometimes ending with the tent's top covering sailing across the field.

4. A smaller, two-family, two-fire shelter, called a bark house (ganosote), was probably the basic structure from which many longhouses were extended. It was flat sided, gabled, and covered with bark held in place with the addition of vertical poles reaching the roof all around.

TOOLS

The native peoples of the Northeast and Southeast made and used a variety of tools and utensils that helped them live easier, more efficient lives. These tools were used in hunting, fishing, farming, and the preparation of food, clothing, and shelter.

FOR FARMING

Digging Stick

Often made of pine or ash, this tool had one round end and the other sharpened to a point that became polished with use. It was about 35 inches long and was used to make a hole in the ground in which to plant the seeds.

Hoe

The farming hoe of the New England area (and of Tennessee) had a shaped flint blade and an (elm) wood handle.

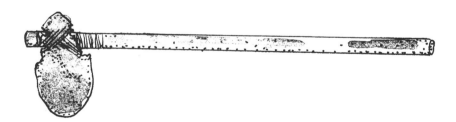

Spade

Oval flint spade blades such as these have been found in the Ohio Valley. The fan-shaped spade blade is from Tennessee.

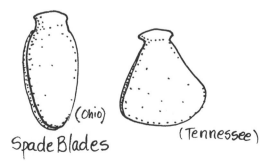

Spade Blades (Ohio) (Tennessee)

Burden Basket

The Woodlands Indian woman supported the burden basket (filled with roots or corn) by a head strap, called a tumpline. This strap was worn across her forehead or upper chest, and ran back around or under the basket itself; some tumplines connected to a cord on the sides of the basket.

Northeast Burden Basket

FOR HUNTING

Bows

Most of the Woodland tribes used bows and arrows. The bows were made of plum, elm, ash, or other hard wood and were often decorated.

Northeastern Bow (from an old print)

The Penobscot bow was unlike any other.

Penobscot Bow

Projectile Points (Arrowheads)

The arrow and spear points made by the early Woodland people (upper Mississippi Valley, 1000 B.C. - 100 A.D.) were held to the shafts as shown in this illustration.

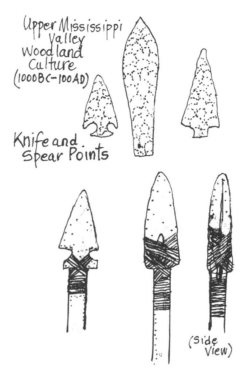

All of the tribes of the North and Northeast formed and used projectile points made from bone fragments, or by chipping flint or other smooth dense stones into a pointed shape.

Points and blades were usually set into a slot at the end of the arrow's shaft. They were held in place with wet sinew that tightened as it dried.

(from a 19th c. school book)

Arrow Shaft Straighteners and Smoothers

The stone straightener was heated and the wooden shaft of the arrow pulled rapidly back and forth along the stone's notch to straighten the shaft.

(Kansas)
Heat Straightener

The stone shaft polisher was used for smoothing the now-straightened arrow's shaft.

Eastern Woodland
Shaft Polisher
7 inches long
(ohio)

Shaft Smoothers

The Blowgun

The Choctaws of Louisiana used a cane blowgun that could be six feet long! The wooden dart, feathered with thistledown, could be propelled to a target up to 25 feet away!

FISHING TOOLS

Fishhooks

Used in fishing, these bone hooks were common tools all through the Eastern woodlands.

Sometimes double hooks were carved, as in this hook found in Arkansas.

Bone hooks
Eastern Woodlands

Double
Hook
(Arkansas)

In Wisconsin fishhooks were often made of copper.

(Bi-pointed)

Copper Hooks
(Wisconsin)

Spears

Harpoons were ground from flat pieces of bone. The Iroquois made harpoons from long thin bones. The Huron and Micmac used barbed detachable bone harpoon points.

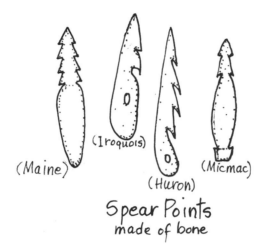

(Maine)   (Iroquois)   (Huron)   (Micmac)

Spear Points
made of bone

Traps

The Menominee women wove fishnets of bark fibers.

Underwater fences, or weirs, were made in the shallows of rivers by sticking tall thin sticks into the mud and weaving branches and brush between them. Fish would swim up to the "fence" and be unable to get around it.

Canoes

The Iroquois used elm bark for building their canoes. These boats could be made in less than a day as elm bark is easy to work and the forests were filled with elm trees.

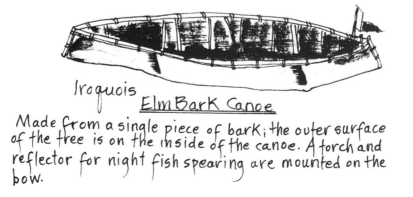

Iroquois Elm Bark Canoe

Made from a single piece of bark; the outer surface of the tree is on the inside of the canoe. A torch and reflector for night fish spearing are mounted on the bow.

To the far North native people made birch bark canoes, which were lighter than elm bark boats and so were easier to carry when making short trips on land. Birch bark canoes were also easier to handle on the water.

Algonquin Birchbark Canoe

Beothuk Birchbark Canoe

It took two weeks to build a 15-foot Chippewa canoe. The men did the woodwork, the women did the sewing, and an expert oversaw the making of the canoe itself.[1]

(from a 19th c. schoolbook)

The Seminoles made a dugout canoe, the pirogue, that was used to navigate the gulf and inland bayous, everglades, and swamps of the deep South. Usually you do not see the fin on the bow as it does not show when the boat is in the water.

Seminole Dugout Canoe

FOR WOODWORKING AND BOAT BUILDING

The Adz

The stone adz was used by woodworkers for splitting, shaving, and shaping wood; its ax-like blade was set at a right angle to the handle.

Chisels

These blades may have been used as picks, scrapers, adzes, or even as wedges. They were made of stone (Kentucky, Tennessee), of bone (Pennsylvania), or of copper (Wisconsin).

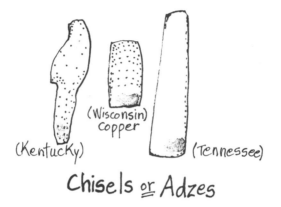

Chisels or Adzes

FOR FOOD PREPARATION

Clay Vessels

In earliest times clay bowls were used for cooking. (In the Southeast, stone bowls were also used in food preparation.) With time, pottery was used to hold water, to store dried foods and seeds, and even for religious purposes.[2]

WOODLAND POTTERY   In Missouri cooking pots had lugs (tiny projections) for easier handling when the pot was hot. The pot on the right, a Mound Builder bowl, has a fish head and tail for handles.

Prehistoric Cooking Pot with lugs

Mound-Builder Bowl (Missouri)

In Arkansas the early people made black pottery and decorated it with curving circling lines.

(Alabama)

The illustration below is an example of a Woodland cooking pot.

Early
Eastern
Woodland Culture Pot

Much of the early Eastern pottery could be seen as rather drab or plain: it is often an overall soft gray without decoration.

Many pots were ornamented with incised designs. These were made by scratching, stamping, by the use of thumb prints, string, or basketry imprints.

(Louisiana)

Some Algonquins made very unusual pots that had round bottoms with square collar rims.

Some Eastern pottery was decorated with sculptures of animals, fish, birds, or people.

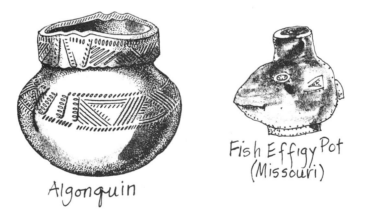

Algonquin   Fish Effigy Pot (Missouri)

Painted pottery has been found in the mud of the Mississippi Basin.

Spoons

These cooking and eating utensils were made of stone (Kentucky), shell (Ohio Valley), deer or bear bone scapulae (Menominee), or wood (Sauk-Fox, Northern Woodland peoples).

Wooden Ladles   Small Spoons

Mortars and Pestles

These grinding tools were used in the Northeast and to the South to break up, mash, or grind food.

A stone was smoothed to an oval shape to make a grinder and a second flat stone was used as the grinding surface.

Stone Mortar and Pestle

The Chippewas carved the side out of a log to make a wooden mortar, while the Algonquins (and the Cherokee) cut out the end of a log for their mortar and used a double-ended pestle.

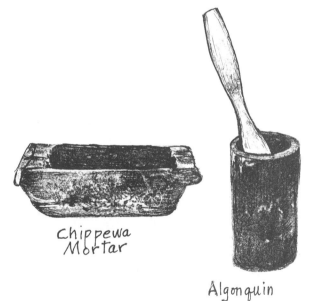

Chippewa Mortar

Algonquin

Miscellaneous Cooking Utensils

WOODEN PADDLE   This utensil was used for stirring the maple sap as it was being made into syrup.

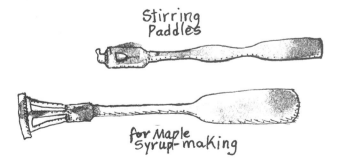

Stirring Paddles

for Maple syrup-making

MAPLE SYRUP STRAINER The Menominee people strained the maple sap through such a strainer as the one shown here.

Menominee
Sugar Sap
Strainer

NUTCRACKER STONES In Ohio small round rocks, called nutcracker stones, were used like a mortar and pestle, having just one purpose.

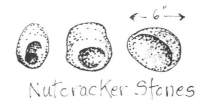

Nutcracker Stones

CORN SHELLERS Corn shellers were cut from deer jawbones in the Great Lakes area.

Deer Jaw Bone
used for shelling corn

CONTAINERS

Baskets

Baskets were used for farming, harvesting and transporting as well as for food preparation.

THE NORTHEAST The Northeastern Algonquin people pounded oak, ash, or hickory logs until the wood separated into layers that they then split to make plaited baskets.[3] They also made coiled baskets of sweet grass, which had a lovely scent from which it has taken its name.

Sweet Grass Coil Basket
(Ojibwa)

The Micmacs plaited baskets with patterns of dyed splints.

Twill Work in Basketry

The Nauset added simple painted designs to their woven work, while the Mohegan used root stamps (like potato prints!) to decorate their flat-sided baskets. The Ojibwa sometimes combined coiled sweet grass with splint plaiting.

Soft bags of diagonally plaited cedar were made in which to store wild rice.

Corn washers, sieves, berry baskets, and pack baskets were made by the Iroquois. (The Iroquois and Cherokee are related by language. Their basket weaving is also similar.)

Iroquois Baskets

Pack Basket

Berry Pickers'
Basket

Sieve

Corn
Washer

The Iroquois twined corn husks to make tobacco and salt containers.

Tobacco
or
Salt
Container

THE SOUTHEAST   In areas of Louisiana, Mississippi, and Oklahoma, the Chickasaw, Creek, and Choctaw made fine plaited cane baskets in twill patterns. These included sturdy pack baskets that each had a buckskin tumpline which the woman wore across her chest.

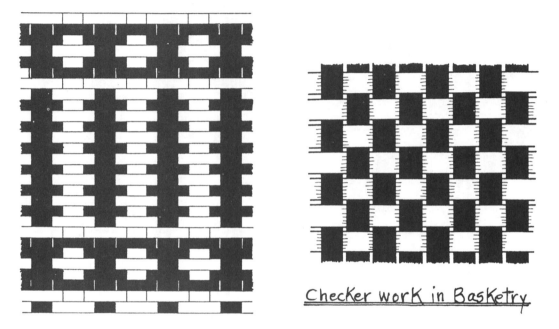

Checker work in Basketry

Some of their baskets had unusual shapes: the winnowing, cow nose, and elbow baskets are among these.

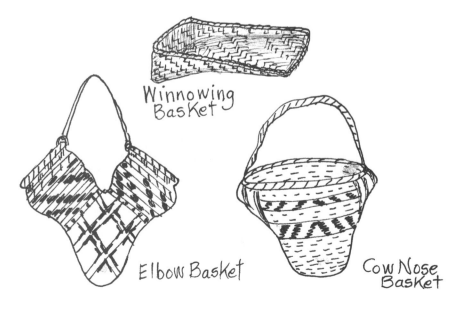

Winnowing Basket

Elbow Basket

Cow Nose Basket

The Chitimacha and Atakapa peoples in Louisiana made cane splint baskets in black, yellow, and rust with zigzag and meander designs.

Chitimacha ZigZag

In Oklahoma, root-runner wicker baskets were made.

The Cherokee and Catawba often used oak splints to weave their baskets, the rims of which were finished with a hoop, bound on with hickory bark.

Hoop Rim with Hickory Bark Binding (Cherokee, Catawba)

Bark Containers

These boxes, bowls, and pots were made by the peoples of the East and Northeast. They served as containers and could be used as drinking cups, trays, pans, and buckets!

There were four main patterns for making birch bark containers, as shown here.

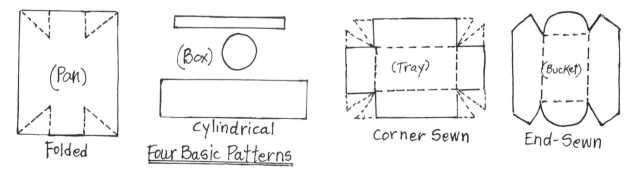

(Pan) Folded

(Box) Cylindrical

Four Basic Patterns

(Tray) Corner Sewn

(Bucket) End-Sewn

HOW THE CONTAINERS WERE MADE   First, the birch bark was cut into the correct shape. Then it was heated to soften, bent into the chosen shape, and sewn with root or wood fiber through holes made along the edge with an awl.

The Chippewa sealed the seams of their "mocoks" or buckets with pitch or balsam gum. They also made birch bark trays for winnowing wild rice.

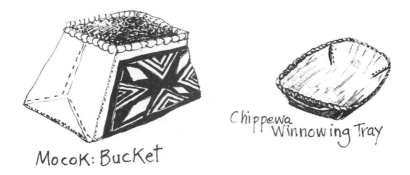

Mocok: Bucket

Chippewa Winnowing Tray

The deep storage containers, made by the Cree, were corner sewn.

Cree

Deep Storage Container

The Naskapi used a strip of bark to make a round box with a lid.

Naskapi Round Box

Watertight pans—folded birch bark with sewn ends—were made by the Penobscot and by the Chippewa, who folded the birch bark and tied off the ends of their containers. The Chippewa also made birch bark boxes with sewn grass edges and decorated the containers with punched designs.

Chippewa Box

The Northwoods Indians engraved designs onto the bark of many of the containers.

Algonquin Birchbark
Container

Quillwork was first used by the people of the Northeast in decorating their birch bark boxes. (For details, see **Arts and Crafts**.)

Northeast Quillwork
on Birchbark

The Iroquois made baskets from rough elm bark.

Iroquois Elm Bark
Container

FOR DRESSING HIDES AND MAKING CLOTHES

Stone Knives

These blades have notches, showing that they were lashed to handles. The "turkey tail" knife blade came from the Mississippi Valley.

A `Turkey Tail' Knife Blade
Notches show it was attached
to a handle.   (Mississippi Valley)

Fleshers or Beamers

Made from bone, these skin-dressing tools were given a serrated edge to help in cleaning the flesh from the hide.

Southeastern
Scraper
made from the
Columellae,
spiral center of a
large bivalve shell
ground down on the end.

Serrated Edge
Flesher
(Beamer)   (Illinois)

DRESSING A DEER HIDE   The skin was laid over a waist-high horizontal log and a bone or flint blade beamer was pulled across the skin to remove the hair.

Then the hide was rubbed with a mixture of deer liver and brains and then soaked in water for three or four days.

Next, it was stretched and twisted around an upright pole to wring it dry. Then it was tied vertically to four poles; this was done to pull it out flat, after which it was beamed again.

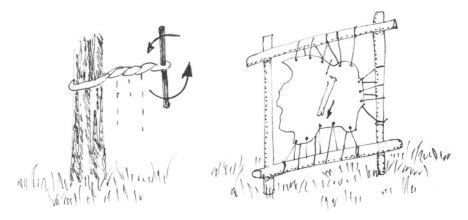

Finally, the deer hide—hung upright in a cone shape—was smoked to give it color and to soften it.

Needles

Bone needles used by Northeastern women were flat with an eye near the middle of the needle. Ottawa needles were double-pointed, while Menominee needles had just one point. A smaller bone needle was used for making the webbing on snowshoes.

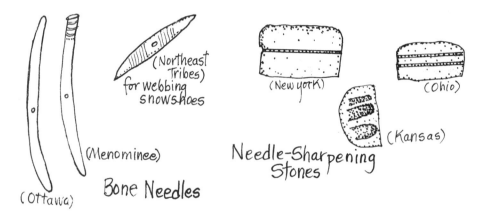

(Northeast Tribes) for webbing snowshoes

(New York)

(Ohio)

(Kansas)

(Menominee)

(Ottawa)

Bone Needles

Needle-Sharpening Stones

WARRING TOOLS

Special weapons were made for fighting. These (along with hunting weapons) were used when battles were being fought.

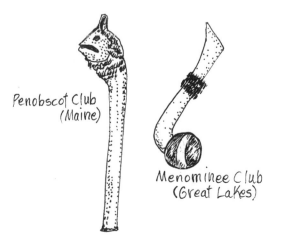

Penobscot Club (Maine)

Menominee Club (Great Lakes)

Clubs included those that were wooden and those that had stone ax blades.

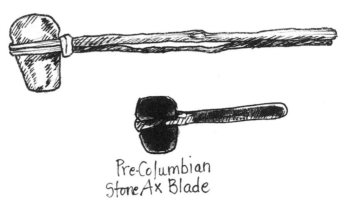

Notes for "Tools":

1. To begin making a birch bark canoe, the main sheet of birch bark was laid out on the ground and a wooden canoe form was placed over it. Next, the sides of the bark were turned up at equal spaces and held up with cedar stays. (See step 1.) Extra strips of bark were added to the top edge of the main sheet of birch bark. (See step 2.) Then the end frames were bent from white cedar. (See step 3.) Next the end frames were placed at either canoe end. The gunwales were sewn in place and then spread with wooden thwarts.

    The seams were sewn up with Jack pine roots and then coated with pitch. Thin cedar boards were soaked in water to make them flexible and these became the floor boards: longer ones were curved to be U shaped to become the canoe ribs. Set in place and left to dry for one day, the cedar boards were then very carefully hammered into place. (See step 4.)

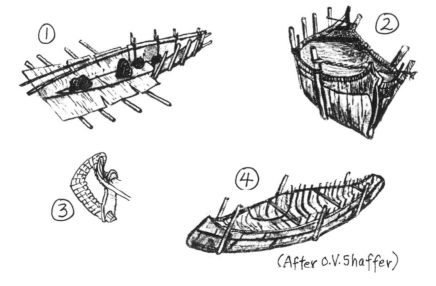

(After O.V. Shaffer)

Finally, all cracks and holes were filled with pine pitch. A guard strap of root was sewn over the gunwales and along the prow seams to protect all the stitching.

Then the Chippewa canoe was completed!

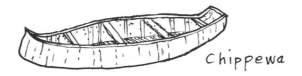

Chippewa

2. Often when early Woodland people were buried, special funeral pots were buried with them.

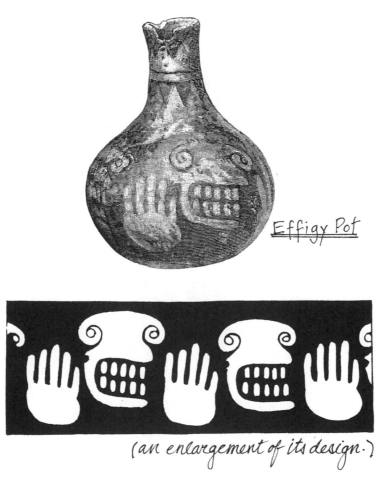

Effigy Pot

(an enlargement of its design.)

3. To plait a basket you have two sets of splints that cross each other, alternately passing over and under those of the other set to produce a checkerboard effect.

Variations are made by changing the number of elements crossed at one time and by using sets of splints of different colored materials.

LANGUAGE

When Christopher Columbus arrived on the shores of the New World, there were three hundred languages being spoken among the people north of Mexico. These were separate languages, not dialects, as speakers of one language could not understand speakers of another. This shows how varied the North American Indian culture was before the Conquest.

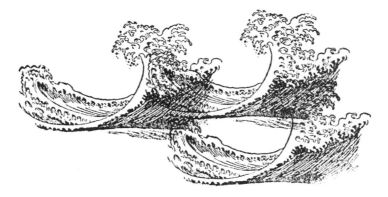

Algonkian[1] is a great language family, one of the most widespread in North America. It (or one of its related languages) was spoken from the Carolinas to Newfoundland and west to the Great Lakes and beyond.

LANGUAGES OF THE NORTHEASTERN INDIANS

The languages of the early Northeastern Indians fell into three linguistic families:

1. Eastern Algonkian included the languages of the Micmac, Malecite, Passamaquoddy, Abenaki, Lenni-Lenape (Delaware), Nanticoke, and Powhatan tribes.
2. Northern Iroquoian included the languages of the Mohawk, Oneida, Onondaga, Cayuga, Seneca, Huron, and Erie living in upper New York state, Pennsylvania, and Maryland.
3. Central Algonkian included the languages of the Ojibwa (Chippewa), Ottawa, Potawatomi, Menominee, Sauk-Fox, Kickapoo, Miami, Illinois, and Shawnee who lived on the lands around lakes Superior, Huron, and Michigan, and west almost to the Mississippi River.

78

LANGUAGES OF THE SOUTHEASTERN INDIANS

When the Europeans came into the Southeast, they found the people speaking languages belonging to four distinct language families:

1. Muskhogean included the languages of the Choctaw, Chickasaw, Creek,[2] and Apalachee. (The Florida Seminoles today speak Mikasuki, which is related to the Muscogee spoken by the Creeks in Alabama.)
2. Algonkian included the languages spoken by Indians of coastal Virginia and North Carolina and the language of the Shawnee Indians.
3. Iroquoian included languages spoken by the Cherokee of North Carolina and other tribes of the Atlantic Coast of North Carolina and Virginia.
4. Siouan included the languages of the peoples living in South Carolina and along the Gulf Coast of Mississippi and Louisiana.

In most of the Eastern woodlands the native people used "Kou-e" (pronounced "quay") to greet one another.

The Iroquois said "Nyah-weh Ska-nok," meaning roughly, "I hope all's well with you!" to which the other person would say "Do-ges!" meaning "Truly!"

To the Iroquois the word "friend," "Gayah-da-sey," really means "a new body" which is a way to say that your friend is a person who always seems fresh and new—never stale—when you are together!

Phonetics to be used with Ojibwa and Cherokee words are:

a = the sound of ah

e = the sound of ay

i = the sound of ee

o = the sound of oh

u = the sound of you

ai = the sound of -igh (as in eye)

au = the sound of -ow (as in cow)

Some Ojibwa Words

Bird	Pe na she
Butterfly	Men' en gaw
Dancer	Na' mid
Daybreak	Bib' a ban
Dreamer	En a ban' dang
Eagle	Mig a ze
Fire	Ish ko da
Lightning	Wa wa' sa mo
Little star	A nou gons'
Moon	Te be ke sis
Owl	Koo hoo ku'ho
Robin	Pee chaw
Star	A nang'
Sun	Ke sis'
Thunder	Ah ne me ke
Wind	No din

Ojibwa Numbers

1	ba shik
2	neensh
3	nis we
4	ne win
5	na nun
6	nin god was we
7	nish was we
8	shous we
9	shang as we
10	me das we[3]

Some Cherokee Words

Hello	Si - yo
Come in!	Gi - yv - ha!
All right	Ha - wa
Do you want (some) bread?	Tsa du li hatsu ga du?
I shout: I want bread!	Ge lu hv ga: ga du a qua du li ha
It is going to rain	Dv ga na ni
It is snowing	U s qua lv hv

Cherokee Numbers (*di se s di*)

1 . . . . sar quoh
2 . . . . tar li
3 . . . . chaw le
4 . . . . ner kee
5 . . . . his ǵi
6 . . . . su da li
7 . . . . ǵa li quo
8 . . . . tsu na la
9 . . . . la na la
10 . . . . lar too

One way that the native people got new words was by borrowing some form of the Spanish, English, or French words they learned from the European newcomers.

Another way was to invent a phrase that described the object. For example, when the Indians of eastern New York State first saw the horse, they called it "One rides its back"; while in the western part of the state, the people called this new animal: "It hauls out logs."

Words and Place Names We Got from the Woodland Indians

The English settlers, on the other hand, took Indian words for many of the creatures and plants they found in "The New World" (persimmon, pecan, squash, moose, raccoon, skunk) and for the totally new things the Indians gave them (hominy, succotash, moccasin, tipi, toboggan, wampum, totem).

Today Native American names dot the maps of the United States; rivers, towns, parks, lakes, and half of our states take their names from Indian words. Here are the eastern and southern state names given to us by the Woodland peoples:

Alabama—from Alabama, a Muskhogean tribal name; the state motto, "Here we rest," is a commonly used translation.

Arkansas—from akansea, the Illinois name for the Quapaw.

Connecticut—from the Mohegan for "long river."

Illinois—French tribal name from Algonkian "iliniwak": "men."

Iowa—tribal name, via French, from the Fox aayahooweewa, translated as "sleepy."

Kansas—from the Kaw name for themselves, via the Illinois and French.

Kentucky—first noted as a river name, but perhaps from an Iroquois word for "planted field."

Massachusetts—from a tribal name taken from the name for Blue Hill south of Boston; literally "big hill."

Michigan—perhaps Ottawa for "big lake."

Mississippi—Illinois for "big river."

Missouri—French use of an Illinois tribal name meaning "those with dugout canoes."

Ohio—French form of the Seneca name for the Allegheny-Ohio; means "beautiful river."

Oklahoma—Choctaw for "red men"; the name "Oklahoma Territory" was used by a Choctaw leader as a translation of "Indian Territory."

Tennessee—from tanasi, a Cherokee name for the Little Tennessee River.

Wisconsin—an Algonquin river name.

Wyoming—Delaware for "big river-flats," the name of a Pennsylvania valley well known in the 19th century from a romantic story of that time.

POETRY

The early peoples often thought of things in terms of pictures (of natural objects or creatures), and then spoke of those pictures rather than the actual feelings or events involved. For example, when an early Woodlands Indian suddenly found himself in a scary situation, he might say, "My heart is a frightened frog in a deep mud hole," comparing his fluttering heart to a cold shivering frog in the dark waters of a murky pool.

The early peoples spoke in very poetic terms and their wording, even when translated into the stiffer English language, kept much of that poetry:

> "I think one way—my way, but when I talk my thoughts in English, it is like passing a flower over the fire to you: what I think wilts, and the flower has lost its perfume."

> —Chief Cornplanter, Seneca

Here is the reply given by the famous Red Jacket to the missionaries who had come to convert his tribe:

"Brother: We do not worship the Great Spirit as the white men do, but we believe that forms of worship are not important to the Great Spirit—it is the offering of a sincere heart that pleases Him, and we worship Him in this manner."

Song to a Baby

What is this
I promise you?
The skies shall be bright and clear for you
This is what I promise you.

—CHIPPEWA,
from Song of the Pima

Song of the Butterfly

In the coming heat
of the day
I stood there.

—CHIPPEWA,
from Song of the Pima

Song of the Child

Throughout the world
Who is there like little me!
Who is like me!
I can touch the sky,
I touch the sky indeed!

—WINNEBAGO,
from The Indians' Book *by Natalie Cole*

Prayer at Nightfall

We wait in darkness!
Come, all you who listen,
Help in our night journey:
Now no sun is shining;
Now no star is glowing;
Come show us the pathway:
The night is not friendly;
She closes her eyelids;
The moon has forgot us,
We wait in the darkness!

—*IROQUOIS, from* Myths and Legends
of the New York State Iroquois
by Harriet M. Converse

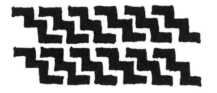

RIDDLES

The Woodland Indian people loved riddles. They had a midwinter ceremony that was all about the importance of "riddling."

Riddling Ceremony (Onondaga of New York State)

During this midwinter ceremony the people of the community help one another in the following way: anyone who has been disturbed by nightmares, bad dreams that show a strong wish or a need, puts one of these dreams into a riddle form and offers it to the group. Everybody tries very hard to guess the answer. When at last someone does, the whole group says: "Wa-o-wa-o-waaaa!" Then a singer, chosen by the dreamer, sings a song of thanks to everyone for their help. Following this, the person who made the correct guess promises to give the dreamer a small gift the next day.

This is a very, very old custom practiced by many other Iroquoian tribes including the historic Huron, the Cayuga, and the Seneca. The Onondagas, in particular, maintain this ritual and will surely carry it into the 21st century!

Most Native American riddles are about one of these three subjects: *nature* (living creatures, plants, soil, sky, wind, water, seasons); *tools*; or *parts of the human body!*

Some Riddles of Eastern Woodland Peoples

Into what black tunnel can a mouse go when a cat chases it? Seneca (*into the cat's throat*)

What I'm looking for has a swamp and many little islands inside it. Huron (*a pumpkin*)

It has holes—and yet it catches, what is it? Onondaga (*the net of a Lacrosse playing stick*)

What goes around your house everyday, and never comes in? Cherokee (*a path*)

The first Eastern peoples loved good jokes and often played tricks or practical jokes on one another. Woodland Indian jokes were based on odd comparisons, huge exaggerations, play on words (puns) as well as funny life situations. They often told jokes with completely straight faces, knowing that this only helped make the joke all the funnier!

Storytelling

Among the Indians, stories became part of the child's psyche through repeated listenings and retellings.

Stories were told to help explain the mysteries of this world: how we got here, what happens to us when we die, why we are born in the first place. Some stories taught children how to live in this world and the importance of kindness, generosity, cooperation, and respectfulness for one's elders and for the Earth.

Sometimes stories were told to amuse and entertain; such stories often featured Manabozo, who could change himself into a rabbit, or Glooscap who was also a trickster!*

In a Winnebago tale, the trickster, Wakdjunkaga, sees the reflection of ripe plums in a pool beneath the plum tree. He dives into the water only to scrape his nose on the stones, so he gets out and dives in again—this time, knocking himself unconscious! His body finally

---

*Many North American Indian tribes have these important traditional tales, that feature a hero-trickster (Coyote in the southwest, Manabozo in the northeast) who has some supernatural powers and who often gets in trouble and then emerges unharmed—and unrepentent!

floats up to the top of the pond and, after a while, the trickster comes to. He looks around, sees the plums in the tree overhead, and says, "You big dummy! You really give yourself an awful lot of trouble!"

11 Stories of the Woodland Indians

How Stories Came into This World (SENECA)

Long long ago there were no stories at all. This made the winter months especially hard. It was also the reason that it was hard to get little children to go to sleep at night. But because there had never been any stories, people just thought life was difficult like that.

Then one day a young Seneca boy went out to hunt and he was lucky: he got three partridges. On his way back to the village, he stopped by this boulder and he laid one of the birds on the big rock while he caught his breath. Right there and then a deep voice rumbled, "Then I will tell you a story!"

"What?" cried the boy who thought he was all alone there in the woods.

"Because you've given me this bird, I, the Great Storytelling Stone, will give you a tale in return!" and the boulder began to tell the boy the story of how the world was made, of how plants and people and birds and animals came to be!

Now it was a cold winter night, but the boy did not feel the cold. The wonderful story made him warm and happy. When the tale was over, the boy got up from where he'd been sitting and he said, "Thank you, Grandfather! I'm going right back to the lodge and share this tale with my people. I will come again soon and bring you another gift."

The boy picked up the other birds and hurried off to his village. When he got there, he called the people together and told them of his adventure and THEN he told them the story of how Earth was first made. The people listened, with open mouths and wide eyes. Because they had heard this story, each person slept deeply that night and everyone had fine dreams.

The very next day the boy returned to the rock and, laying another partridge on the stone, said: "I have come back, Grandfather; please tell me another story."

"I will give you this tale," said the rock and the boy sat down to listen. This time the Storytelling Stone spoke of the great flood and how it covered all the world and what the animals did to survive. The boy listened for a long time and then, as the light was failing, he returned to the longhouse to sit by the fire with his people and again he shared another story with them!

All winter the boy returned each day to the boulder and gave it a gift of food. Then he would receive a story that he would take back and share at his camp. He heard stories of how we got fire and where mosquitoes came from. There were stories of the old days, stories that taught the listener to be kind and hardworking and brave. The boy remembered every tale and shared each one with his people.

Time passed. The days were growing longer and the wind was mild; green buds began to appear on the trees.

One day the boy arrived at the rock as always, laid his gift on the stone and waited, but he heard not a word. The stone was silent.

"Grandfather," said the boy. "I have come. Here is your gift. Please tell me a story!"

In a soft, almost weary voice, the Storytelling Stone replied, "Grandson, I have told you all the stories. Now it is up to you and your people to see that these stories stay in the world. You must tell your children these stories—and with time other tales will appear. Stories will keep the people together. I have finished now. Naho."

So this is the way stories came into the world, and each winter night they were told around the fire in the longhouse. They kept the people warm and they have kept the Senecas together. Each time a tale finished, they gave thanks to the storyteller, just as the young boy had thanked the Storytelling Stone—for giving this world those first stories!

The Great Lake Cranes (Quapaw)

One day in the early beginnings of this world, the Great Spirit said to two cranes, "I want you to go down to the world below and find a place where you'd like to live. When you do, fold up your wings close to your sides and stand on that spot and wait. After awhile something wonderful will happen."

The cranes thanked the Great Spirit and they flew down to the Earth. They began looking to see where they'd like to settle. They looked and looked. They saw a green prairie below.

"Let's live here," said one crane. "It's pretty and green; there are lots of wild flowers and it will be a good place to live." They dropped down to the prairie and began looking around. It was pretty there. Sometimes they found food, but many times they did not.

"Let's leave and go live in the woods. We'll always be able to find food there." So the two cranes flew off.

They went to live in the forest, but hunting was not always easy. So they left those woods.

They flew over the Earth, looking and looking until one day they came to the Great Lakes. These lakes were huge and they were filled with fish.

"Let's try living here," they said. Every day they flew over the lakes, the streams, and the ponds, and they were always able to find fish to eat. So they went and stood on the lakeshore and tucked their wings close up to their sides—and they waited.

The Great Spirit looked down at last and He saw their signal.

Slowly they began to change...one crane became a woman and one became a man. They were the very first people of the Crane Indian tribe and they lived by the Great Lakes.

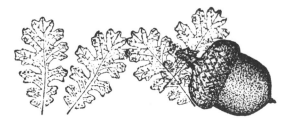

Little Burnt Face (the Cinderella story) (ALGONQUIN)

Once there was a large Micmac village built beside a lake in the Eastern Algonquins. In this village there lived an old man who was a widower. He had three daughters: the eldest was jealous and cruel. The middle girl was somewhat kinder, and the youngest was small, gentle, and meek. Each day when their father left to go hunting, the eldest girl would mistreat her youngest sister and even burn her face with hot coals from the fire. The little girl's face and body were so scarred that the people of the village called her Oochigeaskiv: Rough-faced girl. Whenever their father would ask how she got burned, the oldest girl said it was the little girl's clumsiness, as she was always playing too close to the fire. Then the father would scold the little girl for her foolishness, making her cry.

At the far end of the village there was a wigwam in which there lived an invisible hunter, who was a great Chief, and his sister. She was the one person who was able to see him.

One spring his sister told the villagers that the invisible warrior wanted to marry and that he would take as his bride anyone who was also able to see him. Many were the young women who tried, but each one in turn failed and no one could tell his sister how the great Chief truly looked.

The two older sisters of Little Burnt Face decided that they would go and try their luck at seeing the invisible hunter. They put on their finest buckskin dresses and their most beautiful beads, and they braided their hair with care. Then they went to visit the great Chief's wigwam. His sister greeted them kindly.

Now little Oochigeaskiv decided that she would go and visit the great Chief's wigwam also. She had always gone barefoot, so now she got an old pair of her father's moccasins and put them on. Her clothes were ragged so she went into the woods and cut some sheets of birch bark. These she made into a slip, a loose-fitting dress, and an odd, little hat. Wearing these "new clothes," she set off for the Chief's wigwam.

Her sisters saw her coming and they tried to make her go back home, but, no, the Chief's sister welcomed Little Burnt Face and asked her to come in and join them.

Just then the door flap seemed to pull itself to one side and his sister announced that the invisible hunter was among them. Did they perhaps see him?

"Oh, yes!" both the older sisters said.

"Well, tell me then, of what is his shoulder strap made?"

"A piece of the finest rawhide!" they both shouted.

"And of what is his bowstring made?"

"Sinew," they chorused. Of course they were lying; they did not see the Chief, so very soon they were on their way back home.

His sister now turned to Little Burnt Face and asked if she saw the invisible Chief.

"I do—oh yes, I do and he is wonderful!"

"Of what is his shoulder strap made?" asked his sister softly.

"It is a shining rainbow," cried Little Burnt Face.

"Well," said the other, "of what is his bowstring made?"

"His bowstring is the Spirit's Road—the Milky Way!"

"Ah, indeed you do see him," said his sister, and she took the young girl by the hand and bathed her in dew until all the burns and scars disappeared. The girl's hair became long and as black as ravens' wings. Then her eyes did sparkle like stars as his sister changed her bark clothes into a wedding dress. She was seated in the Bride's Place and the Great Chief, now no longer invisible, turned to her. He was beautiful and he smiled at his bride-to-be.

"So we have found one another!"

"Yes," she answered, "yes!"

Their wedding feast lasted for days and to it came all of the villagers, even her two older sisters. They all marveled at the beauty of the once invisible Chief and of his bride, Oochigeaskiv—Little Burnt Face no more!

The Tale of Manabozo (or The Story of Nanabush) (Menomini)

He came from another time, this Manabozo (Nanabush), and he was a Manitou—a powerful spirit god. When he found himself here on Earth he took the shape of a huge white rabbit. He had a personal servant, a big gray wolf, and together they lived in Manabozo's lodge.

One morning the wolf went down to the lake for a swim and when he did not return, Manabozo grew worried. He went to the kingfisher and said:

"You know everything that goes on down by the lake, dear kingfisher; my wolf has not returned from his swim and I'm worried that a huge fish may have attacked him!"

"It's not likely," said the bird, "but I will say that if it was a fish it would have been the King of all Fish and this is how to get in touch with him..." and the bird gave Manabozo directions.

The spirit god was grateful and in return gave the bird a white wampum necklace which he wears to this day, you can see for yourself: that white pendant on every kingfisher's chest!

Manabozo took his canoe out on the lake. In it he had his war club and—although he didn't know it—a little gray squirrel that had come along for the ride!

Manabozo paddled out into the middle of the lake and threw out his fishing line and called: "Mesh-enah-mah-gwai! King of all Fish, come take my line! I have lost my wolf and I want to talk with you about this. I, Manabozo, command you!"

Well, the King of all Fish rose up, annoyed by the yelling, and furious at being told what to do. He grabbed the fishing line, swallowed it and the canoe, and the rabbit Manabozo, as well as that little gray squirrel!

Once inside the fish's stomach Manabozo began wedging his canoe across its throat so it couldn't spit him out far from shore, and then the spirit god saw he had a helper—the little squirrel!

"A-ji-daumo! I'm glad to see you. Here, give me a hand and we'll get this fish's attention!" and he handed his war club to the squirrel. Then the two began hitting and kicking the walls of the fish's stomach!

"Stop that!" yelled the huge fish! "You can see for yourself that I didn't eat your wolf." But the rabbit and the squirrel kept on until the fish had a heart attack and died. Its body at last washed up on the lakeshore.

In time Manabozo and A-ji-daumo felt the fish's body shake and they knew the gulls were going to set them free.

And so it was. In a while the birds had pecked a hole in the fish's side and one of the gulls screeched: "Hey, look HERE: it's Manabozo and A-ji-daumo!" Out the two crawled, dragging the canoe behind them.

Once he got dry in the sun, Manabozo asked the birds about his wolf. The gulls sadly reported that the serpents in the lake had gotten him.

Oh, then did Manabozo cry and mourn the loss of his gray wolf friend. The Chippewas say that in order to help Manabozo get over his loss the spirits gave him the Medicine Ceremony; it deals with death and rebirth which, in a way, is what Manabozo had gone through: swallowed by the fish and then returned, by the gulls, once more to this world.

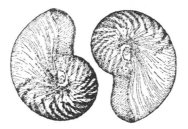

The Seven Mateinnu (Lenni-Lenape: Delaware)

Long ago there were seven men who had spent their whole lives fasting, praying, and going on dream quests. When at last they became old wise men, the Creator, the Great Manitou, gave them special powers: they knew the plants that could cure all sicknesses and they could see the future and know how to get ready for it. With time more and more people heard about the seven mateinnu (wise men), and they came in crowds to ask their help and their advice. From morning until night the old men knew no peace.

"We've got to do something, to get a little rest," said one of the mateinnu.

"Yes, we're just too well-known. We need to find some way to hide ourselves," said another.

And so because they had magic powers, they changed themselves into seven large rocks.

Now in a nearby village was a young man who was really good at seeing things that other people might not even notice. One night this young man had a dream that told him to go to a certain place in the woods and look at these seven stones.

In the morning the young man jumped up and ran right out into the woods. He looked and looked until he found the seven stones that he had seen in his dream. Then he looked long and hard at those rocks until at long last he saw the mateinnu inside each one!

"Oh, my Grandfathers! How are you? I hope you are each well?"

"Yes, quite well, Grandson, thank you for asking!"

Then the young man and the seven stones had a long quiet conversation and the mateinnu shared with him many of their secrets.

So it was that from then on the young man helped his people when they were sick or in trouble. He often went back to that place in the woods and spoke with the seven rocks.

After some time, a few of the villagers began to secretly follow the young man when he went into the woods. They saw him whispering to the stones, so THEY tried talking to the rocks, too, but the seven rocks spoke only to their friend.

After some more time had passed, one day the young man came into the forest and he saw that the seven rocks had each changed into a man!

"Oh, my Grandfathers! I am so happy to see you."

"We have changed back into men because today we are going away. The others just won't give us any peace here. Use the things we taught you to help your people, Grandson."

Then the seven mateinnu went away. Some people say they went deep into the forest where they became seven tall and perfect cedar trees. It's said that after a time people saw how perfect these cedars were and they guessed they were the seven wise men so they began flocking *there* to ask advice and ask for their future to be told. Those poor old men, they just wanted to be left in peace!

Then it was that the Creator, the Great Manitou, took pity on the mateinnu. He lifted them up high into the heavens and changed them into stars. The Lenape people call them The Seven Wise Old Men—The Pleiades; may they have found peace at last!

The Southeast had a strong oral tradition that took the form of fables and legends about animals, men, and gods. In these tales we get to see the peoples' view of themselves, of life, of good and evil, and of death.

How Fire Came to the People (ALABAMA)

In the beginning Bears owned Fire. They took it everywhere they went. Once they went into the woods looking for acorns and they set Fire down while they looked for nuts.

After awhile Fire grew smaller and smaller and at last it cried out, "Bears, come back! I am dying!" but the Bears did not return. Some humans heard the Fire and they came and they took a stick from the North and laid it on the Fire. Then they took a stick from the West and laid it on the Fire. The Fire grew a little and said, "Thank you for feeding me!" Then the people took a stick from the South and laid it on the Fire. Finally they took a stick from the East and laid it on the fire, too. Now the Fire blazed up and when the Bears returned, the Fire said, "I do not know you any more." So the Bears did not get Fire back and the humans have had Fire ever since!

The Wild Roses (CHIPPEWA)

This is another story about Manabozo. This one is about how he taught the Anishinabe a lesson. The elders have always told this story to show the children to be respectful of the Earth's plants, to never take more of anything than you can use.

One spring long ago the people noticed that all the plants were beginning to blossom but that there were no wild roses that year at all. The children were especially sad because they loved to smell the roses and make bouquets and crowns of them and play in and around them.

The people decided to have a big meeting. They asked everyone, old and young, all the people and all the animals. Once everyone was there, they discussed the year's missing roses. They all felt worried because always before there had been so many, many roses. At last they decided to send someone to find at least one rose and bring it back to the meeting so they might question it.

The hummingbird said, "I'll go. I can fly far and fast. I'll go find a rose." She was gone four days. At last she returned with a rose in her beak.

The medicine man spoke to the rose, asking why no roses were growing this year in their land. The rose answered that the rabbits had been greedy and they had eaten every rose bush in sight. This made the people really mad. One of them ran out and caught a rabbit by its short stubby ears. Then he shook the rabbit up and down hard. All the people were amazed to see the rabbit's ears stretch out real long. Then the man slapped the rabbit and its upper lip was split right down the middle!

Manabozo had been watching all this and he didn't like the people hitting the rabbit, even though he understood that it had done something wrong! So he said: "From now on, Rabbit, you will have those long ears and that split in your lip to remind you not to be greedy and to help you think about other people's wants, not just your own."

Then Manabozo turned to the people. "I am also going to put lots of little needles all along the roses' stems: these will protect the roses and they will also remind the rabbits not to overeat or take more of one kind of plant than they should!"

And that's how it's been from that day 'til this.

How We Got Thunder (CHEROKEE)

Once a young Cherokee fell in love with a girl he met at a dance. He followed her when she left and asked her to marry him. She said "Okay" and took him home to meet her mother.

The next morning the young man awoke to a huge roaring sound. He looked out and saw his new wife's brothers. They were coming along and each one rode an enormous rattlesnake. His brothers-in-law were glad to meet him and decided to test his courage.

"Please take our horses to the corral for us," they said.

Well, the young Cherokee was scared, but he didn't let it show and he took the huge rattlers off to the corral.

The next day the brothers asked the young man to play a game of stick ball with them. He said "Sure," and they told him to ride a third snake and follow them to the ball field. He was scared, but he didn't show it and he rode his big rattler to the ball park. Once there, each man took a playing stick. The brothers-in-law decided to test the Cherokee's courage a third time: when they brought out the ball to begin the game, the young man saw that it was a human skull! When this "ball" came flying toward him with its bottom jaw open wide, the young man was scared to death but he didn't show his fear and he played on. In these ways he proved his courage.

His wife's brothers were glad to see how brave he was and they said, "Now you may join us in our work. We travel the world, just ahead of the rain, making huge rolling sounds. You shall travel the skies with us and together we shall be known as the Brother Thunders." The Cherokee joined them as they headed out into the darkening skies—always just a few miles in front of the rain! And so it was and continues to be until this very day!

How We Got Poison (CHOCTAW)

In the beginning of time a very poisonous vine grew along the edges of rivers and streams. Often when the Choctaws would go down to the water to bathe or even to swim they might touch this vine and become badly poisoned and then die.

This vine actually was not evil. It wished that it was not poisoning and killing the Choctaw people, so it decided to try and get rid of its poison! He called together all the snakes, bees, hornets, spiders, wasps, and a few lizards, and told them how he was wanting to get rid of his poison. Up until then no one in the animal world could sting or bite to protect himself.

The snakes and wasps and spiders and other interested creatures agreed to share the vine's supply of poison.

The rattlesnake spoke first: "I will take some poison, but I will try to warn people by making a buzzing sound before I use the poison."

The water moccasin said: "I also will take some of the poison, but I won't use it until somebody steps on me."

Finally, the small ground rattler hissed, "I, too, will be happy to take some of your poison and I will jump at any person or animal whenever I get the CHANCE!" And that's the way it's been from then 'til now.

The Trickster's Talents (CREEK)

Rabbit, the Trickster, went to the Great Spirit and complained: "You have made me with few ways to protect myself. I hear pretty well and I can run fast, but you haven't given me any way to attack. Please think it over and give me some more talents, Sir."

The Great Spirit listened to Rabbit and then he said, "Go, Rabbit, and bring Rattlesnake to me." So the Trickster ran off.

When he came to Rattler, the snake was angry and coiled to strike.

"Oh, Rattler, the Great Spirit has asked me to measure your considerable long length. Please lie down along this stick so I may see exactly how very long you are!"

Well, Rattlesnake was flattered, so he stretched out to his full length beside the stick. At once Rabbit grabbed a rope, tied the snake to the stick and carried it to the Great Spirit!

"Well done, Rabbit. Now go and bring all the wasps to me!" So the Trickster ran off.

When he came to the wasps they were playing ball with their Queen. Rabbit sat down, holding a hollow gourd, and he called out: "Oh, Wasps, the Great Spirit has asked me to count your huge numbers. Please fly into the hollow gourd and I will count you one by one as you enter."

Well, the wasps were flattered, so they followed their Queen into the gourd. At once Rabbit took a stone, plugged the hole in the gourd, and carried it to the Great Spirit!

"Well done, Rabbit. See what you can do with the talents I have given you? You need no more powers. Go and use your talents and you will gain the very destiny I have meant for you!" and this the Rabbit did.

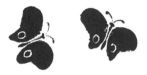

The Song that Comes from the Sea (BILOXI)

Long, long ago, far back in time, the Biloxi were a great tribe. They were farmers, hunters, and artists. And they lived in peace and did not go to war.

The tribes around them were not peaceful. Of them all, the Choctaw were the most fearful warriors.

One day a Choctaw war council decided to go and raid the Biloxi village. Now the Biloxi were not cowards, but they did not want war—and yet they had to defend their village.

The night came when the Choctaw attacked! Both sides fought ferociously, but little by little, the Biloxi were pushed back until they came to the edge of Pascagoula Bay which leads into the deep black sea. The Biloxi hurriedly built a wooden fortress at the bay's edge and the whole tribe went behind this.

Days passed. They fought long and hard and at last their food ran out. They couldn't go out to gather plants or hunt game...What could they do? They would not give up. If they did, the Choctaw would kill every man and make slaves of the women and children. The elders talked it over and in the end they saw only one way out. They must all walk out into the waves of the ocean; there the Choctaw could not attack them and they would never know hunger or war again. They would all be at peace forever.

The Chief led his people. He was followed by the elders, all proudly singing the Song of the End. Next came the young men chanting their death songs. The women and children followed, all chanting and singing the Song of the End.

The Biloxi people walked straight out into the waves until the waters of the bay covered them, each and every one.

So it was that the peaceful Biloxi showed the fierce Choctaw how a people could leave this world without showing fear.

Today in Alabama they say that when the sun rises over the waters of Pascagoula Bay, if you listen carefully, you may hear the death songs of this fearless people, the Biloxi, who are living peacefully now at the bottom of the bay.

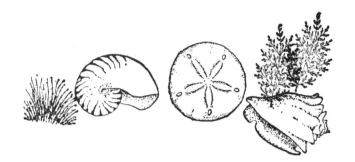

Notes for "Language":

1. For purposes of clarity, "Algonquin" refers to the people, whereas "Algonkian" refers to the language.

2. The Creek spoke several different, but in some ways similar, languages.

3. The Ojibwa vocabulary words are found in *The American Indian Craft Book* (pages 368 and 386) written by Marz and Nono Minor (Lincoln: University of Nebraska Press, 1972).

ARTS AND CRAFTS

MUSIC

The early Woodland people danced both for religious purposes and socially. They sang to their music, playing drums, blowing whistles, shaking rattles. Music was a part of the daily life of the Woodland Indians. Their music was not written down; each song was memorized individually. There were songs for every part of life: work, play, falling asleep, being in love; songs of competition, hunting, war, and death; as well as songs to celebrate being alive on this very beautiful day!

Native American music has rhythm, melody, and harmony. Rhythm is felt in our breathing and our heartbeat, in the dripping of water, in our very pulses. Life is rhythmic. Melody is a series of sounds of different pitch: bird songs, the howl of a wolf, the laughter of a young woman. Harmony is the blending together of several sounds; in nature we hear combined sounds when the wind blows through the boughs and leaves of the trees, and when rain falls on the wigwam as we warm ourselves by the crackling fire inside.

Singing was believed to have the power to put a person in perfect balance with all of nature.

Their music was extremely personal and was made as prayers for ancestors, for good hunting, safety, rain, and to note the changing seasons.

Musical Instruments

RATTLES   Menominee Indian rattles were each made of a rawhide box-like holder with a wooden handle. Here a turtle claw has been attached.

Menominee

The Iroquois would make a rattle out of a turtle shell and use this in False-Face Society ceremonies.

The Iroquois also used animal horns and gourds filled with tiny stones or corn kernels for rattles.

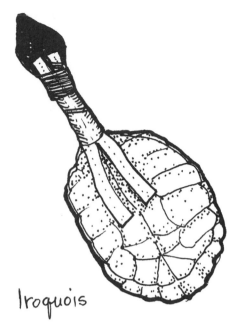

Iroquois

FLUTES AND WHISTLES made and played. In the Eastern Woodlands slate as well as pottery whistles were

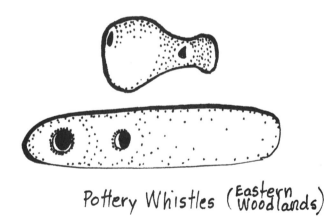

Pottery Whistles (Eastern Woodlands)

In the Mississippi Valley flutes were carved from bones or from wood. Sometimes these even had vent regulators!

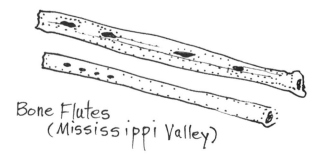

Bone Flutes
(Mississippi Valley)

END FLUTES   These two-chambered flutes were often used for playing love songs.

DRUMS   The large Chippewa ceremonial drums were made from hollow logs. The Iroquois made water drums that had plugs so they could change the level of water inside and, in so doing, change the tone of the drum itself!
They also used turtle shell "mallets" to beat on hollow log drums.

Choctaw Drum   (Louisiana)

VISUAL ARTS

Clay

EARLY POTTERY   Here are three examples of early pottery.

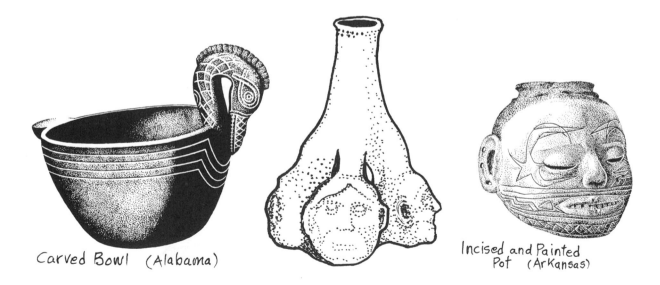

Carved Bowl (Alabama)   Incised and Painted Pot (Arkansas)

SCULPTURE   In Oklahoma and Tennessee the early Hopewell people made large clay figures.

Hopewell Figure

Stone Carving

NORTHEAST   There was little stone carving done in the Northeast except for birdstones, slate spear points, and knife blades, and pipe bowls. Carved from stone or clay, such pipe bowls were made by the Iroquois as early as 600 years ago.

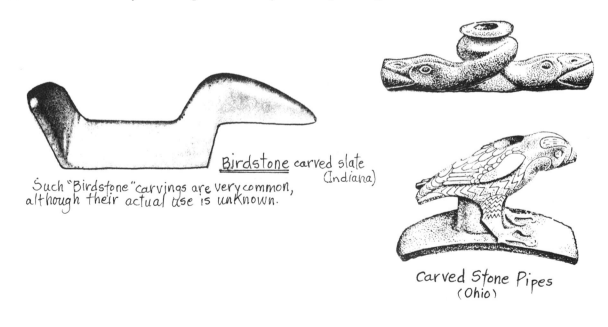

Birdstone carved slate
(Indiana)
Such "Birdstone" carvings are very common, although their actual use is unknown.

Carved Stone Pipes
(Ohio)

The effigy pipe was remarkable. Its bowl was the carved or molded figure of a person or an animal that was usually looking back at the smoker. Such a pipe was buried alongside the body of its owner. (For effigy masks, see **Religion**.)

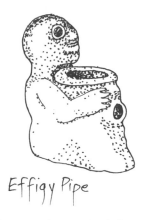

Effigy Pipe

SOUTHEAST   Unlike the North, the Southeast had fine stone carvings, including pipes of human and animal forms, large realistic figures, carved bird bowls, and plaques with religious symbols engraved on them.

(Mississippi)   (Georgia)   (Arkansas)

Carved Pipes

Incised Pottery Designs
(Arkansas)

(Alabama)

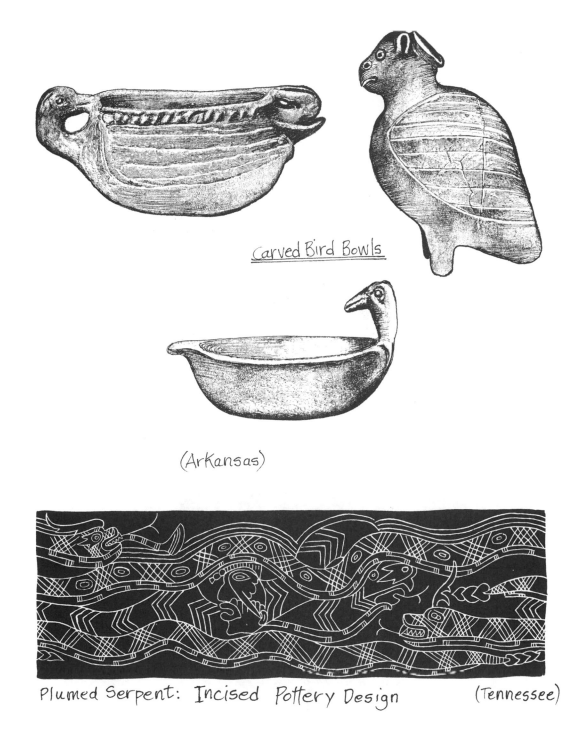

Carved Bird Bowls

(Arkansas)

Plumed Serpent: Incised Pottery Design   (Tennessee)

A large group of prehistoric carved and inlaid wooden sculptures and objects have been found at Key Marco, Florida. These show us that the early people who lived there were artists of the highest quality.

One of these wooden objects is a mask or a figure-head of a deer. Another is a seated cat carved of wood.

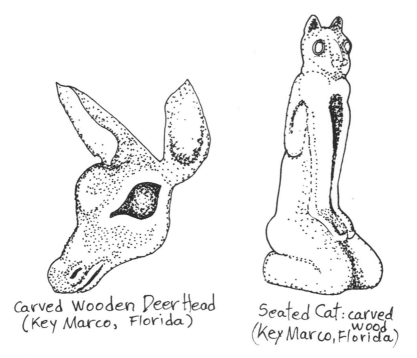

Carved Wooden Deer Head
(Key Marco, Florida)

Seated Cat: carved
(Key Marco, Florida) wood

Weaving

Hand weaving is an ancient craft. The Hopewell and Adena peoples made textiles with their fingers—without the use of looms.

We know that the Eastern Woodland Indians wove baskets because small basketry pieces, or their imprints, are found in the mounds. However, by the time the Europeans

arrived, basket making in this area had pretty much died out. (For more details on basket weaving, see **Tools**.)

The Natchez tribe of Mississippi is now extinct, but in the 17th century, these people wove clothing of buffalo and opossum hair, and with the fibers of mulberry and nettle plants. They also wove huge mats (6 feet long and 4 feet wide) decorated with geometric designs.

Another material used in weaving was moosehair. In the North the Iroquois decorated their clothing with sections of woven moosehair.

Woven Moose hair

(Iroquois)

(Mohawk)

Quillwork

In North America this craft was practiced primarily by Iroquois, Huron, Algonquin, Micmac, Ojibwa, and Winnebago women. The men were responsible for hunting the porcupines that provided the quills. In some tribes the men prepared the dyes from roots, bark, buds, and plants, while the women sorted, flattened, and applied the colorful quills to the deerskin, hide, or birch bark.

The largest porcupine quills (up to 5 inches long) came from the tail of the animal; somewhat smaller, though still big, were the quills that came from its back. Small quills were taken from the neck and the finest were found on the rest of the animal's body.

PREPARING THE QUILLS   First, the quills were soaked and softened in water. Then they were dyed; red, yellow, green, blue, and black were the usual colors.

In the next step, a woman would hold several quills in her mouth to again soften them. She would draw each one out between her teeth to flatten it. The flattened quills were then ready to be sewn or woven into clothes, including belts, garters, leggings, wrist guards, shirts, moccasins, and dresses.

APPLYING THE QUILLS   One method was to apply the decorations to clothing, belts, or bags using the wrapping technique.

The woman would wrap the quills around a single thread, which was then sewn to the hide or skin.

Northeastern Wrapped Quillwork

Another method was to fold the quills around the thread, which was next sewn to the skin.

Folded Quills around a single thread which was sewn to cloth

The Algonquin, Huron, and Iroquois covered moccasins and bags with linear designs. Solid designs were often made by the Winnebago to decorate ceremonial belts.

Iroquois Quillwork

Quillwork on Leather Bag (Ojibwa)

Quillwork on Hide (Delaware)

The people of the Northeast were the first craftsmen to use quillwork on birch bark boxes. (See **Tools**.) They pushed each quill through a tiny hole in the bark and folded the ends over on the inside of the bark. Once the design was done, an inner lining was put over the quill ends to cover them and hold them in place. The Micmac made round-topped boxes as did other Northeast tribes. Quillwork on birch bark spread to the Great Lakes later when Chippewa and Ottawa made quill designs on round or rectangular boxes. These designs included flowers, animals, or solid patterns.

The designs they used had deep religious meaning for them. They believed that each thing in the world had a spirit—a source of power. They also thought that power could be given to the artist when he or she used certain symbols or designs.

Quillwork is an art invented by Native Americans and is produced nowhere else in the world!

Quillwork on Birch
Bark Box
Lid
(Ottawa)

Prehistoric Jewelry

In all times and in all cultures people have made and adorned themselves with jewelry. It makes the wearer more beautiful, more handsome, and it draws attention to the wearer.

Seven thousand years ago (5000 B.C.) the people of the Old Copper Culture (as scientists call them)—in present-day Minnesota, Wisconsin, and Michigan—hammered and rolled copper into thin beads. They knew that this metal, which would become brittle after a good deal of hammering, would grow pliable again if it were heated in a fire.

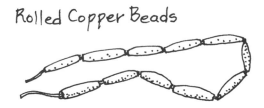

Rolled Copper Beads

Later, the Hopewell people of Illinois (A.D. 200) beat copper into sheets and made jewelry of this metal.[1]

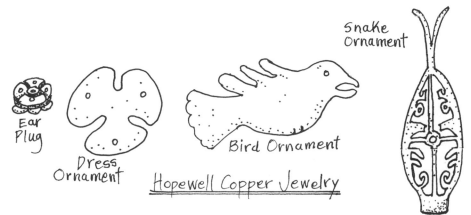

Ear
Plug

Dress
Ornament

Bird Ornament

Snake
Ornament

Hopewell Copper Jewelry

Early Northeastern people would often make necklaces from little seashells and small bird bones.

The early Mound Builders also made slate ornaments and pendants and etched two-holed shell ornaments called gorgets. These have been found in Georgia, Illinois, and Tennessee.[2]

(Tennessee)

Engraved Shells
(Gorgets)

(Georgia)   (Illinois)

Later the Eastern Woodland people made large beads from slate, pipestone,[3] and hard sandstone. They also carved beads of magnesite, shell, bone, quartz, and animal teeth.

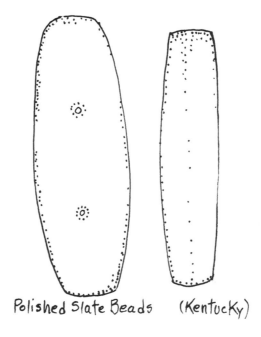

Polished Slate Beads   (Kentucky)

Bear claws were prized by the Northern tribes and were worn as collar necklaces. Seminole necklaces were usually a mixture of beads of clay, stone, shell, and claws.

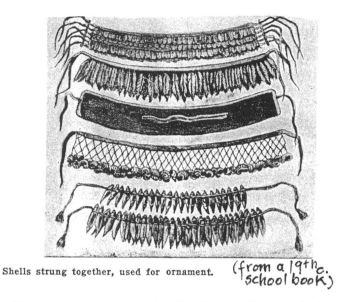

Shells strung together, used for ornament.   (from a 19th c. school book)

Bracelets made of bone were worn in the Southeast. Copper hair ornaments have been found in Spiro Mound, Oklahoma.

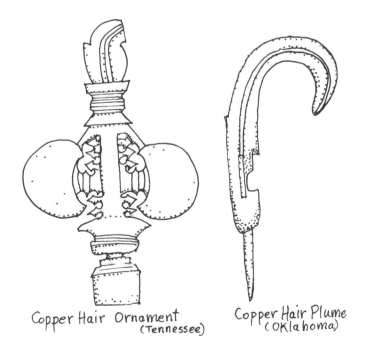

Copper Hair Ornament (Tennessee)

Copper Hair Plume (Oklahoma)

COMBS   Combs were carved from bone or antler by the Iroquois 400 years ago! They were used as decoration and to hold their hair in place.

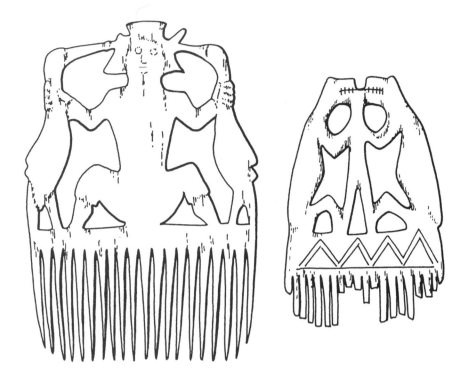

Notes on "Arts and Crafts":

1. The Hopewell people also cut copper into sheets from which they carved outlines of bird talons or of human heads. They also used copper to make tools such as awls, axes, fish hooks, and jewelry.

   The Mississippi Mound Builders cut out shapes from flattened copper and added embossed designs to them.

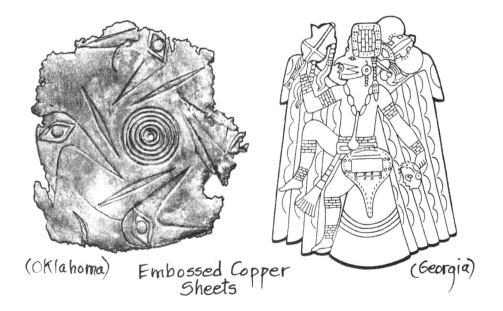

(Oklahoma)   Embossed Copper
                    Sheets   (Georgia)

2. The early Mississippi Mound Builders, who lived at present-day Cahokia, Illinois, etched designs into shells. These designs included snakes, vultures, and eagles, and were often involved with death—such as the "weeping eye" symbol seen in their art. (They shared some designs with Mexican artists of that time.)

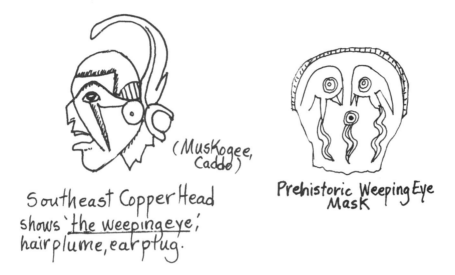

(Muskogee, Caddo)

Southeast Copper Head shows 'the weeping eye', hairplume, earplug.

Prehistoric Weeping Eye Mask

3. Many Eastern Woodland pipes were carved of steatite; some were carved from catlinite, a reddish-brown or pinkish-gray mineral named after George Catlin, famous 19th-century painter of early American Indian life. It comes mainly from a quarry in Minnesota. Through the ages native peoples all have shared this mine.

    When catlinite is first taken out of the ground, it is rather soft and easy to carve. With time, it hardens. Often it was used to make a pipe bowl that was then fitted to a wooden pipe stem.

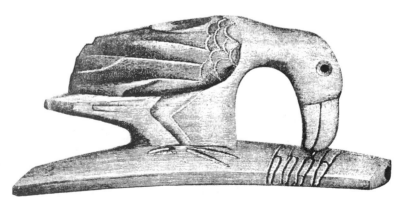

Prehistoric Carved Pipes

CHILDREN AND PLAY

CHILDREN

From the time of birth the Seneca child had a close relationship with corn. A fine powder made from dried corn was put on the newborn baby's navel. The young child slept on a mat woven of corn husks and played with dolls with cornsilk hair. Boys were encouraged to make war on other boys using "war clubs" made from cornstalks. Childhood illnesses were remedied with corn: for intestinal worms, a purifying tea made of corn ashes; for nosebleed, a distracting corn husk ring was wrapped around the distressed child's finger. When it came time to wash up, dried corn cobs were used to scrub off the dirt and grime of a busy day.

Seminole Baby Hammock

Children continued to be breast-fed until they were 3 or 4 years old. Mothers were loving in their treatment of youngsters, but were careful not to pamper them in a way that might weaken or soften them. Right from the first, all children were cautioned not to overeat: "If you ate too many corn cakes smothered in maple syrup, the bogeyman, Long Nose, would come and get you!"

Even very small children had chores that helped prepare them for being grownups. By the age of 8, every child knew what chores were expected of him or her. Girls helped in the longhouse or went into the fields and worked with the women. Boys went into the woods, often with a group of friends, and stayed there living off small game they could catch or roots and berries they gathered. During free time, girls and boys played together.[1]

Young boys all looked forward to going on a deer hunt with their uncles. But before this could happen (in the Northeast) the boy had to learn to shoot straight. An Iroquois boy's first lessons were with a tiny little bow; only a boy who never aimed at a person would be trusted with a larger bow and arrow. Next, a young boy had a series of challenges to meet.

First, he practiced shooting at a bear's paw that was hung from a tree branch. Then he had to shoot a flitting chickadee. He was next allowed to hunt a rabbit or a squirrel and, once he was successful, he would go out to shoot a grouse or a turkey. Only after shooting a large bird was he *then* taken on a deer (or a beaver) hunt! No wonder young boys all loved learning to use their hunting tools!

Once a boy had succeeded in killing a deer with his bow and arrows (with no outside help), he was allowed to come on adult hunting parties.

A young Southeastern boy practiced hunting and going to war; this was because until he had gotten a war title he was always thought of as a child and only fit to do chores. Once he had been on a battle and showed his bravery by killing, or at least hurting, an enemy, he joined the council, was treated as a man, and was given a new name. This name was often that of an animal that the boy seemed to resemble in some way. He also got a war title that spoke of his actions in battle.

Woodland Indian children learned through play. Their toys were miniatures of the tools and objects that their parents used. Often these tiny toys and dolls were lovingly made by a father or an aunt or uncle of the child. As the child played with his or her toys, the child learned to be neat and orderly. Each child had a certain place to put these toys. If a child failed—over time—to put away these playthings, they were swept into a trash hole and it was a long while before other little toys were made for this youngster.

Miniature Clay Pots

Children were taught never to yell in order to "get their way" and crying was not rewarded. Once a child could talk, she or he was shown that to ask for something in a nice way—rather than demanding or crying for it—would quickly bring attention and approval.

All children were taught "good manners." When a playmate was rude or impolite, he or she was rejected by the other children and left to play all alone until good behavior had returned.

Children of the Northeast and Southeast were not whipped or spanked. The only physical punishment commonly used was throwing water on the child or plunging the child into water (to stop a tantrum and bring the child to his or her senses).

GAMES

Both girls and boys played games. Lacrosse was played by most Eastern tribes. In the south, stickball, similar to Lacrosse, was played sometimes on the very chunkey (ball) yards of their ancestors.

Southeastern Lacrosse: Istaboli (or Tolik)

Of all the games they played, this was the favorite of all the Southeastern peoples, including the Choctaw. A big game between two villages of neighboring tribes might bring out a thousand people to watch! The spectators began arriving two to three days before the game, loaded down with skins, furs, and jewelry to bet on the match.

The night before the big game, both sides met with their medicine men, drank holy medicine, sang, and danced—to give their team strength and to weaken the other team.

The next morning the game began as the two teams (of hundreds of players) came toward each other from opposite directions, each shouting promises of strength, fleetness, and victory over the opponent. When an old man threw the skin-covered ball onto the field, the play was on!

So began a bloody struggle that could last for hours. Each player had two net sticks.[2] The object of this game was for one team to try and throw a ball into their opponent's goal and for the other team to try and keep it out of its own goal, throwing it into the other goal! Each team tried very hard to get the ball as it was flung through the air or carried on the net stick by a runner. In order to get the ball, almost anything was allowed: kicking, tripping, tackling, hitting, stomping on a fallen player—no wonder this game could end in serious injuries, and even death.

When a point was made, the successful ones would scream insults at their opponents and make fun of them by gobbling like turkeys! This would enrage the other team and the battle would go on. The game ended when one team scored a certain number of points—usually 12.

Iroquois Lacrosse Stick

The Winnebago players used single sticks to play lacrosse. The Iroquois used a long hook-shaped stick with netting over the end, and the Southeastern tribes played with two sticks that each had a small net on one end.

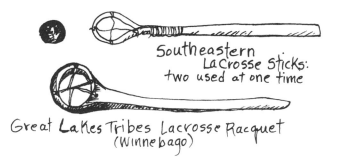

Southeastern Lacrosse Sticks: two used at one time

Great Lakes Tribes Lacrosse Racquet (Winnebago)

Ground Hockey

This game was played by both girls and boys. In fact, there were mixed teams among the Sauk and the Assiniboin.

The idea was for the player to drive the ball into the opponent's goal; the opponent, of course, tried to prevent this. Sticks with curved ends were used to move the ball.

Bowl Guessing Game

The Algonquins and the Iroquois played this guessing game during certain hours of religious ceremonies. They used a small round bowl and four to six round flat playing pieces, one side black and one side natural.

Stakes were put up by each side.

An equal number (70 to 80) of red-bean (point) counters went to each team.

To play: All the round pieces were turned, natural side up, in the bowl. The first player on a team took the bowl, shook it hard, and—with a whack—overturned it onto a pile of hides. If all the pieces showed the same color, the player got 10 points (ten red beans were given to him by the other team). If all but one piece showed the same color, the player got 5 points (five beans); if two pieces showed the same color, the player got two beans. Play continued until one team got all the beans—although sometimes the game had to be given up by agreement because it was lasting more than four days! The winners took the stakes[3] of their opponents.

A variation was played by the Iroquois using two-sided peach pits in a bowl. The player struck the side of the bowl causing the pits to "jump"; the number of dark sides showing provided the player with points.

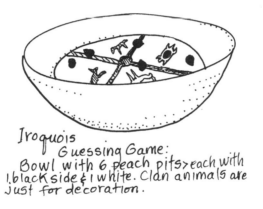

Iroquois
Guessing Game:
Bowl with 6 peach pits, each with
1 black side & 1 white. Clan animals are
just for decoration.

TOYS

During winter months children played inside the Northern wigwam where

> "...the winter evenings were social and pleasant. The fire burned brightly...a favorite pastime was the making (and playing with) birch bark transparencies... The young men reclined in the wigwam and always had a drum conveniently near them...Winter was a time for enjoying story-telling and many old women were experts in this art. One old woman used to act out her stories running around the fire and acting while she talked."

> —Frances Densmore, 1929

These little toy transparencies were held up to the light, which illuminated them and gave them life.

Birch bark
Cut outs
(Transparencies)

Early Woodland parents loved their children and gave them miniatures of their own adult tools and utensils with which to play. Tiny bowls and baskets, little bows and blunt-nosed arrows, tiny axes and grinders were each carefully fashioned and beautifully decorated.

Algonquin

Choctaw

Iroquois

Miniatures for Children to Enjoy   Cherokee

Catawba

A toss-and-catch toy was played with, in some form, by all the Woodland groups. The Chippewa toy shown here has a long bone needle tied by a sinew to several bone cones and a buckskin flap with holes that it could pierce and catch.

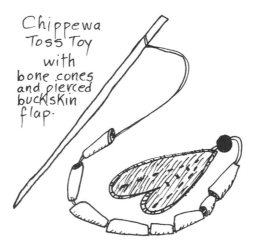

Chippewa
Toss Toy
with
bone cones
and pierced
buckskin
flap.

The Winnebago child tossed hollow deer bones up in the air and tried to catch them on a long bone pin. This game helped to improve a child's hand-and-eye coordination—as well as his ability to be patient!

The Chippewa made a child's toy that was naturally soft and cuddly. They stuffed an entire gray squirrel's skin, tail included, with wild rice!

Notes on "Children and Play":

1. Often this play could be erotic or suggestive in its actions.

2. These net sticks differed among the tribes. The Huron and Iroquois used a racquet much like the one used today except that it didn't have a flattened net end. The Chippewa used a small netted ring tied to, or bent from, the end of the handle. The Southeastern tribes used two sticks with nets.

3. Gambling games were enjoyed by people of all tribes of the East and South. Some popular playing pieces included painted bone counters, dice made from deer ankle bones, and marked bone chips (these were tossed from a basket onto a hide).

    Once in awhile gambling "got out of hand," as may happen in any culture, and it did sometimes happen that a player would bet—and sometimes lose—the very clothes "off his back"!

RELIGION AND BELIEFS

To the Woodland peoples religion was not a separate part of their lives; it was present at all times, in all things. This unseen force was stronger than humans and people needed its power to find game, win battles, and change bad luck.

There was a Great Spirit who created everything: this all tribes believed. Many tribes saw the Sun as being a special power or force. There were living spirits in all natural things as well: They warmed a person, led you, healed you; they answered your prayers with rainfalls or sunrises.

The Mohawks believed there was an energy or force, called "orenda" that was available to each of us. It could be collected and saved up, to later be used to help a person overcome hard times.

These early people believed that one way to be in touch with this powerful unseen world was through the help of a guardian spirit.

A wooden carved
Personal Dream Guardian
(Wisconsin)

Each tribe had its own creation stories to explain how the world and their people came to be. Each tribe performed ceremonies following the instructions given in their sacred stories. (Dancing was a very important form of worship.) Such rituals healed the sick, renewed ties with spiritual beings, brought rain and success in growing crops and hunting, and gave thanks for the harvests. Some ceremonies were performed to insure that the natural world

116

and all life would continue; these were known as "renewing the world" and were usually involved with restoring balance.

Religious practices were closely linked to natural formations: sacred lakes, high and isolated sites, where the people would go to fast, pray, receive guidance, and be in touch with spirits—of plants, animals, and their ancestors.

COMING-OF-AGE RITES

Most tribes had special rites for marking the time when young boys and girls became young adults.

At the age of 12 or so a Seneca boy might go into the woods with an old man of his tribe; there he would test his strength, his manliness. The older man made the boy throw himself against rocks until he bled. He then had to rub his whole body with dirt and ashes. Each night he would remember his dreams so that he could report them in detail to the old man. This elder would explain their meanings to the boy and tell him, from these dreams, who his guardian spirit was. When they returned to their village, the boy would find a rock or a piece of bone that reminded him of his guardian spirit and he would carry this fetish (symbol) with him from then on.

When a Delaware boy reached the age of 12 or 13, he took part in a ritual that brought him officially into manhood. This rite was called the Youth's Vigil. It required that he spend many days alone in the woods, without food. This tested his self discipline and forced him to feel the comforting—as well as challenging—forces of nature. At the end of his stay, the boy was expected to have visions, dreams that would prepare him for, and protect him during, his adult life.

Girls might also have dreams of special spirit-helpers. Among the Great Lakes tribes a young girl, at 12 or 13 (when she had her first menstrual cycle) went into a hut outside the village. She fasted and waited. She prayed for help in finding a good husband, having good health, and lots of children; if she were lucky enough to be visited by a guardian spirit, that was especially fortunate!

Sculpted Stone Effigy
It may represent an
ancestor, a guardian spirit.
Found from Mississippi to
Georgia.   (Prehistoric)

MEDICINE MEN AND WOMEN

A strong vision could lead someone to become a medicine man or a medicine woman.[1] This was a person with special gifts for telling the future, understanding sickness, preventing trouble, and bringing victory in battle. Each was trained in the use of healing plants, and how to set bones and drive out evil. Because of their vision, their knowledge, and powers, they were seen as bridges between this world and the world of the spirits.

There were three types of medicine persons: the conjurer or magician, the sucking doctor, and the Morning Star Man. The conjurer used the shaking tent to cure illness (he could also cause sickness and death), to tell the future, and to find lost people and objects. (Also see **Shelter** for more about the shaking tent.)

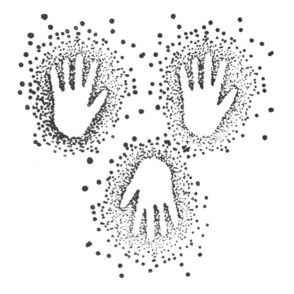

Inside the tent it was believed that the *conjurer* spoke with the spirits that had come in through the hole in the top of the tent. Their arrival was seen when the tent began shaking.

The *sucking doctor* only had one job: to cure the sick. This was done by sucking from the sick person's body the object that was causing the sickness. The sucking doctor used a thin bone tube to suck out the object magically.

The *Morning Star Man* or wa-pano was a very important shaman at one time long ago. He supplied hunting medicine and love powders (to bring the desired one to you at once) and he practiced feats of magic such as holding red hot stones or plunging his hands into boiling liquids such as maple syrup. (This wa-pano medicine person no longer is a practicing shaman among the Eastern tribes.)

NORTHEASTERN BELIEFS

The Iroquois have two kinds of religious ceremonies: one to honor and mark the growing of crops, and the other involved with curing and preventing sickness. This was handled by the so-called medicine societies.[2]

The religious life of the Western Lakes tribes (the Chippewa, Menominee, Sauk-Fox, Winnebago, Kickapoo, and Potawatomi) was centered on the ceremonials of the Midewiwin, the Medicine Lodge Society. This important group taught that good behavior (kindness to women, calmness in actions and speech) would lead to a long life, while evil actions (loudness, lying, stealing, drunkenness) would eventually have bad effects on the wrong-doer.

The Midewiwin Society and Ceremony

In the late spring or early fall the Midewiwin ceremony was usually held, and it lasted for as long as five days. The purpose of this ceremony was to lengthen life, cure and ward off illness, or to bring someone into the Society who may have had a dream telling him to become a member. To belong to the Midewiwin was believed to bring the soul eternal life.

To join the Midewiwin Society (once you had your dream telling you to do so), you had to pay a high fee—many blankets, robes or vessels—which were later given to the priests or Midewiwin helpers; you were also expected to give several feasts to which the priests and helpers came. Then you were given a cowry shell that you always had to wear and the priests gave you special lessons in the secrets of the society. Finally you went through the ceremony itself.

An important part of the Midewiwin Ceremony was the Grand Medicine Dance. Members danced around a lodge that had been draped with mats. They chanted as they danced, throwing cowrie shells at the brand new members.[3] If a shell should hit a new member, he would believe the shell had gone *into* his body and he would fall to the ground, twist-

<u>Mide Bag</u>
Made from an otter skin, it held curing charms, herbs, and shells. It belonged to a member of the Midewiwin Society and was, on his death, buried with him.

ing and turning until he lost consciousness. Then as the magic of the shell began to work, the man would rise up, healthy and completely renewed in energy.

Next he was given a Mide (medicine) bag. There were four levels of importance in the Midewiwin Society and each had its own type of bag: first level was a beaver, mink, otter, or muskrat skin bag; second level, an owl or hawk; third level, a snake and fox or wild cat claw; fourth level, a bear paw or a bear cub. The special secret things inside the bag would bring power and energy to the owner.

Once the new members had been brought into the society, they all marched around the Mide lodge, "shooting" each other with cowrie shells, and left by the west door, each carrying his Mide bag with him.

SOUTHEASTERN BELIEFS

In the Southeastern early people's world opposites were always at war. Their world was balanced between the perfection and order of the Upper World (which included known boundaries and a complete purity) and the chaos and threat of the Lower World (where things were always changing, fertile, and on the brink of misfortune *and* of invention!).

In the very beginning only the Upper and Lower Worlds existed. Once This World was made, some of the animals and superhumans tried living here on Earth, but they were uncomfortable because of the lack of complete order, so they went back up to their world. This left people to live in This World along with some good friends (the plants) and some natural enemies (the animals). Among the enemies was a monster called Uktena, who was completely evil; it looked like an enormous horned snake with bird wings and a huge diamond on his forehead. Just to *see* it was to bring on disaster to oneself and one's loved ones![4]

UKtena

Their greatest god was the sun whom they saw as a female. On This World her symbol was fire, which the Cherokees saw as an old woman to whom they always gave a bit of each of their meals. This sacred fire was always burning in the main building of each village. Women went to it to get fire for their individual homes.

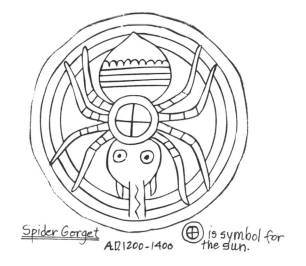

Spider Gorget A.D. 1200-1400 ⊕ is symbol for the sun.

In order to try and find a path and a life that could balance between the energies of the Upper and Lower Worlds, the Southeastern tribes tried to use good to counter evil whenever they could. This is one of the reasons they always used plants and herbs to treat illness, disease, and injury.

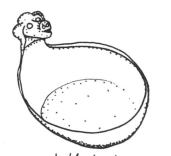

This carved Medicine Bowl was used in the Midewiwin Ceremony. It was 7"x13" and had a bear carved as a handle.

The Green Corn Ceremony, or the Busk

In the Southeast early people each year held a puskita (the Busk), a green corn festival to honor the ripening and harvesting of the second corn crop and to celebrate the renewal of life on Earth. It was a feast of thanksgiving, marking the beginning of the new year. Each Northeastern group celebrated this time in its own way.

To begin the Busk, the women put out their fires, cleaned their houses and cooking utensils, and remained apart from any of the men in the tribe. The community buildings were repaired by the men and no one was allowed to eat any of the just-ripened corn. It was the time for making new pots and new fires and getting rid of the old ones. Longstanding fights and disagreements were also set aside.

Among the Creeks only a few men and women could take part in the main ceremonies: these were Chiefs, wise elders, or young warriors who had been outstanding in their bravery. The elders and the chiefs drank a special tea made from the leaves of the cassina plant; this cleaned out their bodies and made their minds more clear. This was followed by a meal and then the lighting of the holy fire by the high priest.

The honored dancers all carried branches, and the women wore shell rattles on their legs; they circled the sacred fire to the sound of drums and chanting. Those not dancing sat and watched from open three-sided shelters. The Chief sat in the middle with his advisors around him and the elders sat in their own shelter; across from them the most important warriors—faces and chests painted red—watched from their own structure.

Once the Green Corn Dance was finished, the rest of the villagers came to the square. Coals from the sacred fire were used to relight the fires in each of the homes and the women now began making a huge meal.

Finally everyone in the village went to a nearby stream where they all washed to clean themselves for the new year. From there they gathered together at the feast!

MASKS

Masks were an important part of religious ceremonies because they replaced the human face with a supernatural one.

The Native American has always believed that to wear a mask was to become the spirit of the mask—to have his own personality become part of the character he is representing.

This large shell mask (which may have been a pendant) was of a type that was often made in prehistoric times; it probably was used for religious ceremonies.

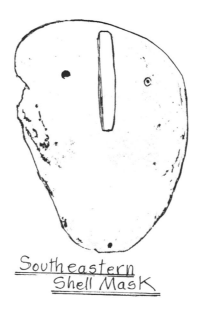

Southeastern
Shell Mask

The Iroquois believed in a world in which good and evil were both a part of all nature. They thought that invisible spirits were everywhere. Some of these were the False Faces,[5] scary devil-like spirits that could cause disease. It was lucky that these powers could be reversed, and even used by medicine men who knew the secrets of the False Face Society.[6] They used the power that *caused* the illness to bring about its *cure*!

False Faces cured people by yelling, repeating secret sayings and sprinkling ashes around the sick person. The Iroquois understood the power of the mind and the influence it had over the body and its health.

False Face Masks in these illustrations show the features common to this kind of mask: deep wrinkles, twisted eyes and mouths, and shaggy hair.

Iroquois

The Cayuga-Onondaga "divided mask" is very, very old.

Cayuga-Onondaga Divided Mask

The Great One is often shown in mask form. The Seneca made masks from woven corn husks that were worn by members of the Huskface Society. They cut corn husks into strips, braided these, and sewed them into flat coils that they wet and molded to form face-like shapes.

Seneca Corn husk
Mask

When the Huskfaces performed their sacred dances in the fall and winter, they carried hoes and digging sticks.

The Cherokee "booger mask" was most unusual. Carved of wood, it was meant to show an evil being.

(Bogey Man)
Booger Mask
(Cherokee)

Gourds were also used by the Cherokee for masks.

Gourd Mask
(Cherokee)

In 1896 F. H. Cushing discovered a large group of more than twenty prehistoric carved wooden pieces in Key Marco, Florida. Twenty were face-sized masks; around the edges were little holes through which fibers or feathers were inserted. These masks show how advanced those early artists were.

Painted Wooden Masks
(Key Marco, Florida)
Two of the 20 full-sized face masks found by F. H. Cushing in 1896. They had holes for attaching feathers or string and dated from prehistoric times.

THE SACRED PIPE AND TOBACCO

The pipe—and the tobacco for it—had a very important place in Woodland Indian ceremonies. The Ojibwa tribe offered smoke from their pipes to the Great Sky Spirit. The Iroquois scattered crumbled sacred tobacco on their holy fires during religious ceremonies. There were strict rules as to who could light the pipe and how it was to be done. There was a certain way to hold the pipe, to pass it, and to store it when it wasn't being used.

Here the Natchez carry their calumet to the shelter where the Europeans are waiting. There they will smoke the peace pipe together.

The calumet, or sacred pipe, was named by the French who first saw it, calling it *chalumeaux,* "a tube or reed." In the mid 1600s Jacques Marquette, a French explorer, wrote of the calumet:

> "There is nothing more mysterious or respected...less honor is paid to the crowns and scepters of kings...It has to be but carried on one's person and displayed, to enable one to walk through the midst of enemies,...who in the hottest fight, lay down their arms when it is shown."

Not every man had his own pipe. A chief, however, would have several, with one that was especially powerful and used only when the most difficult decisions had to be made. This calumet was the tribe's most sacred belonging; it was cared for by a special attendant who was responsible for its correct use.

DEATH AND THE AFTERLIFE

On the whole the Woodlands people saw death as part of the cycle of nature.

> "Thus a man is born and for a time becomes a cannibal, eating and taking energy from his fellow creatures; when his soul and shadow leave his body, Earth Mother takes it back to nourish the plants which in turn feed both animals and men. His debt is repaid, his spirit freed, and the cycle of life complete."

> —from *Art of the Great Lakes Indians*
> by Charles E. Cleland, 1973, Flint Institute of Arts, Flint, Michigan

They mourned their dead and respectfully prepared their bodies for the funeral ceremonies to make sure that the spirits of the dead could make the journey to the Next World and to the afterlife it promised.

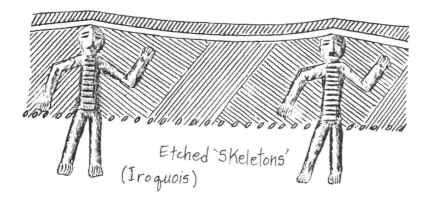

Etched `Skeletons'
(Iroquois)

The Ojibwa buried each body dressed in its best clothing and surrounded by a supply of food and tobacco for the four-day journey to the Land of Souls where Nanabush ruled. This was, they believed, a place of contentment where the souls hunted, enjoyed good food, and danced together joyously.

Carved effigy figures have been found in burials. The Chippewa often placed small wooden owls or hawks in with the body when it was put into its grave.

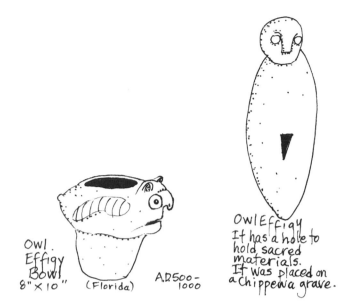

Owl.
Effigy
Bowl
8" x 10"   (Florida)   A.D.500-1000

OwlEffigy
It has a hole to
hold sacred
materials.
It was placed on
a Chippewa grave.

Funerals

The Iroquois buried objects such as tools and jewelry with their dead. Following a death, the family fasted for ten days; the widow(er) could not marry for a year.

The Hurons held a feast of the dead during which the men literally carried on their backs the corpses of those who had died in the last year. They brought them to a common burial pit; the Hurons believed that this mingling of ancestral bones insured that the people of the tribe would all live together at peace with one another.

The Algonquins believed that death set one's spirit free. After death the spirit went to a place where there was no sorrow or pain. The dead person's body was put in a shallow grave[7], without any casket, as a coffin might keep the soul from traveling to the next world. Dead souls lived, they believed, in a place to themselves that was like this world except that *there* was no sickness or sadness of any kind. (See Photo 16.)

The Natchez of the South, now extinct, believed in life after death. Their idea of heaven was a place where everyone enjoyed every physical pleasure including eating, drinking, laughing, dancing, and singing. Hell for the Natchez was a boggy swampland filled with swarms of mosquitoes and the only foods available were rotting fish and crocodile meat!

Notes on "Religion and Beliefs":

1. The Iroquois believed that dreams were very important and that when you understood your dreams, then you would understand yourself! If an Iroquois had trouble with a dream, he or she could go to a special seer, usually a woman, who was skilled in understanding and explaining dreams and who would listen carefully and patiently. Such Iroquois wise women were said to be able "to see right into one's soul."

2. Scientists have found that words involved with healing ceremonies are much older than those that are concerned with crops. This seems to suggest that the Iroquois have lived in the Northeast—where medicine societies are so important—for a long time (and that they did *not* come from the South, bringing farming with them, as was once thought).

3. These shells, called "midis," were often in medicine bags. They were believed to bring the spirit power into the man whose body they had struck!

Photo 16. 1725 sketch of Natchez funeral ceremony. The bier with Great War Chief Tattooed Serpent's body seems to have spiraled up from the mound at the bottom for its burial in the earthwork at top. *Courtesy Smithsonian Institution.*

4. This idea of a horned serpent may very well have been influenced by the Mexican "plumed serpent" images brought by trading groups.

5. The Iroquois have two stories to explain how they first got the False Faces:

A. As the Creator walked around the earth looking at his works, suddenly an enormous stone head came flying up to him. It said "You seem to think that you made all this— well, I'm here to say that I am the one who made this earth and all that's on it!"

The two decided to have a magical contest to decide the question: a mountain stood in the far-off distance and each would try to move it, and the one to move it closer would be the winner.

The Stone Head went first and he moved the mountain a little closer to the two of them. Then it was the Creator's turn, but the Stone Head lost his attention for a minute (that's the way he was) and looked away; when he turned back to watch, the mountain was rushing right *at* him and it smashed him in the face!

The Creator saw the now-twisted head and recognized that it did have some power, so he gave it the job of curing sickness. From then on men would always carve his crooked face and use it to heal illnesses.

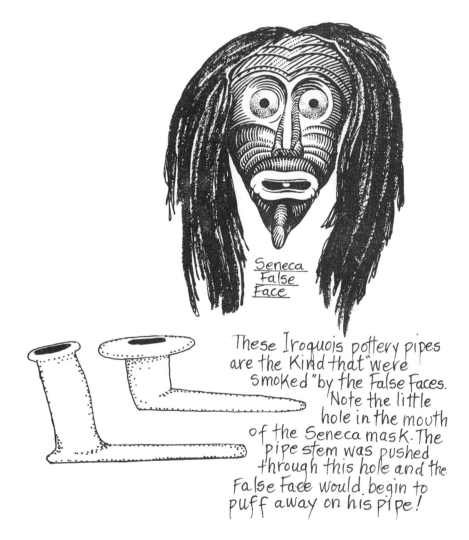

Seneca
False
Face

These Iroquois pottery pipes are the kind that were smoked "by the False Faces. Note the little hole in the mouth of the Seneca mask. The pipe stem was pushed through this hole and the False Face would begin to puff away on his pipe!

B. Long ago when hunters camped in the deep woods, they would sometimes catch sight of weird spirit beings with long scraggly hair. When the hunters returned to their camps at nightfall, they'd find the fire's ashes scattered about and big hand marks on the lodge pole.

One day a hunter decided to stay in camp while his buddy went out hunting. During that day he saw a twisted-faced fellow come into their camp, pick up hot ashes, and scatter them around. That night in his sleep the hunter saw the weird creature and it asked for an offering of tobacco and corn mush.

The next day the hunters put out this offering and the twisted-faced beings came and taught them their songs as well as how to cure illnesses by blowing on hot ashes.

Then the hunters carved masks of these creatures, each from the living trunk of a basswood tree. They always treated these masks with the greatest care and respect.

False Face CLOWN Mask

In this tale we see an upset of balance, a solution, and an agreement reached between the spirit world and the humans. Wearing the False Face masks is the symbol of this agreement/pact; it is also a magical prescription.

6. Their name came from the masks they wore; each mask was carved on a living basswood tree in order to receive the spirit it stood for. This spirit was drawn to the tree by the medicine man's chants; it went into the tree and found its face. Then the tree was spoken to by the carver as another man cut the tree down, sending the tree's life into the face—giving the mask life as well as spirit. The false face was then taken back to camp where it was completed.

7. When a chief of the Algonquins died, his skin was removed whole from the body. Then the meat was cut from the bones and these, still connected together by ligaments, were inserted back into the treated skin. This "body" was laid out in a special temple wigwam with other treated bodies of earlier chiefs. A *kewas*, a carved god figure, crouched beside the remains and protected them from harm. Under the platform was a deer skin, a place for the shaman to rest as he prayed for the chief's spirit.

TRADE

Trade between the Woodland tribes was very common. Most of it took place between the farming people and the hunting people and this was good for both groups. (There was little reason for a crop-growing tribe to trade with other farmers.)

The hunters offered dried meat, tanned skins, robes and clothing—often decorated with quillwork. In exchange they might receive beans, nuts, corn, squash, pumpkins, or wild vegetables—and depending on the season, these foods would be fresh or dried.

Once good weather arrived there was a steady stream of traders from the west (inland) and traffic up and down the Atlantic coastline. Each traveler carried at least one pouch of items for trade. When he entered a village, the trader was usually greeted warmly and, after silently sharing a pipe of tobacco (symbolizing the beginning of friendly relations), he would be feasted and there would be lots of conversation and laughter.

Iroquois Pipes

For centuries the Menominee of the Lake Michigan area traded with the Winnebago to the south. The Winnebago were buffalo hunters and farmers, raising corn, beans, squash, and tobacco. They would trade their extra buffalo hides, tobacco, and corn to the Menominee for wild rice and baskets or finger-woven sashes. These handicrafts often had striking geometric designs and were valuable trade items much prized by all the Great Lakes tribes.

Trading was direct and easy-going. You would spend a day or two in pleasant bargaining and return home with the goods—both parties happy with the outcome.

The spot where two rivers met was always a natural place for a permanent village to be built. Also natural is the fact that such a village would become a trading center, serving traders who arrived from either direction, along each river. This was true in prehistoric times in the woodlands—and continued to be so even after the Europeans arrived.

Riverways and forest trails crisscrossed the Eastern woodlands. Trade (and with it, unhappily, disease) flowed along these trails. In 1568 David Ingram, an English sailor shipwrecked in Mexico, was able to follow the native system of roads and walk all the way from Mexico clear up to the Atlantic seacoast in "about eleaven monethes in the whole!"

(Panther Pattern)

(Thunderbird Pattern)

Menominee Woven Patterns

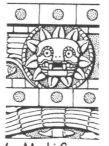

(Sash: Finger Woven)

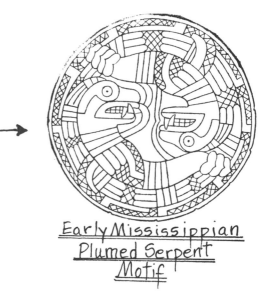

Mexican Plumed Serpent Motif
    Through trade this image—
and religious concept— was
brought up to the Woodlands
Indians where they changed it
a bit to suit <u>their</u> needs.

Early Mississippian
Plumed Serpent
Motif

SOCIAL ORDER AND GOVERNMENT

In early times the organization of the Woodlands tribes varied a great deal from group to group. For example, the early Chippewa-Ojibwa had a classless society that was very loosely organized. A man got a place of power or importance by being a fine warrior, having a good speaking style, or strong supernatural powers. On the other hand, the Huron had male Village and War chiefs while the Miami had both male and female chiefs.

Some Eastern Indian tribes were patrilineal (children inherited through the father), while other tribes were matrilineal (the children inherited through their mothers).

SOCIAL UNITS

The first unit was the *family:* mother, father, unmarried children. The second unit was the *band:* several families living together. Usually 20 to 50 people were in a band. The leader of a band had powers and duties that were based on family ties.

Together, several such bands would make up a *tribe,* which also was loosely organized, the members having a language and customs in common, as well, perhaps, as political views.

In the Southeast the people lived in rather wandering settlements. The town had a main square around which were the public and religious buildings. These included: the chief's house and other houses of important people, the temple or community center and, sometimes, storage buildings for the village's produce. The villages were often at a little distance from the square. Each town was self-governing and was really very much like a tribe.

Within each tribe would be several *clans:* groups made up of people who had special family ties to one another. Most often these clans had animal names. The Seneca clans, for example, were called Turtle, Bear, Beaver, Wolf, Snipe, Hawk, Deer, and Heron. The clan animal or "totem" (from the Algonquin word for "kinsman") was a special helper to each person in his clan.

Clans were useful within a tribe because their members were close to one another and they worked well together. Also, one clan could have members living among several different tribes and that helped tribes bond with one another.

In the Southeast, clans were important as a method of social control; it was often the duty of a clan to take revenge for a serious crime committed against one of its members.

Members of a clan could not marry within it. Among the Iroquois, Huron, and Delaware, clans were matrilineal: a child at once belonged to the clan of his mother. Patrilineal clans were found among the Miami, Winnebago, and many other upper Great Lakes (Central) Algonquin tribes; a child in these tribes belonged to the clan of his father.

In some groups (e.g., Winnebago and Iroquois) the clans were grouped into *moieties* (halves) that shared certain responsibilities. For example, among the Iroquois, the members of one moiety buried the dead of the other moiety. The men of one moiety also would marry women from the opposite moiety. Some tribes such as the Chippewa-Ojibwa did not have moieties.

SOCIAL ORDER

Northeast

Among the Delaware, and this was usually true of the Woodlands peoples, everyone had a certain role in tribal life. The men hunted, fished, cut down trees, cured sicknesses, and protected the tribe. The women planted and harvested the foods, made clothing, cared for the children, and did the cooking. Even young children helped with household chores. (See **Children and Play**.)

Among the early Beothuk, except for hunting which was done by men, there were no "women's jobs" or "men's work." All tasks were shared by everyone.

Southeast

In the Southeast the idea of balance in social affairs was also important. It was strengthened by bringing opposing groups or clans together to go on hunts, trading trips, or to play in ball games with each other.

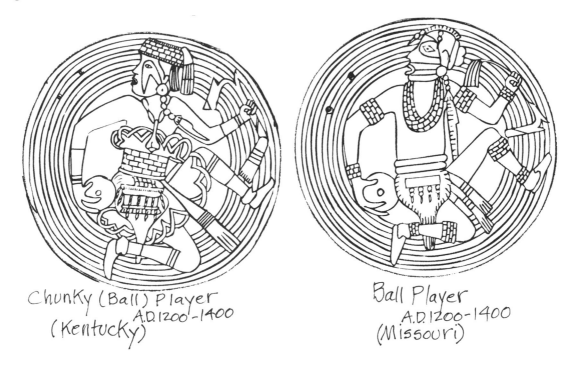

Chunky (Ball) Player   Ball Player
A.D. 1200-1400   A.D. 1200-1400
(Kentucky)   (Missouri)

As far as wealth was concerned, there was little "property," almost no stored wealth, and only a little trading was done by these southern people.

Inheritance was, as a rule, through the female side of the family—from mother to daughters: or if there were no girl children, from mother to her sister's daughters.

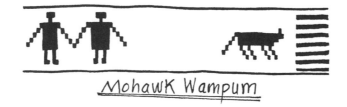

Mohawk Wampum

MARRIAGE AND DIVORCE

Northeast

Social arrangements, marriage, and divorce were often simple. To marry, a man and woman just began living together. Perhaps the parents had arranged for this to happen. The young man might give his new in-laws a few gifts, but this was about all of the wedding formalities that there were.

In some tribes, such as the Huron, a man had just one wife; in others, a man had as many wives as he could support—usually two or three.

To divorce, the couple just stopped living together. The woman kept the children and the house.

Southeast

Marriage was marked by the man giving his bride a gift of game and the woman presenting her new husband with vegetables. Then the man would move in with his wife's family. From that time on he was expected to bring game home for everyone. After a few years the couple might move out into their own home.

Divorce was quite common and almost casual. A man might take a second wife but only with the consent of the first wife. Often a widow would marry her dead husband's brother. (In time this custom came to be very practical as men were more frequently killed during the wars with the Europeans.)

Skull (Death) Design
found on pottery

LEADERSHIP

Tribal Chiefs or Sachems

Chieftainships were often passed from father to son or, if there were no son, to a nephew.

Usually each clan had a Peace Chief (Village Chief) and a War Chief, so the several Village Chiefs took care of village concerns and peace affairs.[1]

The several War Chiefs handled the village's affairs of conflict. (For more on the roles of the War Chiefs, see **War.**)

In the Southeast chieftainships were usually inherited. The degree of a chief's power varied from the godlike power of the Natchez's Sun to the soft-spoken, peace-making Ukus of the Creek, Cherokee, and Choctaw.

When signing treaties with the
Europeans, the Seneca drew their clan
totems as shown above: turtle, bear,
and 3 birds — which may be hawk and
snipes.

There was a balance of power in all aspects of governing in the Southeast. The War Chief was young, active, and assertive. The Peace Chief, twenty years older, was more measured in thinking and action. In the village the Peace Chief was the most important leader, while the War Chief was the more important when the people had concerns or dealings outside the village.

Councils

Tribal councils could be political or religious, as American Indians did not see a big difference between the two.

Often village affairs were run by two councils, each with different members and duties. No women were in these councils.

A council opened with the smoking of a pipe.[2] In the Midwest this practice became the Calumet Ceremony used to greet strangers.

Early Woodlands leaders were extraordinary speakers: poetic, intelligent, sarcastic by turns. Each chief, or sachem, had to speak well—as no action could be taken until every council member was in agreement. If complete agreement was not reached, there would be no action. It was through persuasive speech that consensus could be reached.[3]

CONFEDERACIES

Confederacies were groups of tribes that came together for a common purpose, whether to fight a war against a shared enemy or to keep the peace among themselves. The Huron Confederacy was made up of four to five tribes of the same general territory. The clan system with its various chiefs helped cut across any possible tribal divisions.

In the Southeast, villages could come together to form confederacies (e.g., the Creek and Choctaw) that were directed by councils. Such confederacies were loosely formed and might break apart and then recombine at some later time.

On the other hand, some confederacies lasted for centuries, as was the case with the most famous of them all, The League of the Iroquois. (See Photo 17.)

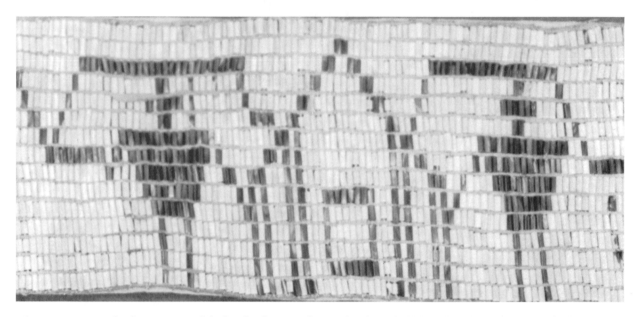

Photo 17. Detail of ceremonial belt of white and purple clamshell beads. This wampum belt honors a peacemaking council between the Iroquois League (the longhouse on belt) and the American colonies (the 13 fires). *Courtesy New York State Museum.*

The League of the Iroquois

The five nations of the league—the Seneca, Mohawk, Onondaga, Cayuga, and Oneida—were geographically connected by the Iroquois Trail in upper New York State. To show how close they felt as a group, they always spoke of themselves as "a Longhouse of Five Fires."

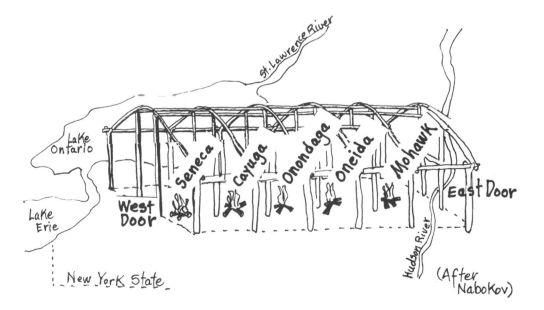

Their territory *was* their Longhouse: the eastern "door" was guarded by the Mohawk; the Seneca were keepers of the western "door"; the southern "walls" were watched by the Cayuga while the Oneida kept guard over the northern "walls." In the middle of their great shelter were the Onondaga, the symbolic "keepers of the Longhouse's fire."

This confederacy was founded to make and keep peace among these five Iroquois-speaking tribes.[4] (See **War**.) The legendary founders were the holy man Dekanawidah and Hiawatha.[5] Until recently it was thought that the league was founded in the 16th century; scholars have found evidence that may prove the league is at least 300 years older![6]

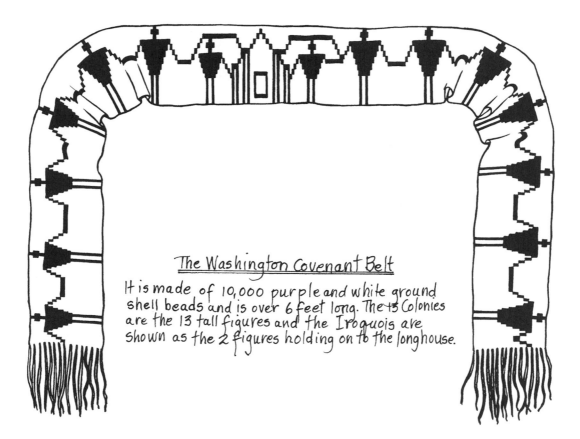

The Washington Covenant Belt

It is made of 10,000 purple and white ground shell beads and is over 6 feet long. The 13 Colonies are the 13 tall figures and the Iroquois are shown as the 2 figures holding on to the longhouse.

The members of the League together created a formal constitution that, among many subjects, stated the specific prices for committing murder:

10 strings of wampum beads for the life of a man

20 strings of wampum for the life of a woman

These fines were paid by the family of the murderer to the family of the victim. The actual cost was: 20 strings of wampum for the killing of a man: 10 for the victim's life and, since the murderer was considered as good as dead, 10 additional strings for *his* own life. (The murder of a woman actually cost 30 wampum strings, to pay for her death and to buy back the killer's life.)

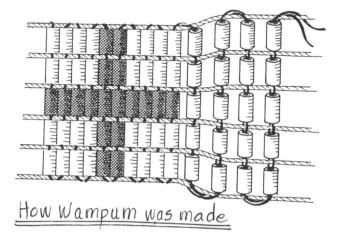

How Wampum was made

Before the League was formed, tribes would go to war whenever they felt the price offered for a murder was not a fair one. The fixing of the price kept the members of the League, from then on, from warring with one another over such a concern.

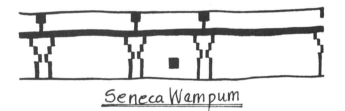

Seneca Wampum

HOW THE LEAGUE OF FIVE NATIONS WORKED   The five nations, or states, all spoke the same language and had similar cultural traditions. Each tribe governed itself and there was very little, if any, League interference.

Once a year the Great Council met at Onondaga, the main Onondaga tribal village, and there decided and discussed larger problems of government. Traditionally this meeting was held on a hill beneath the Tree of Great Peace; the Great Council Fire burned nearby, the rising smoke of which told everyone that the council was meeting and responsible men were taking care of tribal questions.

Forty-nine tribal members sat each on a thistle-down cushion: 14 Onondagas, 10 Cayugas, 9 Mohawks, 9 Oneida, and 8 Senecas. The numbers did not refer to the size or power of the tribe and did not change resolutions—since agreement on any question had to be unanimous.

There were actually 50 thistle-down cushions under the Tree of Peace. Hiawatha was seen as so irreplaceable that no one would ever take his position; because he had been a Mohawk the empty pillow was a part of that delegation.

Although the Council was all men, the 49 seats were filled by men chosen by women (just as was done by the mothers of the first chiefs who were brought together by Hiawatha) who also briefed them before each meeting, watched their progress and behavior and, if necessary, removed them from office.

The council meeting lasted for more than two weeks, until every member had his (often very lengthy) say. No action could be taken until all the members had reached agreement.

With time The Iroquois League became so powerful that it controlled the valleys and forested hills from the St. Lawrence River to Lake Champlain. Although founded to bring peace to its members, it also brought war to other tribes. When beaver (the most valuable fur used in trading) became scarce, the Iroquois went to war with their neighbors over trapping grounds. Between 1649 and 1675, they attacked and defeated the Tionontatl, Neutral, Erie, and Susquehanna. During the 17th century, the League of Five Nations was all powerful and remained so until the time of the American Revolution. (See **The Europeans Come**.)

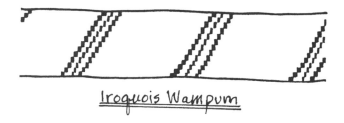

Iroquois Wampum

Ceremonial belts of purple and white clam shell beads (called wampum belts) were made to honor important historical or religious events.

The Hiawatha Belt was made to honor the forming of The Iroquois League. The inter-connecting squares are joined to the tree (of Great Peace) or the heart in the middle of the belt. This was to show the unity of the five Iroquois tribes (See **The Europeans Come** for more information on wampum belts.)

The Hiawatha Belt
This wampum belt honors the formation
of the Iroquois League; the squares are
the tribes, the tree linking the tribes
together.

Notes for "Social Order and Government":

1. Among the Miami the Peace Chiefs could not go on war parties or show anger! Their property was available to anyone who needed it. Each spring these sachems received gifts of game and furs from the people of their village.

2. Smoking was sacred or part of Native American religious practice for at least 4,000 years. Stone pipes are often found in graves of Eastern Woodland peoples. Pipes were smoked to seal a peace agreement or an intertribal bargain.

3. Early American Indian leaders were often wonderful public speakers. They used wit, irony, and poetry in their speeches. The very name "Iroquois" used first by the French to describe this great confederacy came from their practice of ending their speeches with the words "hiro" and "kone." The first meant "I speak" or "I have spoken" and the second was an exclamation of joy—or of sorrow—depending on the content of the speech that had just been given. These two words were joined together and given a French pronunciation to become "Iroquois."

4. In the late 18th century, a sixth Iroquoian tribe, the Tuscarora, moved into the territory and joined the confederacy, making it into the League of Six Nations.

5. An early American Indian legend tells how the first person to speak out against the warring among the Iroquois tribes was a holy man named Dekanawidah. He was, the story says, born in the early 16th century of a virgin mother. In about 1570 he had a vision in which he saw the coming together of the Five Iroquois Nations. His message was the Iroquois warriors must stop fighting among themselves and come together and live in peace under the protection of the symbolic Tree of Great Peace.

   The Mohawk Hiawatha heard Dekanawidah's words and was so touched by them that he personally took them from tribe to tribe, paddling his white canoe from village to village. Hiawatha convinced the various Iroquois groups to "clasp the hands of their sister tribes so firmly that a falling tree should not sever them." This is how, according to tradition, the League of Five Nations came to be.

6. According to the research of Barbara Mann and Jerry Fields (of Toledo University, Ohio), which uses a combination of documentary sources, solar eclipse data, and Iroquois oral history, The Iroquois Confederacy's body of law was adopted by the Seneca (the last of the five nations to ratify it) on August 31, 1142. The ratification council convened at a site that is now a football field in Victor, New York. This site is called Gonandaga by the Seneca.

Delaware Wampum

WAR

In the east summer was the time for raids and war. As a rule this meant small conflicts—raids on other tribes, each of which gave the young men a chance to show their bravery, improve their rank, and get revenge for past wrongs. Generally this was a one-on-one kind of fighting or band-to-band warfare at most. Men died, but not in huge numbers.

War was a kind of ceremony, a ritual activity with accepted rules. There was far less killing and financial expense than was the case with the European wars of that time.

Etched Copper Plate, Etowah, Georgia

In most tribes each clan had a war chief. These men handled all the affairs of conflict. An outstanding warrior could be made a war chief. Some hereditary war chiefs, not suited for leading raids, may have mainly spent their time dealing with ceremonies and rituals of war. War chiefs were almost always men, but among the Miami a woman could inherit the position of war chief. In such a case she was responsible for preparing the supplies for war parties; she could demand the end to a blood feud or to a war that had gone on too long.

142

After agreeing in a war council to go on a raid, and before leaving for battle, the Huron would have a war feast prepared by the women. During this feast there would be singing and dancing by the young warriors and many war cries and insults to the enemy would be shouted.

Often in summer several hundred Huron would leave to attack an Iroquois (Seneca) village. The warriors would hunt and fish along the way. Once near the village they built temporary forts and they would take prisoner any children or women they came across. Then they would split up into small groups and sneak up to the village. During the attack that followed, the wooden ball-headed club was the main weapon used.[1] There weren't many deaths or injuries; this was mainly an opportunity for the young men to show their bravery. Soon the attackers would leave with their prisoners, going back to the forts they had made.[2] If help came from a nearby Iroquois village, the Hurons would leave for home.

Any wounded were carried home to the Huron village in basket slings, each on the back of a warrior. The wounded sat on the woven seat, legs under his chin, tightly bound in place. A tumpline ran across the carrier's forehead and back down under the seat of the sling. It was a *very* uncomfortable ride for the wounded man!

Iroquois means "terrifying man" in Algonkian.[3] The Iroquois warrior was well-trained and loved to fight. His tomahawk was "two foote and a halfe long" with a wooden ball on the end "as round and bigge as a football."

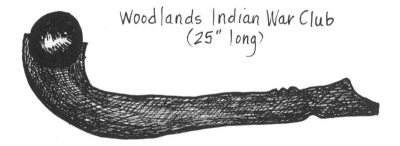

Woodlands Indian War Club
(25" long)

Many early Iroquois villages had tall wooden walls or stockades—and sometimes even moats—surrounding them. The tall fences were made of two tight rows of very tall tree trunks driven into the ground. These trunks crossed overhead and any spaces left below were filled in with logs. Where each two trunks crossed overhead, a plank was laid to make a walkway for the Indians. Each of these walks was protected by bark slabs. A ladder led up to the walks so the Iroquois warriors could climb up and shoot their arrows at the enemy down below.

When the Iroquois were returning in victory from a raid, they displayed scalps on poles as they entered their camp. Their prisoners were hand-cuffed with slave-straps and each was led by a leash from a collar around the neck.

A prisoner was tortured on the trail back to the Iroquois village; he was beaten, burned, jabbed, and bitten. Once at the village, the captive was stripped and was forced to run between rows of women and children who hit him with sticks and whips. If he was very brave during this beating, he might be adopted by an Iroquois family. Captive women and children were almost always adopted. If, however, the Iroquois women were very bitter about deaths of their men during the earlier battle, the prisoner was marked for death and faced hours of agony at the hands of his enemies.[4]

The prisoner was expected to meet his torture with silence and, near the end, with the singing of his own death songs.

Falcon Warriors
important to southern cult
A.D. 1200-1400
(Georgia)

Warrior with Apron Pouch
Holding ceremonial mace & a
severed head. A.D. 1200-1400
(Tennessee)

War Song[5]

Here on my breast have I bled!
See-see! There are fighting scars!
Mountains tremble at my yell!
I strike for life!

—OJIBWA

Before the Iroquois League was formed, most wars in the Northeast were about personal injuries. These revenge raids were at first small, but with time each side "needed" to kill more and more "enemies" until over the years there were so many scores to be settled on all sides that the tribes lived in a time of ever on-going war.

The Iroquois leaders realized that the Iroquois, though fierce fighters, were fewer in number than their neighbors, the Algonquin. The Iroquois elders saw that such constant warring, if it went on, could bring about their very end.

It was with this understanding that the five Iroquois tribes joined together making the Iroquois League of Nations—bringing peace to their tribes, if not to their neighbors. (See **Social Order and Government** for more information on the League.)

The early Southeastern peoples were made up of between 150 to 200 separate tribes and these were often at war. But fighting usually only happened on small raids between groups and few men were killed.

The Southeastern Indians believed strongly in taking revenge for any wrong-doing.[6] Even if it took years of planning and miles of travel, a murder had to be avenged. Many of the wars between chiefdoms were clan wars fought to gain revenge!

Before the warriors headed off to war, the members of the men's council of a chiefdom—the wise elders—met with the chief to discuss and debate what should be done. Once it was decided that they must go to war, the meeting was turned over to the Great Warrior who, with other older warriors, would begin to whip up the courage and anger of the young men.[7] A red

Roach Spreaders

Made of elk antler: the teeth of the spreader kept the porcupine roach spread out, the sockets & holes held feathers.

Porcupine Quill Roach: worn down the center of a warrior's scalp & held in place by Roach Spreader(s).

war club and red flag were displayed. Speeches were given; the women sang high-pitched war songs.

For three days the warriors stayed in the war leader's hut. There they fasted and drank teas to clean out their bodies. Always they heard war tales told by older men. They ate only deer meat (for swiftness in battle) and dog meat (for loyalty to their leaders).

The warriors painted themselves black and red and wore just loin cloths and moccasins. Then in single file, twenty to forty strong, they left their camp shouting war chants![8]

The warriors each kept a sharp eye out for any bad luck sign: an oddly shaped tree trunk, an unusual looking animal. If one were spotted, the war party would return to the village at once!

If no bad luck signs were observed, the war party would move on. As they neared the enemy camp, they became completely silent—in word and movement.

"They come like Foxes through the woods. They attack like lions. They take flight like birds."

—Written by a French Jesuit about 17th-century Indian warfare

Surprise was the main plan of attack used in war. The party split into small groups so they could reach the camp from several directions, surround the enemies, and trap them. The small groups used bird calls and animal cries to be in touch with one another. At the sound of the war leader's bone whistle, the war party attacked!

First they sent a rain of arrows; then—howling and screaming—they clubbed and stabbed their enemies. It could all be over in a matter of minutes; the winners left with scalps, an enemy head or two, and their prisoners.

Once back home, the warriors returned to the war leader's house, there to fast again to cleanse themselves after having shed human blood. After three days the men came out and decided what to do with the prisoners. There was no set rule. A captive could be adopted into a clan or he might be made a slave; if so, he was lamed or blinded so he could not ever run away. If a prisoner was an enemy feared for being a great warrior, he would be slowly killed by torture—and expected to show his courage by singing his death song until the very end.

Warrior with Roach, Gorget
(Alabama) A.D. 1200-1400

Warring between the Woodlands tribes continued even after the arrival of the Europeans, but the new enemy and the introduction of firearms would have terrible consequences.

Notes on "War":

1. The Huron wore special armor made of wood covering the front and back. Also worn were heavy leather leggings and a woven head-covering. They used both bow and tomahawk when in battle.

2.   "As soon as the Huron had an enemy in their power they tore out his finger nails and bit or cut off the fingers he used to draw the string of a bow."

                                     —from *The Huron: Farmers of the North*
                   by Bruce G. Trigger (Holt, Rinehart and Winston, 1969, page 48)

3. Even in the 20th century native peoples in Labrador used the word "Iroquois" to scare their children!

4. An early European observer reported:

Huron warrior wearing
wood slat armor.

"(They) delight to tormente men in the most bloodiye manner that may be; flaying some alive...cutting off members and joynts...by peesemeale and brorling (them) on the coles, eate...their flesh in their sight while they live."

(The wisdom and strength of the victim was believed to enter the body of anyone who ate his flesh.)

5. From *Ojibwa Songs* by H. H. Schoolcraft.

6. If someone was murdered, his clan had to kill the murderer. (This was done by someone related to the victim through the mother's side of the family.) If, for some reason, the murderer could not be killed, a member of his tribe had to die in his place.

7. No one was forced to go into battle, but the young men wanted to be able to prove their bravery—and fighting was how this was done!

8. When a war party set out, it always carried a collective medicine bundle that included crystals that could be used to tell the future.

THE EUROPEANS COME

The native people of Northeastern and Southeastern areas had their lives and their cultures changed forever by the coming of the Europeans. The dates of contact varied, but similar consequences resulted everywhere.

The Europeans claimed the land each for his own king, who wanted the natural resources of this New World: safe harbors, fur pelts, free labor—and gold, if there was any to be had. Often these white men also wanted to "save the souls of the natives and turn these 'primitives' into 'civilized beings.' "

From the time of de Soto the Spanish—when they met southeastern Native people— killed them, took them as slaves, or left them with European diseases from which they would later die. Every Indian tribe was at some time overwhelmed by European disease. Many Southeastern tribes which were thriving in the 17th century today no longer exist.[1]

The Eastern coastal Indians (Micmac, Passamaquoddy, Abenaki, Lenni-Lenape [Delaware], Nanticoke, Powhatan, in particular) were the first to feel pressed by the Europeans' desire for more land.

These native groups were small in number and not organized to cooperate or work together against the forces of the newcomers. A few battles broke out between the Indians and the colonists (Pequot War in 1637 and King Philip's War, 1675-76) but, generally speaking, the Eastern coastal native peoples began to take on European ways as a way to survive.

With time, most of the native people on the East coast either sold their land (as the Delaware did in the 18th century), were killed by European diseases, or began slowly moving west.

CHANGES IN EVERYDAY LIFE

The coming of the Europeans brought about changes in the day-to-day life of the Woodland people.

148

Food

The Native people learned to enjoy coffee, sugar, and tea, all of which they got through trading with the newcomers.

On the other hand, the Eastern American Indians introduced the Europeans to many foods[2]—hominy, cornbread, clams, cranberries, wild rice, many kinds of nuts, and sweet potatoes—which we enjoy to this day!

Clothing

Calico and flannel cloth became very popular among the Woodland people for making clothing.

In the early 1900s the Seminole women began sewing together horizontal strips of cotton cloth in contrasting colors to make their skirts. Patchwork clothing was just beginning to be made at this time.

Elaborately beaded clothing often took the place of quillwork-decorated garments worn on special occasions by the Chippewa, Micmac, and Seneca.

Silk ribbons and appliqués began to ornament leggings, skirts, dresses, and shirts of the Sauk-Fox and Potawatomis after the Europeans arrived. (See "Arts and Crafts" section of this chapter.)

European buttons became a kind of quick decoration for some American Indian seamstresses.

Shelter

Following the Revolutionary War, log-walled and bark-roofed houses began to take the place of traditional longhouses in the northeast. European furnishings, rugs, tables, chairs, and trunks became very popular among the native peoples.

Notched log cabins were built by the Creek and Cherokee from the mid-18th century on. The Native people saw the early pioneer buildings and used many of those construction ideas when building homes for themselves.

Tools

Metal tools of all kinds: fish hooks, needles, kettles, knives, ax heads, guns—and later, sewing machines—were trade items that were popular with all the Woodland Indians.

Woodland Indian war clubs changed after the Europeans' arrival. Warriors used metal balls, as in the Sauk-Fox ball head club, and the (shape of) gunstocks for later war clubs.

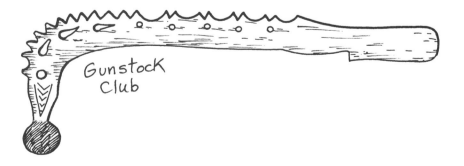

Gunstock Club

Arts and Crafts

BEADWORK   The Europeans began trading their mass-produced glass beads to the Native Americans in about 1675. The best beadwork seems to have been done in those places where quillwork was traditional.

Beadwork was woven, netted (lace-like), and spot-stitched (laying threaded beads in a design and sewing them in place).

Each tribe had a distinctive way of doing beadwork. The Penobscot and Iroquois could do lacy beading; the Micmac did abstracted flower designs; the Chippewa did flowing realistic flowers, leaves, and berries; and the Sauk did bold symmetrical designs.

Potawatomi

Sauk-Fox Beadwork

Winnebago Beadwork

The flower designs used in beadwork may have been influenced by the embroidery on European church vestments.

Centipede

Storm Clouds

The Milky Way

Otter

Rainbow

Clouds and Moon

Yuchi Beading

Seminole

Mohegan

Micmac Beadwork

Penobscot

Menominee

Eastern Cree Beadwork

Ojibwa Beadwork

SILVERWORK About 1800 the Iroquois began hammering silver coins into flat pieces of metal and decorating these by stamping them. They had traditional shapes. (Around 1825 they began using "German Silver," a mixture of copper, nickel, and zinc as a substitute for silver.)

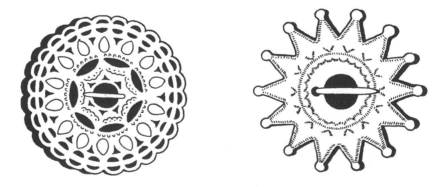

Eventually gorgets and dangling earrings, worn both by men and women, were made from sheet metal.

Silverwork in the Great Lakes area began in the 1820s when the Oneida, an Iroquois tribe, moved into northeastern Wisconsin. The Menominee made flatter, plainer pieces including round pins, hair ornaments, wide bracelets, earrings, and silver hatbands complete with buckles.

RIBBON APPLIQUÉ   This method of decorating clothing is done by sewing intricately cut pieces of silk or satin onto cloth or leather.

Ribbonwork was first done by the Great Lakes people in about 1780. The Iroquois combined ribbonwork with beaded designs.

Menominee women's robes and skirts had a center panel of appliqué. Winnebago and Sauk, among many, decorated their moccasins and leggings with ribbonwork.

Some ribbon appliqué was done in the Southeast. The Seminole replaced appliqué with patchwork in about 1910. Incidentally, the Seminole have been using the sewing machine since 1890. The men wore patchwork "big shirts" that came down to the knees. In the 1930s they shortened these shirts and began wearing trousers with them. Seminole women wear very long, very full patchwork skirts and overblouses with mounds of bead necklaces.

Religion

French Catholic missionaries were among the very first Europeans to come to this "New World." The white men believed it was their duty to convert the Woodland Indians to Christianity. They preached the benefits of their religion and way of life.

Many of the Woodland leaders and prophets warned their people against becoming used to European goods—especially alcohol—advising them to stay pure and keep in touch with their tribal way of living.

Many American Indians did convert to the European religions, however, raising their children according to these new teachings.

Trade

From the first the Europeans changed the centuries-old relationships among the tribes. The European traders ignored some tribes (weakening them) and favored other tribes with guns in exchange for trade goods—usually furs. The very first European fur traders on the eastern coast were French. In 1608 explorer Samuel de Champlain and his small party moved up the St. Lawrence River looking for beaver pelts. The next spring he met the Algonquin, and to gain their favor, he joined them on a raid against their long-time enemies, the Mohawk of the Iroquois League. Because of Champlain's guns, the Algonquin easily defeated the Mohawk, but Champlain did not realize that he and his guns had made bitter enemies of the powerful Five Nations of the Iroquois.

In addition to metal tools, the European trader brought beads,[3] red dye, blankets, cotton cloth, and household furnishings. In return the Europeans (French, Dutch, and English) wanted furs, beaver fur in particular as it made a fine felt fabric and beaver-skin hats were very fashionable in Europe at that time.

So it was that once the beavers had all been taken from an area of land, the Indians needed to find new sources. This led to fighting over fur-rich areas. (In the mid 17th century, the well-organized Iroquois had defeated so many other tribes that they held control over lands from New England to Illinois!)

The *influence* of a frontier travels ahead of the frontier itself. Diseases spread before the body of settlers even arrived in an area. Because of the oncoming wave of newcomers, tribes were forced to make new partnerships with other groups, trade patterns became changed, and whole tribal economies were reshaped.

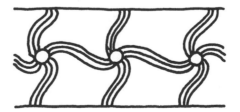

LANGUAGE AND EDUCATION

In 1865 the U.S. Government gave contracts to Protestant Missionary Societies to operate Indian Schools. At such schools the children were made to eat, speak, dress, worship, and live as white children.

In 1879 Richard Pratt founded the Carlisle Indian School in Pennsylvania. It was the philosophy of the school to do everything necessary to make Indian children become an accepted part of the white culture. English was the *only* language allowed.

Until well into the 20th century, it was the policy of the U.S. Government to do everything possible to destroy native languages and cultural ties so that these people would become a part of the "white American society."

GOVERNMENT

It is seldom acknowledged but the Europeans learned a great deal about politics and government from the Iroquois! The way in which the League was organized—with its built-in systems of checks and balances—influenced and strengthened the American Articles of Confederation as well as the United States Constitution![4]

WAR

When the Europeans introduced firearms into North America, warring was changed forever for the Woodland peoples.

At first the American Indians and the Europeans fought one another. These exchanges were brutal.[5] Then the various Europeans began making pacts with specific tribes.[6]

In the 200 years between 1636 and 1858 there were at least fifteen major wars between the Woodlands people and the Europeans.[7]

REMOVAL AND RELOCATION

In 1735 the Menominee, Iowa, Fox, Sauk, Ojibwa, Winnebago, Ottawa, Sioux, and Potawatomi tribes formally agreed that the United States could make an amicable and final adjustment of their various land claims. In 20 years the "adjustments" had been made: the tribes had either been forced to live on lands far to the west or made to stay in cramped reservations within their once ample and ancient homelands.

After the American Revolution, the new states of Alabama, Mississippi, Georgia, and South Carolina began forcing the Southeastern Indians to move far off to the west.[8]

From 1830 to 1833 thousands of Choctaws set out on foot, walking from October until February or March until they finally reached The Indian Territory, present-day Oklahoma. More than one-fourth of the Choctaw people died on the way.

From 1836-1837 more than 14,000 Creeks journeyed to their new territory, arriving in a wretched condition.[9]

Between 1838 and 1843 most of the remaining Creeks, Cherokees, and Chickasaws were forced to leave their homes and travel for months in freezing or in stifling hot weather; they crossed six states before reaching their relocation camps. "The Trail of Tears" was the name earned by the route these native people were forced to take.[10]

Talequah OK.

Cherokee N.C.

The Eastern Seminoles' story was different. Many were forced to go west, but large numbers of them hid out, forming small armies that waged bloody warfare against U.S. troops for over 20 years. Many young men on both sides were killed. The fighting finally stopped in 1856 when the U.S. Army saw that continuing such warfare was fruitless.

Thirty years later, white settlers pressed the Seminoles farther into the Everglades. There they live today—1,350 strong—in or around four reservations.

Notes for "The Europeans Come":

1. Among them were the Ais, Apalachee, Atakapa, Calusa, Chakchiuma, Chatot, Cusabo, Keys, Mikisuki, Mobile, Natchez (survivors blended with Creek and Cherokee), Tekesta, Tutelo, Tocobaga, Tohome, and Yamasee. These tribes are gone and their cultures and spoken languages with them.

2. Fourteen years before the Pilgrims' arrival, an English ship anchored in Plymouth Bay. It took on fish, beaver skins, and some native people whom they kidnapped to serve as their slaves. One of these was a young boy, Squanto. He went to England, became a house boy, and learned English. The years passed. Then as a young man he sailed back to New England as an interpreter. Once near his coastline, Squanto jumped ship and ran to his village—only to find it empty, his people dead of smallpox. A few months later he saw the Pilgrims searching for food and they were amazed to hear him greet them in English. Squanto gave the Pilgrims seed corn, taught them to cultivate it, and make and use corn cribs and husking pins. Squanto made it possible for the Pilgrims to survive.

3. The Woodland Indians used ground clamshell beads (wampum) for jewelry, presents, or to mark important historical moments—*never* for money. The early people did not use money. The Europeans soon understood the value of wampum to the native people and set up wampum factories on Long Island and in New Jersey.

   Soon wampum became the coinage—not only between Indians and European traders, but also among the settlers. Because at that time there was a wide variety of moneys being used—Spanish, French, Portuguese, English, and Dutch—it was easy enough to take wampum as another method of payment.

4. Both Thomas Jefferson and Benjamin Franklin were impressed by the way the Iroquois governed themselves. Some scholars believe that the U.S. Constitution owes as much to the Iroquois Law of Peace as it does to European ideas.

5. Scalping may very well have been introduced to North America by the Europeans. In 1613 in response to a shooting attempt on one of their tribesman by a Frenchman, the Beothuk Indians in Newfoundland killed 37 fishermen. As a reaction to this, the French armed the Micmacs, enemies of the Beothuk, and offered bounties for scalps—which led eventually to the complete extinction of the Beothuk tribe!

   In 1664, in reaction to the killing of a Staten Island farmer by some Raritans, the Dutch offered bounties for Raritan scalps or heads.

   On the other hand, scalping may have been an outgrowth of the old Indian custom of taking a piece of hair or clothing of the killed enemy as a trophy of that event. Did the

Europeans, in asking for proof of kills when paying bounties, take the Indian custom beyond its original state? We do not know.

6. The Iroquois power helped the British against the French in the wars that won Canada for Great Britain. In 1776, during the American Revolution, the Cherokees sided with the English and this eventually may have influenced President Jackson to take the Cherokees' lands from them. (Several hundred Cherokee were able to hide from the U.S. troops who herded the people west to Oklahoma. The descendants of these few hundred Cherokees live on today in North Carolina.)

At the start of the Revolutionary War, the League of Six Nations was divided as to which group to back—the colonists or the British. The majority of the League members chose to fight for the British. Only the Oneida and the Tuscarora did not. Once the war was over, George Washington sent his general, John Sullivan, to "not merely overrun, but destroy..." the tribes that had sided with England. This General Sullivan did; his troops burned 40 villages and hundreds of corn crops and orchards. The Iroquois were totally defeated.

It must be noted here that the tribes that did not join the British forces were not treated, in the long run, much better than those that did.

7. Time Line:

1636-1637	*Pequot War* during which 600 Pequot women, men, and children are killed by the colonists on a surprise attack, in what the settlers believe is a retaliation for the murder of a colonist by a Pequot.
1640-1685	Beaver and otter are nearly gone from Iroquois lands so until around 1685 the Iroquois League wars on and defeats the Huron, Tobacco, Neutral, Erie, Mohican, and Susquehannock for their lands and furs.
1655	*Peach Wars* begin a 9-year period of violence between Dutch and Hudson River Indians.
1675-76	*King Philip's War* between the Wampanoag, Narraganset and Nipmuc and the New England Confederation of colonies. Metacom (King Philip) is killed in 1676.
1689-97	*King William's War*, the first in a series of colonial wars between France, and their respective Indian allies.
1702-13	*Queen Anne's War*, between England and France in the Northeast, and between England and Spain in the Southeast, and their various Indian allies.
1715-28	*Yamasee War* in South Carolina, between the British and Yamasees.
1720-32	Chickasaws fight French and Choctaws in the Southeast.
1744-48	*King George's War* between the French and British, and their respective Indian allies.
1760-61	*Cherokee War* on Carolina frontier, between colonists and Cherokees.
1763-64	In 1763, because of frontier attacks by Indians, the *Paxton Riots* occur in Pennsylvania; peaceful Conestoga Mission Indians are massacred by settlers.
1769	*Pontiac's Rebellion* against the British in the Great Lakes region. Pontiac, a chief of the Ottawa, is assassinated in 1769.

1774	*Lord Dunmore's War* in Virginia, between settlers and Shawnees.
1778	Iroquois Indians under Joseph Brant and British regulars attack American settlers on the western New York and Pennsylvania frontiers (Cherry Valley and Wyoming Valley massacres).
1809-11	*Tecumseh's Rebellion:* Tecumseh, a Shawnee chief, endeavors to unite Tribes of the Old Northwest, South, and the Mississippi Valley against the United States. His brother, Tenskwatawa, is defeated at Tippecanoe in 1811.
1812-15	*War of 1812* between the United States and England. Tecumseh, brigadier general for British, is killed in 1813.
1813-14	*Creek War* in the Southeast. In the Treaty of Fort Jackson, Andrew Jackson strips Creeks of their land.
1817-18	*First Seminole War* in Southeast. Andrew Jackson invades Florida in a vengeful expedition against the Indians.
1827	*Winnebago Uprising* in Wisconsin.
1825-42	*Second Seminole War:* Osceola dies in prison in 1828.
1855-58	*Third Seminole Uprising* in Florida.

8. The whites rationalized that the tribes were uncivilized and not worthy of the lands that the Christian farmers wanted. Odd that the Southeastern tribes—Choctaw, Chickasaw, Creek, Cherokee, and Seminole—were known as the Five Civilized Tribes, having adopted both European farming methods and Christianity.

9. The Trail of Tears also had a water route: from Ross' Landing (Chattanooga), TN on the Tennessee River up to Paducah, KY, down the Mississippi to Montgomerey's Point, AK and up the Arkansas River to Fort Gibson, OK—a journey of 1,200 miles!

10. Private John G. Burnett of the U.S. Mounted Infantry took part in the Cherokee Indian Removal, 1838-1839. Years later, on his eightieth birthday, he wrote a lengthy recollection of that hideous experience. Here is an excerpt:

"The long painful journey to the west ended March 26th, 1839, with four thousand silent graves reaching from the foothills of the Smoky Mountains to what is known as Indian Territory in the West. And covetousness on the part of the white race was the cause of all that the Cherokees had to suffer."

—Courtesy of the Museum of the Cherokee Indian

THE WOODLAND INDIANS TODAY

We have seen in the previous chapter how destructive the European diseases were to the indigenous peoples—even threatening them with extinction. But the Native Americans continued to struggle for life and they survived: in the last fifty years their populations have been steadily increasing.

What of the lives of these Native Americans today? How do they fare in the contemporary United States?

The statistics can seem bleak[1]: less than 10 percent of American Indians still speak their native language; their unemployment rate is 45 percent—the average Native American worker earns less than $7,000 a year; and 45 percent of all native people live below the poverty level.

The Native American who lives in a city is often disconnected from other people there. Alcohol is a serious problem in urban settings as well as on the reservations.

Native American teenagers often feel as if they don't "belong," that the future is without promise: half finish high school, only 4 percent complete college, and the rate of teenage suicide attempts (one in six has tried suicide) is four times higher than that of other teenagers in the United States.

These figures are sobering, but they do not tell the entire story. In the Northeastern and Southeastern states native people are working hard to change such statistics by recapturing old traditions and starting new business enterprises.

POPULATION

The 1990 census tells us that there are about 1,800,000 American Indians living in the United States today. About 400,000 (23 percent) live on reservations and 1,400,000 (77 percent) live in cities[2] and suburban areas.

The American Indian population in the present-day states of the Woodlands is as follows, according to the 1990 census:

State	Native American Population of State	% of Total Population of State
Alabama	16,506	.8%
Arkansas	12,773	.7%
Connecticut	6,654	.3%
Delaware	2,019	.1%
District of Columbia	1,466	.1%
Florida	36,335	1.9%
Georgia	13,348	.7%
Illinois	21,836	1.1%
Indiana	12,720	.6%
Iowa	7,349	.4%
Kentucky	5,769	.3%
Louisiana	18,541	.9%
Maine	5,998	.3%
Maryland	12,972	.7%
Massachusetts	12,241	.6%
Michigan	55,638	2.8%
Minnesota	49,909	2.5%
Mississippi	8,525	.4%
Missouri	19,835	1%
New Hampshire	2,134	.1%
New Jersey	14,970	.8%
New York	62,651	3.2%
North Carolina	80,155	4.1%
Ohio	20,358	1 %
Oklahoma	252,420	12.9%
Pennsylvania	14,733	.8%
Rhode Island	4,071	.2%
South Carolina	8,246	.4%
Tennessee	10,039	.5%
Texas	65,877	3.4%
Vermont	1,696	.1%
Virginia	15,282	.8%
West Virginia	2,458	.1%
Wisconsin	39,387	2%

RESERVATIONS

Long ago, an Indian reservation could be defined as land that the U.S. government assigned to a tribe and reserved for it when it gave up its larger land areas to the United States through treaties.[3] More recently Congressional Acts, Executive Orders, and administrative acts have formed reservations.

Today there are about 275 Indian land areas in the United States that are administered as Indian reservations; some reservations have non-Indian residents and land owners. About 140 reservations are entirely tribally owned lands. In the Northeast and Southeast regions there are approximately 60 U.S. Federal and State Reservations. The following is a list of U.S. Federal and State Indian Reservations of the Northeast and Southeast areas.[4]

State	Number of Reservations	Tribes on These Reservations
Connecticut	3	Pequot, Mohegan, Schaghticoke
Florida	5	Miccosukee, Seminole
Iowa	1	Sauk-Fox
Kansas	4	Sauk-Fox, Kickapoo, Potawatomi
Louisiana	1	Chitimacha
Maine	2	Penobscot, Passamaquoddy
Massachusetts	2	Hassanamisco-Nipmic
Michigan	5	Saginaw, Chippewa, Huron, Potawatomi
Minnesota	11	Chippewa (Eastern/Mississippi Sioux)
Mississippi	1	Choctaw
New York	9	Seneca[5] (Nation of Indians), Oneida[6], Onondaga, Poospatuk, St. Regis Mohawk, Sinnecock, Tuscarora
North Carolina	1	Eastern Cherokee
Oklahoma	27	Cherokee, Chickasaw, Choctaw, Potawatomi, Delaware[7], Kickapoo, Missouria, Sauk-Fox, Seminole, Seneca-Cayuga, Muscogee

Some 20 areas of land were set aside in Oklahoma for tribes that were orginally from the eastern United States.

State	Number of Reservations	Tribes on These Reservations
Texas	2	Alabama-Coushatta, (Tiqua)
Virginia	2	Mattaponi (Powhatan), Pamunkey
Wisconsin	10	Chippewa, Oneida, Potawatomi, Munsee, Mahican, Winnebago, Menominee[8]

There are 8,000 Algonquin Indians today and they live in Canada: nine groups in Quebec and one in Ontario.

American Indians born on reservations usually stay on the reservations; although they may leave sometimes, they often return. When an American Indian is born off the reservation, there is only a remote chance that he or she will go live on a reservation later in life. The most recent census figures show there are today more native people living in urban settings than in rural ones.

As a general rule, only American Indians living on a reservation get U.S. Government help in the form of housing, utilities, health care, and educational aid.

Finding a stable source of income on a reservation has always been difficult. The number of businesses located on the reservations and owned by Native Americans grew in the 1980s; there was growth in construction companies, car sales, food and goods stores, farming, and trucking.

Most native people today live in two worlds; many want to continue their traditions and their cultural ties, while at the same time work (and live) in the modern world. Even traditional people living on reservations have adapted to parts of 20th-century white culture and values. Televisions, telephones, modern clothing, modern housing, cars—have all made their appearance on the reservations.

Nevertheless, American Indians continue to face harsh problems on and off the reservation.

Modern concerns of Eastern American Indians include:

- Saving their Native languages
- Solving sovereignty questions
- Preserving fishing and hunting rights[9]
- Solving questions of economic development including Indian gaming, the building of casinos on tribal lands
- Dealing with drug-and-alcohol related problems
- Protecting sacred burial grounds and ceremonial sites

Each of these are accomplished by the use of legal strategies as well as activist demonstrations.[10]

HEALTH ISSUES

One hundred years ago, the Northeastern and Southeastern peoples were attacked and killed by smallpox, measles, and diphtheria—diseases brought to this continent by the Europeans. Present-day Native Americans continue to be challenged by serious health problems. Among the native people, the death rate due to drinking alcohol is ten times higher than that of all other races combined. Tuberculosis is seven and a half times more frequent among Native Americans than it is among non American Indians, and diabetes affects Native Americans seven times more than it does the rest of the population.

EDUCATION

Just about half (52 percent) of all Native Americans finish high school; 20 percent go to college and, of these, only four out of every hundred graduate.

Many Native Americans feel that the best way to improve the lives of their people is through education:

"Today the Native Americans must get ready to take control of their lives: this can be done through education.

"The next battles will be won by warriors whose weapons are the briefcase and the computer."

—George Russell, *The American Indian Digest*

RELIGION

Ancient traditional religions remain strong among some Eastern native peoples, while others practice Christianity, or a mixture of the two.

Many Eastern Native Americans continue the tradition of ceremonial dancing, as it is by dancing that the old ways are kept alive; they continue to dance so that they might be connected to their ancestors.

As was mentioned in the **Religion and Beliefs** chapter, sacred sites are a basic part of traditional religious practices. In this century sacred sites have been destroyed by mining, logging, and the construction of dams, houses, roads, and power plants. Tourists and thieves have also spoiled many holy places. Since the 1970s U.S. Government officials have made narrow rules restricting the use of public lands and forests—preventing Native Americans from reaching some sacred sites. Whenever such a site is ruined or restricted, the religious rituals connected with that place are also destroyed. This is because native people cannot substitute another site for an ancient holy place. So the loss of access is a threat to their very religion.

Today ancient Indian graves are at risk also. Erosion, flooding, farming, urban development, and logging have all exposed skeletal remains and burial goods. Grave robbers deliberately plunder burials. Recently, because of the efforts of Native Americans, laws have been passed to protect ancient gravesites and give these people legal avenues for reclaiming skeletal remains and religious artifacts.

JOBS AND INCOME

As early as 1886 the Mohawk Indians of Caughnawaga Reserve were trained in high-steel construction to build a bridge across the St. Lawrence River. The high-rise construction work by Iroquois men in New York City continues to be a tradition to this day.

Many of the Cherokees and others who were removed to Oklahoma have taken up farming and ranching. Some benefited from the discovery of oil and gas on their lands.

However, almost one-half of all Native Americans are out of work; of those with jobs, three-quarters earn less than $7,000 a year. (The average household income in the U.S. in 1992 was $30,786.)

Many tribal leaders believe that only jobs can solve the serious problems of poverty and alcoholism on and off the reservations.

> "...until very recent years the trend has been for both reservation and non reservation Indians of the Southeast to leave their homes seeking work in the urban areas of the South and mid-Atlantic states. These urban Indian communities, in Baltimore and elsewhere, have not tended to fare well in cities packed with competing minority populations. There is even talk among the Indian leadership, like James Billie of the Seminoles, that the time is drawing near when even the strongest of the Southeastern tribes will no longer exist as independent entities. Indeed, there appears to be no consensus among either Indian or white about what the future does, or should, hold for the Southeastern Indians."
>
> —*Native North Americans: An Ethno-historical Approach*,
> Daniel L. Boxberger, ed. (Dubuque, Iowa: Kendall/Hunt Publishing, 1990)

Arts and Crafts

The Eastern native people continue to produce fine traditional crafts. For example, in the far north Cree and Chippewa make a woven quillwork—the finest quillwork of North America.

The band is woven on stretched fiber wraps, then soft flattened quills are woven in and out of the wefts. The quills are pushed very close together and look, at last, like tiny round beads. Geometric designs often appear on white backgrounds and decorate bags and belts.

The Eastern people are learning how to mass market their art and handiwork. They form cooperative craft shops on the reservations and often, due to the draw of casinos, more tourists are coming there to spend their dollars.

Indian Gaming

Recently the development of gambling casinos on reservation lands has become a concern in the Eastern states, as well as in the rest of the United States. The right to determine their own economic development on the reservation is a very important issue of sovereignty to American Indians today.

Some tribes are counting on the gaming business to provide income and capital for their people, but this brings up both economic and political concerns and questions.

"The issue of Indian sovereignty hangs in the balance as Indians cautiously negotiate the maze of overlapping state and federal jurisdictions and control."

—George Russell, SAGINAW-CHIPPEWA, *The American Indian Digest*, page 54.

In recent years high-stake bingo and gambling casinos have become a way for tribes to attract tourists, to make money, and bring jobs to the reservation. Because these operations are on American Indian land, where local and state laws don't apply, they can offer forms of gaming not allowed off reservation. Their federal tax-exempt status gives Native Americans a definite advantage over other gambling establishments in so far as gambling receipts are concerned. Often the profits are used to fund health clinics, to offer housing for the elderly, and to build classrooms for the reservation schools.

There are questions concerning the casinos, however. How should the profits be shared: should they be distributed to individual tribal members or should they be earmarked for investments and social services? Should the casinos give a percentage to the Native American housing and educational services located in cities where their tribal people work and live? These are not simple questions and each tribe must find its own answers.

Federal Moneys

Occasionally an Indian tribe will receive moneys from the federal government to make up for unfair treatment the tribe suffered in the past. For example, in October 1989 the Seminole Nation was awarded more than $35,000,000 for land payments in Florida. With interest and time, this amount has grown to over $53,000,000. The Seminoles are now developing human service programs for their people and have the chance today to develop a powerful economic Indian Nation.

LANGUAGE

It is estimated that about one-third of all Native Americans still speak their tribal language.

The use of native languages was once forbidden in U.S. schools. In 1990 the Native American Language Act was signed into law by President George Bush. It states that it is U.S. policy to "preserve, protect and promote the rights and freedom of Native Americans to use, practice, and develop Native American languages."

"Language is the basis of every culture. I think we should know our language even if we only know a few words. It's still something. You can still identify with being Indian.

"I think it's too late to revive the language through education. That's why I started a program with just (memorizing historic) speeches. I didn't want anything to do with the Secretary of State, with the Band Council or Department of Education—nobody. We wanted to be independent. It was going to be run by the community themselves because they know what they want.

"My concern now, is that the culture and the religion goes on anyway—even if that's all they know."

—Reginald Henry, CAYUGA Nation

Photo 18. Standing at the men's doorway to the Sour Springs longhouse are singer Willie John and Bill Johnson wearing an Iroquois false face mask. *Photo by Gertrude Kurath, 1962.*

Storytelling by the elders continues (see "Storytelling" in **Language**). Today, when children spend so much time watching television and videos, we can only wonder if retelling the old stories can compete with the dazzle of the media.

One thing that all Native Americans have in common is what one could call "Indian humor." This humor causes laughter that may be bawdy one minute, sacred the next. But whichever it is you can be sure it is a humor that makes its points clearly to Native Americans—and those points include the importance of humility and the affirmation that laughter leads to learning and survival.[11]

Communication

In recent years many tribes and reservations have begun using the Internet as a way to communicate with one another and to give and receive information around the world. Many have put home pages on the World Wide Web[12] to publish information about tribal history and culture, to announce upcoming events (such as pow-wows), and to coordinate political action. These sites are also used to promote tourism and to market goods and services.

SUMMING UP

The Native Americans are a sturdy and inventive people. They have lived through a 400-year struggle with the Europeans, during which their very existence was at stake. They have lived through one hundred years of BIA and U.S. Government control. Yet they survive. Many of them have strong ties to the Earth and to nature, and these have given them strength over the years.

Today, with a population of more than a million[13] and with an annual birth rate twice that of the general population, the first Americans seem to be in no danger of disappearing!

Many eastern tribes are rebuilding their economic bases, preserving tribal traditions, reviving their culture, language, crafts and art as well as working to provide health care and education for their people. They are not simply surviving, they are moving into the future!

Notes for "The Woodland Indians Today":

1. The statistics quoted here are from *The American Indian Digest*, 1995 edition, by George Russell, a member of the Saginaw-Chippewa tribe. To order the latest edition of this very informative book, as well as American Indian history maps, call Thunderbird Enterprises at 1-800-835-7220.

2. Because census-takers have had different ways of judging who is an American Indian, it is difficult to know how many live in the larger cities. In any case, we do know that the numbers are rising:

   1940—about 5% lived in cities

   1950—almost 20% lived in cities

   1960—nearly 30% lived in cities

   1970—44 1/2% lived in cities

   1980—49% lived in cities

   1990—51% lived in cities

3. This definition is from the Bureau of Indian Affairs and appears on their Web page: *Answers to Frequently Asked Questions.* (To access the BIA's web site, search for U.S. Government, Department of the Interior.)

4. These statistics are taken from the Appendix, pages 233-239, of *Atlas of the North American Indian* by Carl Waldman (New York: Facts on File, 1985.)

5. There are four Seneca Reserves in Western New York (60,000 acres in all). There was a fifth Seneca Reserve, the Complanter, in Pennsylvania, but 8,900 acres of it were flooded by a dam project in the 1960s—leaving just 100 acres above water.

6. Most of the Oneida (11,000 of their total 1,600,000) live on or near their 2,200-acre reservation west of Green Bay, Wisconsin. Seven hundred Oneida still live near Oneida, New York, but since their reserve there is only 32 acres, many must live in nearby Onondaga.

7. The Delaware have been forced by white settlement to relocate at least 20 times. By 1900 they had lived in Delaware, New Jersey, New York, Pennsylvania, West Virginia, Ohio, Ontario, Michigan, Indiana, Missouri, Arkansas, Louisiana, Texas, Wisconsin, Kansas, and Oklahoma. Today the majority of the Delaware are in Oklahoma.

8. The Menominee have had an interesting relationship with the U.S. Government.

> "The Menominee in 1872 began operation of their own tribally-owned saw mill which competed directly with private American timber companies in the area. The Menominee began a program of sustained yield harvest in 1908 to assure an income for future generations. The enterprise was a success, and became the primary source of income for the Menominee. By 1955 the United States Treasury had accumulated over $10 million in a Menominee trust account from their timber operations.

> "However, the government apparently did not always fulfill its obligations to supervise the mill in their best interest, and after a lawsuit initiated against the federal government, the Menominee won a $9.5 million judgment for mismanagement between 1954 and 1959. Not too coincidentally, in 1961, the federal government unilaterally terminated the Menominee's tribal status, and their reservation became a Wisconsin county. The saw mill could not provide enough tax base to pay for all of the services a county government was required to provide and the Menominee instantly went from being one of the most self sufficient tribes in the United States to the lowest standard of living in Wisconsin. To meet their obligations, the Menominee were forced to sell part of their reservation as lakefront lots for vacation homes. Federal recognition was restored in 1973."

> —*Menominee History*, Lee Sultzman

9. Fishing rights have been a problem between whites and American Indians since the 1600s. For example, the Ottawas of High Island, Michigan, have always gotten wild rice from the marshes and fish from the surrounding rivers and lakes. The Europeans have believed that this land should be developed for settlements. Some treaties and land cession agreements have included specific tribal fishing rights. Today these rights are challenged sometimes by environmentalists and those who want to end the special position that Native Americans have in relation to the U.S. Government.

10. Today those remaining Southeastern Indians are involved in specific ongoing problems with federal, state, and local governments. These battles are in part a result of the fact that in the 1930s the few Native people who remained in the Southeast were encouraged by the federal government to organize into tribes with political structures modeled after the U.S. Constitution. Once the tribes were organized ("reorganized" as the government put it), they could petition the Indian Claims Department of Justice for lands that they had had taken from them.

This line of action resulted in forming tribal governments where none had existed originally, and each of these—whether Florida Seminole, the Seminole tribe of

Oklahoma, or the Miccosukees of Florida—could agree on little, battling over every court-awarded judgment.

11. Joseph Bruchac, Parabola, Vol. XII, No. 4, 1987, *Striking the Pole, American Indian Humor*, page 29.

12. A set of links to the tribal Web pages may be found in the "Native American Home Pages" site maintained by Lisa Mittenat at the University of Pittsburgh. The URL (as of April 1997) is: http://earth.library.pitt.edu/~lmitten/indians.html

13. It should be kept in mind that this is still less than 1 percent of the total U.S. population. Here we can mention that American Indians have served in the U.S. armed forces in such numbers that today they, who are less than 1 percent of the population, are 8 percent of all living U.S. veterans.

HISTORIC NATIVE AMERICANS
OF THE WOODLANDS

MASSASOIT, WAMPANOAG CHIEF (C. 1590-1661)

Massasoit was born near the present-day city of Bristol, Rhode Island. The peace treaty that Massasoit and the Pilgrims signed on March 22, 1621 was never broken. Because of this agreement, the Wampanoag and Pilgrims lived side by side peacefully.

The Pilgrims' Peace Treaty with Massasoit, 1621

1. That neither he nor any of his should injure or do hurt to any of our people.
2. And if any of his did hurt to any of ours, he should send the offender, that we might punish him.
3. That if any of our tools were taken away when our people were at work, he should cause them to be restored; and if ours did any harm to any of his, we would do the like to them.
4. If any did unjustly war against him, we would aid him; if any did war against us, he should aid us.
5. He should send to his neighbor confederates, to certify them of this, that they might not wrong us, but might be likewise comprised in the conditions of peace.
6. That when their men came to us, they should leave their bows and arrows behind them, as we should do our pieces when we came to them.

   Lastly, that doing thus, King James would esteem of him as his friend and ally.

POCAHONTAS, POWHATAN (1595-1617)

The English explorer Captain John Smith was something of a bully and a blowhard. He expected the native people in Virginia to follow his orders—whatever they might be. Eventually he was taken captive by the native people. Legend says that just as he was to be put to death, Pocahontas[1], the daughter of the chief of the Powhatan tribes, came forward and begged for his life. Her pleas were heard, the story says, and Captain Smith's life was saved.

Whether this actually happened we do not know for sure.[2] But it is a fact that later the English kidnapped Pocahontas and held her hostage for over a year. While their prisoner, she met John Rolfe, a 28-year-old widower, and they were married. Two years later she went with her husband to England where she was called a princess and treated as royalty. She gave birth to a baby boy whom they named Thomas. Then Pocahontas became ill with smallpox and—in 1617—died at age 22 in far-off England.

Her father, Chief Powhatan, died the following spring. In the next twenty years Pocahontas' people were killed off or driven from their lands.

171

Pocahontas and John Rolf (from an old print)

JOSEPH BRANT, MOHAWK (1742-1807)

When the American Revolution broke out, there was deep disagreement among the tribes of the Iroquois League. The British promised to help the Iroquois protect their lands against white settlers and offered to pay for American scalps; the Americans simply asked the Iroquois to stay out of the war. Four tribes offered to help the British, but the Oneida and the Tuscarora chose to take no part in the war at all.

The leader of the Iroquois, who decided to help the British, was a Mohawk Chief whom the colonists called Joseph Brant. He was very unusual in that he had gotten an English education as well as complete training as a Mohawk warrior. In 1775 he made a long visit to England and when he returned to America, he was made an officer in the British army!

During the American Revolution he led the Iroquois war parties that brought terror to the European settlers in the Mohawk Valley. When the British lost the war, Joseph Brant took what remained of his tribe to Canada. There they were given land and Brant eventually became a Christian. He spent his last years translating religious books into the Mohawk language.

Joseph Brant

RED JACKET, SENECA (C. 1756-1830)

Known as Red Jacket because he had once been given a red coat by an English army officer, this young man had little heart for fighting wars. Even though the Iroquois highly valued a man's bravery in battle, they honored Red Jacket and made him a chief because he was such a powerful speaker. He became an important leader because he could fight with his words. Even the white men whom he always spoke against respected his ability to debate and to persuade. Here is part of a speech he gave about the Christian missionaries who were forced on the native peoples:

> "(These missionaries) do us no good...If they are not useful to white people, why do they send them among the Indians; if they are useful to white people, and do them good, why do they not keep them at home? (The white people) are surely bad enough to need the labor of everyone who can make them better."

Up until his death Red Jacket was bitter about the treatment his Iroquois people received from the United States Government. But Red Jacket greatly valued one thing that came from the white men—the large peace medal that President George Washington had personally awarded to him at a conference held to work out better relations between the Iroquois and the new American republic. Red Jacket is usually seen in his portraits wearing this large medal.

Red Jacket

TECUMSEH, SHAWNEE (1768-1813)

The constant movement to the West of the American settlers worried this young Shawnee chief. He decided that there should be a strong Indian state, powerful enough to keep the whites in the East and stop them from moving westward.

Tecumseh traveled tirelessly along the frontier from Wisconsin to the Gulf of Mexico speaking to tribe after tribe of his plan for a war to end all wars between Indians and the white men—and even among the native peoples themselves. He gained the support of the British who still hoped to recover the colonies they had lost.

But while Tecumseh was organizing different groups, his brother, known as the Prophet, went against his orders and started a battle with American soldiers at Tippecanoe, Indiana, before Tecumseh's men were ready.

"These lands are ours. No one has a right to remove us because we were the first (to live on them). As to boundaries, the Great Spirit above knows no boundaries nor will his red children acknowledge any...You and I will have to fight it out."

—Tecumseh to General Harrison[3]

The battle was waged and Harrison won a huge victory, causing Tecumseh's organization of tribes to fall apart.

Then the War of 1812 broke out and Tecumseh joined the British in the sad hope that he might somehow in this way help his people. Tecumseh died in battle in 1813 while leading his warriors against their enemy, the U.S. Government.

"So live your life that the fear of death can never enter your heart. Trouble no one about their religion; respect others in their view, and demand that they respect yours. Love your life, perfect your life, beautify all things in your life. Seek to make your life long and its purpose in the service of your people. Prepare a noble death song for the day when you go over the great divide. Always give a word or a sign of salute when meeting or passing a friend, even a stranger, when in a lonely place. Show respect to all people and grovel to none. When you arise in the morning give thanks for the food and for the joy of living. If you see no reason for giving thanks, the fault lies only in yourself. Abuse no one and nothing, for abuse turns the wise ones to fools and robs the spirit of its vision. When it comes your time to die, be not like those whose hearts are filled with the fear of death, so that when their time comes they weep and pray for a little more time to live their lives over again in a different way. Sing your death song and die like a hero going home."

—from an oration by Tecumseh

SEQUOYAH CHEROKEE, (1783-1843)

Born of a Cherokee mother and an English father, Sequoyah was sure that "their talking leaves" were what gave the white men their power. He believed that to be able to save men's thoughts on paper was like "catching a wild animal and taming it." He decided to create an alphabet for the Cherokee language.

First he tried using animal figures and symbols to stand for Cherokee words, but the list just grew too long. Then he broke the words into syllables and tried to find a different symbol for each of the many syllables. For twelve years he struggled, sometimes writing with a knife or charcoal on bark or scratching symbols onto stones.

At last, in 1821, he put his Cherokee syllabary[4] to the test. He told a group of men who had come to his house to go to another room (far away from his) and tell his child something in Cherokee, anything—and to make sure he, Sequoyah, couldn't hear a word of it. The men

Sequoyah

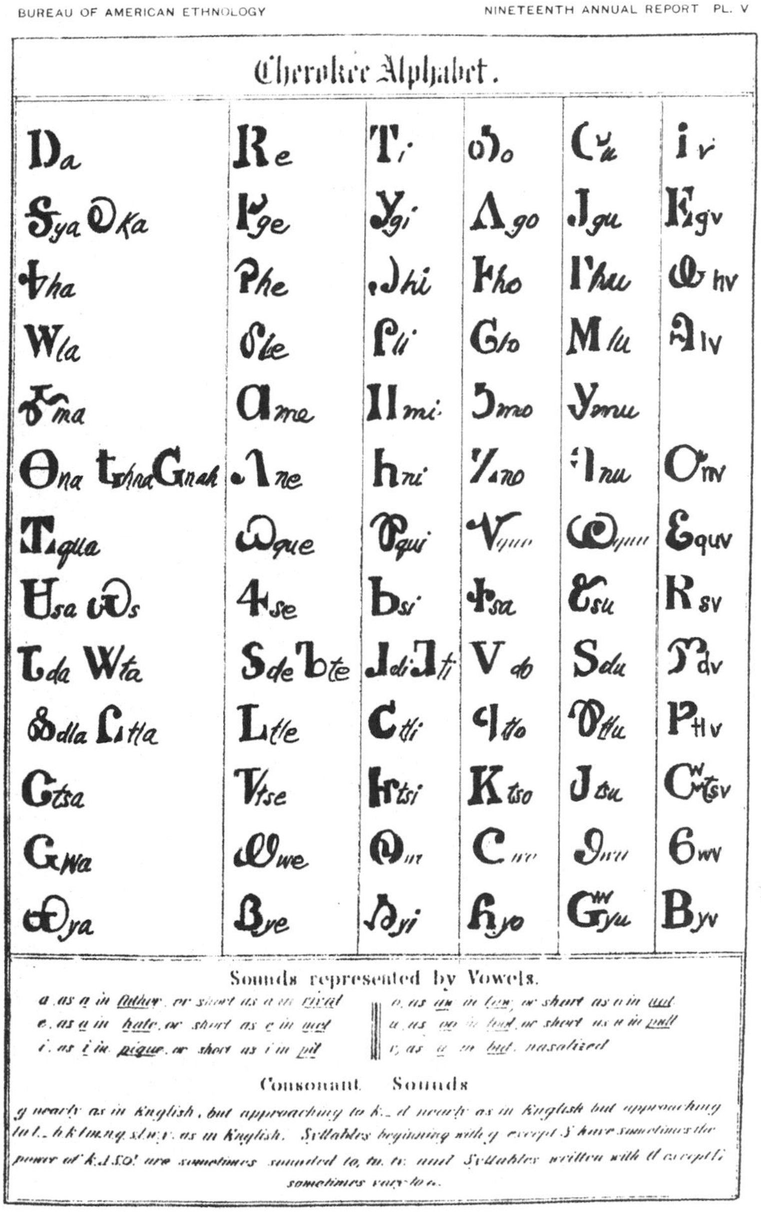

THE CHEROKEE ALPHABET

did this and Sequoyah's child wrote down what they said; then the men took the paper to Sequoyah who read back their own words to the amazement of the visitors!

In the 1820s hundreds of his tribesmen learned these 86 symbols. By 1824 parts of the Bible had been translated into Sequoyah's letters; in 1828 a bilingual newspaper, *The Cherokee Phoenix*, was being published!

Sequoyah is the only person in history known to have created a written language single-handedly!

OSCEOLA, (SEMINOLE C.1803-1838)

In the 1820s the U.S. Government decided to move all Eastern Native Americans to lands west of the Mississippi River. At that time a large group of Creeks known as Seminoles (which means "runaways") fought a desperate war for their right to stay in Florida. A tall thin young man called Osceola was their leader.

In 1835 he made his stand: when federal officials handed him a removal treaty to sign, he slashed it to ribbons with his knife. There followed an uprising of the Seminoles that lasted for seven years—costing the U.S. the lives of 1,500 U.S. soldiers and $20,000,000!

When Osceola agreed to attend a peace conference under a flag of truce, General Jessup of the U.S. Army grabbed Osceola and threw him into prison. There he grew sick and within a year died, "cursing the white man...to the end of his breath!"

Most of the Seminoles were finally made to leave and go live in Oklahoma. A few avoided being captured and they are the ancestors of today's Florida Seminoles.

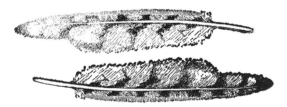

WILL ROGERS, CHEROKEE (1879-1935)

Born in 1879 on a large ranch in the Cherokee Nation in Oklahoma, Will Rogers was taught by a freed slave how to use a lasso in order to work Texas longhorn cattle on the family ranch.

Although he dropped out of school after the tenth grade to become a cowboy on a cattle drive, he always regretted not finishing his studies. However, he made a point to keep on learning by reading, thinking, and talking with smart people.

As he grew older Will Rogers's roping skills became so exceptional that he was listed in *The Guinness Book of World Records* for throwing three lassos at once: One rope caught the running horse's neck, the other would loop around the rider, and the third swooped up under the horse to loop all four legs!

Will Rogers

His extraordinary roping skills won him jobs trick-roping in Wild West shows and on America's vaudeville stages. There, he began telling small jokes and tales of growing up in Oklahoma. Soon his clever stories and one-liners were even more popular than his expert roping.

He was seen as a very smart and thoughtful observer of life in America—telling the truth about things in simple words for all to understand.[5]

Will Rogers became a star on Broadway...he made 71 movies...he wrote six books. He was a popular radio personality and wrote over 4,000 syndicated newspaper columns. He was a friend to senators, U.S. Presidents, and kings.

He traveled around the world three times covering wars, raising money for the Red Cross, and talking about peace. Still he stayed a simple person, often saying: "I never met a man I didn't like." His was a real love and respect for humanity and for all people everywhere.

On a flight to Alaska with a daring one-eyed Oklahoma pilot named Wiley Post, their plane crashed and both men lost their lives. The world mourned Will Rogers's death and considered his words:

"Live your life so that whenever you lose, you're ahead."

"If you live life right, death is a joke as far as fear is concerned."

JIM (JAMES F.) THORPE, SAUK-FOX (1888-1953)

Jim Thorpe was born in Oklahoma in 1888, descended from the famous Chief Black Hawk. His Indian name was Wa-Tho-Huk, which means "bright path." As a boy he went to school at the Carlisle Indian Academy near Harrisburg, Pennsylvania.

In 1912, at age 24, Jim Thorpe took part in the World Olympics held in Stockholm, Sweden. He broke one record after another and won more total points than any other athlete in the history of the modern games. Thorpe won every event but the javelin throw in the pentathlon. In presenting the gold medals, King Gustav of Sweden told Jim, "You, sir, are the greatest athlete in the world."

After the Olympics, a newspaper reporter discovered that while Jim was in school at Carlisle he had played six months of professional baseball for $360. Thorpe insisted that he had not realized that he had broken any rules by playing ball while in school, but the Olympic Committee stripped him of his gold medals saying he had given up his amateur standing when he played that season of baseball.

Over the years Jim Thorpe kept taking part in professional sports, playing for the New York Giants baseball team and with the Canton Bulldogs football team.

In 1950 Jim Thorpe was named the greatest male athlete of the half century by the sports writers of America. But by now Jim was sick and without funds. In 1951 he was a charity case in the cancer ward of a Philadelphia hospital. His wife, when interviewed, said, "We're broke. Jim has nothing but his name and his memories. He's spent money on his own people and has given it away. He has often been exploited."

Jim Thorpe died in 1953. After his native state of Oklahoma would not accept his body for burial, he was laid to rest in a mausoleum in the town of Mauch Chunk, Pennsylvania, renamed Jim Thorpe in his honor.

In January 1982, Jim Thorpe was officially given an amateur standing for the 1912 Olympics. In January 1983, replicas of his gold medals were presented to his family nearly 30 years after his death—and 70 years after his amazing athletic achievements.

WINONA LA DUKE, CHIPPEWA (1959-)

Winona La Duke was born in 1959. Today she lives on the White Earth Reservation in Minnesota with her two children.

She started working for her people at an early age, speaking in front of the United Nations on behalf of native peoples when she was 18 years old. While at Harvard she began research on how health is affected by uranium mining on the Navajo reservation.

Winona La Duke

Since her graduation from Harvard, La Duke has worked to recover lands taken by the federal government and the logging industry from the White Earth Reservation. To date, the Land Recovery Project, which she founded, has purchased 1,000 acres and expects to obtain another 30,000 in the next few years.

In the 1980s she was a leader of the successful fight against the James Bay hydroelectric projects and was named "the most prominent Native American Environmental activist" by several publications.

She founded the Indigenous Women's Network which, among other projects, researches small industries (e.g., rice production) and wind and solar energy sources for use on the reservation.

In October 1994 La Duke was arrested while protesting the cutting of both old and new growth trees to be used in the printing of phone books.

In the 1996 elections she ran as U.S. Vice Presidential candidate on the Green Party ticket. At present she is writing a book on Native Environmentalism to be published by South End Press.

Winona La Duke is an activist for the Chippewa people of Northern Minnesota. She has often said, "Spirituality is the foundation of all my political work." *Time* Magazine named her in 1995 as a Crusader for the Future.

OTHER IMPORTANT WOODLAND INDIANS

- Arsene Thompson, Cherokee Christian minister, who recited this prayer before the Cherokee people began their trek on the Trail of Tears:

  "I will lift up mine eyes unto the hills, from whence cometh my help. My help cometh from the Lord, which made Heaven and Earth."

  —Psalms 121:1-2

- Tammend, Lenape sachem of Pennsylvania
- Black Hawk, Sauk chief

Black Hawk

- Wilma Mankiller, chief of the Cherokee Nation
- Pontiac, Ottawa chief of the Great Lakes region
- Alexander McGellivray, Creek chief of Alabama and Georgia
- Kateri Takakwitha, Mohawk of the 17th century, declared blessed by Roman Catholic Church—a step closer to sainthood
- Louise Erdrich, German-American and Chippewa prize-winning author

Notes on "Historic Native Americans of the Woodlands":

1. Pocahontas was a nickname meaning "the naughty or spoiled child." Her real name was Matoka.

2. The first time John Smith told this story about being rescued by Pocahontas was 17 years after it was supposed to have happened, long after her death. It was just one of three tales he told of being rescued by an important woman. He didn't mention anything about Pocahontas (who was very young at the time) in a letter he wrote soon after his stay with Powhatan's people. He did, however, describe the friendly way in which Powhatan treated him.

3. There's a story that at this heated meeting, Harrison and Tecumseh drew their weapons. Harrison calmed Tecumseh and invited him to come sit at his bench. As the meeting went on, Tecumseh nudged Harrison further and further until Harrison asked him why he was pushing him off his bench. Tecumseh replied: "Well, that's what you're doing to *us*."

4. He created a written Cherokee in this way. He took Cherokee words and divided them into sounds. For each sound he chose a symbol (often based on an English or German letter which he found in books)—86 symbols in all. In this way a three-syllable Cherokee word, for example, would need just three "letters." Of the symbols, five stand for vowels, one for the letter S, and the other 80 stand for syllables, each made up of a consonant plus a vowel.

   It is interesting to note that because this writing system was not brought to the people by missionaries, it was often used by the Cherokees for recording magical formulas, charms, and prayers used in curing illnesses.

5. See the Will Rogers's reproducible page for more of his wise words and clever observations.

THE WOODLANDS INDIANS

Activities for the Classroom

ACTIVITIES

FOOD PREPARATION

While we can neither duplicate the conditions under which Native Americans did their cooking and food preparation nor the methods (an open pit fire, a birch bark bag of hot rocks, grinding jerky in a large stone mortar), we can encourage our students to experience and understand the processes involved in early Woodlands' food preparation.

You can have the fun of making, and then tasting together, some of these early Native American foods.

Dried Squash

You will need: 2-3 large firm squash (butternut or summer squash); string; *optional:* chicken broth, salt, butter.

Wash, dry, and peel the squash. Slice squash horizontally in 1/4" slices, so that the middle hollow forms a hole within each slice. Remove the seeds.

String the squash slices on a piece of sturdy cord and tie this like a clothesline in a dry sunny place. Separate the squash slices so air can circulate between them.

Once dried, squash slices can be kept in a closed or covered container and then added to soups, stews, or chicken broth as it simmers. Serve warm with salt and butter.

Beef Jerky[1]

1 1/2 lbs. brisket of beef or a large flank steak

1/4 cup soy sauce and 1/2 cup water

1 tsp. garlic, freshly squeezed

1/2 cup onions, finely minced

1 Tbsp. brown sugar

(*Note:* This is a two-day process.) Partially freeze the meat to facilitate cutting. Remove all fat. Slice the meat across the grain into *thin* slices. Combine the remaining ingredients in a big bowl and place the meat strips in this liquid overnight, turning occasionally. The next day remove the meat from the liquid and shake off any excess moisture.

Place these strips directly across the racks of your oven. Heat oven to 150° to 200° for 3-7 hours until the beef slices are thoroughly dried or jerked.

Beef jerky may be stored in a closed covered container (or a birch bark box...), but the children will probably want to begin chewing on it at once—just as Native Americans did long ago!

Leather Britches Beans (24 servings)

Cherokee women took fresh green beans, strung them on a plant fiber cord and sun dried them into Leather Britches Beans. *Note:* This recipe is authentic and may take two months to make.

4 lbs. green string beans, washed well

8 quarts water

1 lb. salt pork, cut into tiny pieces

2 Tbsp. salt *optional*

Have the students snap off the ends of the beans. Next, they use big needles and heavy thread to string the beans like long necklaces. They then hang these strings in a dry sunny place for two months—or until the beans are well dried.

When thoroughly dried, soak beans in 8 quarts of water for 1 hour.

Add salt pork, (salt), and bring to a boil. Reduce heat, simmer, stirring once in a while, for 3 hours. (Add more water if necessary). Serve with corn muffins or corn-pone.

Indian Pudding (16-20 small servings)

3 cups raisins	2 tsp. salt
6 cups scalded milk	1 cup honey (or sugar)
3 cups cold milk	2 Tbsp. fresh ginger root, grated fine
2 cups cornmeal	1/2 tsp. grated fresh nutmeg
1 cup molasses	1/2 cup butter

(Have students) add the raisins to the hot milk and then mix 2 cups cold milk in with the corn meal. Next (students) stir this into the hot milk. Add remaining ingredients.

This mixture is then heated very slowly, stirring constantly with a wooden spoon, until the mixture becomes thickened (10-15 minutes).

Sunflower Seed Cakes (30 cakes)

6 cups shelled sunflower seeds

6 cups water

4 1/2 tsp. salt

12 Tbsp. (white) cornmeal

1 cup cooking oil

Put sunflower seeds, water, and salt in a big pan. Cover and simmer for 1 hour, stirring once in a while. Cool mixture. Purée mixture in a blender.

Mix in cornmeal, a tablespoon at a time, to stiffen dough so that it can be shaped with the hands. Cool to room temperature. Shape into firm flat cakes about 3 inches in diameter.

The following step must be CAREFULLY SUPERVISED, or the *teacher* may do this step:

Heat oil in heavy skillet (until a drop of water sizzles) and brown cakes on both sides. Drain on paper towels. (Add more oil as needed while browning cakes.)

Sassafras Tea (1 1/2 quarts)

4 sassafras roots, each 2 inches long (available at health food stores)

1 1/2 quarts water

Scrub roots well, rinse, and scrape away the bark. Place the roots and bark scrapings in a big pan. Bring slowly to a boil, reduce heat, and simmer gently for 15 minutes. Turn off heat. Let tea steep for 10 minutes, then strain and serve.

Fresh Roasted Peanuts

2 lbs. blanched green peanuts

1/4 cup butter or margarine

salt

Place nuts and butter in a big shallow pan and roast in a slow 300° oven for 2 hours. Stir often. Remove from oven, drain on paper towels, and sprinkle with salt.

Sweet Potato Bread (20 servings)

4 large sweet potatoes	3 tsp. salt
2 cups cornmeal	4 tsp. honey
2 cups flour, unbleached	4 Tbsp. melted butter
2 tsp. baking powder	2 1/2 cups warm milk
4 eggs, lightly beaten	

Parboil sweet potatoes until tender; then cool, peel, and cut into 1/4-inch cubes. Sift dry ingredients together and place in bowl. Combine honey, milk, butter, and eggs, and mix into dry ingredients. Fold in tiny cubes of sweet potato. Pour into two 8" x 8" baking dishes and bake in 350° oven until a paring knife inserted in the center comes out clean—about one hour.

Cut into squares and serve hot with butter. Eat with a fork.

CRAFTS

These craft-making suggestions have been included because each provides a sense of what it was like to deal with situations met by early people. Each craft is educational and fun to do, and is possible to complete in a relatively short amount of time.

Sand Clay Projects

SAND CLAY RECIPE   This is a terrific recipe for clay as it produces a material that is clean to use and easy to form; it is fast drying and, once dry, rock hard! This recipe will provide a lump each for 10+ students. You will need:

2 cups sifted sand

1 cup cornstarch

1 1/2 cups cold water

Always use an old pan (from Goodwill) when preparing this recipe. Cook over medium heat, stirring constantly for 5 to 10 minutes, until mixture is very thick. (When doubled, the recipe produces a mixture that is, near completion, difficult to stir; so use a big [wooden] spoon.)

Turn onto a plate and cover with a wet cloth. Cool.

Sand clay should remain moist. It may be kept for a day or two if double bagged in plastic (tightly wrapped and tied off).

Knead a bit before dividing into separate lumps.

A THREE-DIMENSIONAL MAP   Prepare two double batches of Sand Clay, and cover tightly with plastic wrap. Divide the class into pairs so that two students work together on constructing each map. Each pair of students is then given:

a large piece of foam core or heavy cardboard (scraps are often free from frame shops)

a copy of the map from the "How the First People Came Here" reproducible

white glue

toothpicks

2 plastic picnic knives

2 pencils

2 balls of Sand Clay

(watercolors or poster paints)

Tell the students: Study the map and, using pencils on foam core, make a large outline of the land masses shown. Next, apply a small amount of white glue to the middle area of your drawing to help anchor the clay once it is applied.

Smooth out one ball of clay onto your land-mass drawing. Stay within the boundaries and smear the clay so that it is thinner near the edges of the map outline and thicker in the interior of the map.

Now, use the second ball of clay to build up the high areas, such as the Black Hills, as you refer back to the map for accurate information. Use the plastic knives and toothpicks to create crevices, rivers, plains, and lakes. Cooperate in constructing these maps; both of you should be involved in the molding of the map contours.

Put the maps out of the way (near a heat source) and check periodically to note dryness. Once your map is dry, give it a light coat of watercolor; the river and lakes can be painted by using poster paints or watercolors. (Use a toothpick to apply white glue under any area that may have pulled away from the cardboard.) Finally, make a neatly printed title on your map that includes the "signatures of the two cartographers."

EFFIGY MOUNDS AND EARTHWORKS   Using the approach described above, have the children create three-dimensional examples of the various prehistoric earthworks and mounds. Have them label each neatly and with approximate dates of their creation.

Effigy Mounds
Wisconsin

(Hopewell? c.100 B.C. – c.A.D. 500)

Snake
Mounds
Mississippi
Valley

(Adena? c. 800 B.C.- c. A.D. 400)

Shelters

FOLDED PAPER LONGHOUSE OR CHICKEE   Each child will need a piece of tan or white 9" x 12" construction paper and marking pens or crayons.

Show the children how to fold their papers in half crosswise and then in half vertically. Next take the top flap, left handside, and fold it in to meet the center (fold) of the top flap. Repeat this proceducure with the righthand side top flap.

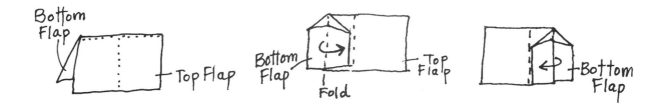

The outside of the longhouse (chickee) is formed when the paper is folded down flat as shown. Have the children each draw the elm bark and the door (or palm fronds) on their paper.

Longhouse
Exterior

Two Chickees

Then when the top flaps are opened out, "we can see inside the longhouse or chickee." Have the children draw the interior of the building and what and whom we might see there.

When a variety of miniature shelters made out of paper and Sand Clay have been created, ask for volunteers to form a committee that will be responsible for organizing the student-made shelters into a classroom exhibit. Explain that you will provide any materials they request, free time in which to set up the exhibit, and that they will earn extra-credit points (if these are offered in your class).

Longhouse Interior   "Inside" a Chickee

Tool-Making Ideas

Provide a supply of the following: little sticks, dead wooden matches, small scraps of wood, lots of sandpaper, scissors, white glue, markers, thin leather scraps, waxed carpet thread, cotton string, small pieces of netting, needles, thread, small round rocks, shells, and long reeds (for atl-atls). A supply of Sand Clay may also be helpful.

Have the students study pictures of prehistoric tools (see **Tools** section earlier in this book). Provide the materials listed above and encourage the class to bring in specific sticks or pieces of wood, shells, leather, etc., that they think would work well as (part of) a tool.

Finally, when a wide selection of materials has been collected, ask each child to select a tool to faithfully and carefully reproduce in miniature. Give the class adequate time for this project so students will not feel rushed.

When (a selection of) the tools has been completed, ask students to come up with suggestions for exhibiting their work and sharing these handmade tools with other classes. Ask for a volunteer who (for extra credit) will lead the group discussion and oversee the selection of an ultimate solution for organizing, labeling, and exhibiting these prehistoric tool replications.

Sand Clay can be used by the children to form realistic-looking bird points, "arrowheads," scrapers, drills, small ax heads, small mortars and pestles, or small stone bowls.

Encourage the students to include every detail of the original prehistoric tools.

Tennessee   Florida   Tennessee

Pipestone Pipes

Have the children look at many pictures of different carved Catlinite (pipestone) pipes.

Mix some rust-colored tempera powder—*not* liquid poster paint—into a batch of Sand Clay as it is cooking in order to achieve the color of pipestone or Catlinite.

Ask the students each to draw a simple pipe, based on the pictures they have seen. The Sand Clay is used to model the short pipes, not the long stems that were sometimes attached to the pipe bowls.

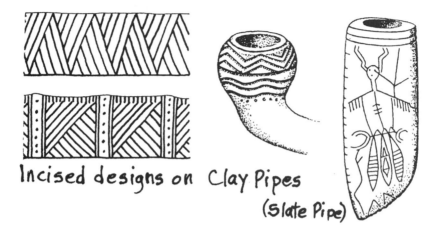

Incised designs on Clay Pipes
(Slate Pipe)

Masks

Masks are worn for many different reasons: to disguise the wearer, to lend a sense of mystery, to give the wearer the power of the creature the mask portrays. Masks are used to celebrate, to tease, to honor, to ridicule.

Use library books to study pictures of Northeastern and Southeastern masks. Have each student find a mask that he or she would like to replicate. Encourage the child to examine the proportions of the mask and how the features were constructed and then to make a simple drawing of it.

PAPER CLAY RECIPE   (Have the students) tear newspapers into thin strips and then into squares. Soak all these in water overnight. Squeeze out the excess water from the paper pulp. Rub the wet pulp back and forth between your hands to form a smooth uniform mass.

Put nine pints of lukewarm water in a plastic pail. Sift 1 pound (one package) Golden Harvest® wallpaper paste (sold at paint stores) into the water, stirring constantly until the paste is smooth. Let paste stand for five minutes and then add it, little by little, to the paper pulp until a malleable modeling material is created. (Add Elmer's White Glue-all® to the pulp to give it added strength.) The Paper Clay should not be too wet or sticky; if it is, add more paper pulp that has been squeezed very dry.

Make sure to add enough wallpaper paste so that the resulting Paper Clay will dry hard and not crack or be brittle. It should hold its shape when wet and you should be able to attach small pieces (eyelids, noses, ears) to the basic head shapes without having them come off. (If some appendages should come off during the drying period, just use Elmer's White Glue-all® to adhere the dried piece in place on the dried head once again.)

MAKING THE MASKS   Each student lays a rather thin slab of the Paper Clay over half a large plastic cottage cheese or yogurt container, as shown in the illustration.

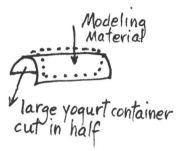

Using the mask drawing he or she made as a guide, the student molds pieces of the clay to form the nose, chin, lips, and facial creases, and attaches these securely to the flattened slab. Then, using a plastic picnic knife, the child carves out eye holes (and the mouth opening). The features of the face should be carefully formed and then the mask left to dry, which takes 2 to 4 days depending on the thickness.

Carefully remove the mask from the plastic container and allow the underside to dry also. Use tempera or acrylic paint (in historically authentic colors) to decorate the mask as illustrated in the reference books.

Birch Bark Projects

The Northeastern Indians—especially the Passamaquoddy of Maine—used birch bark for making canoes, wigwam covers, containers, baby carriers, dolls, drums—and emergency raincoats!

They cut new winter bark, which is heavier than summer bark, and were careful not to harm the still growing (cambium) layer underneath. Next, they turned the sheet of bark over so they could draw into this softer part using a sharpened bone or knife. This left a light line against the darker bark. The early people scratched geometric designs, flowers, leaves, maps, birds, and animals into the bark. Sometimes they made a design in relief by scratching away the background, leaving dark lines against a light background.

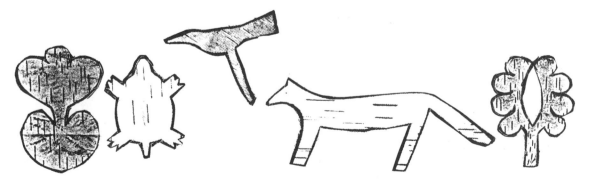

Use heavy brown butcher paper (on which the children will draw with white crayons) or heavy tan butcher paper (on which the students will make designs in brown). If the paper you have available is not heavy, use (wallpaper) paste to completely adhere two sheets of light-weight paper together to form a thickened sheet on which the student will emboss a pattern, outline, or design. Once the glue is dry the outline of the hand or bird or flower can be cut out, if the student wishes.

BIRCH BARK DOLLS (CHIPPEWA)   Make a few posterboard patterns of these figures—or get some older students to do this for you! Distribute them to the students and let them trace these authentic shapes or make up variations of their own. Once the figures are cut out, have students use white crayons to color on birch tree veining and then add a light wash of tan or brown watercolor over the entire figure for a sense of added authenticity and effect.

You may want to encourage students to use these figures to act out a folk tale for a group of younger children.

BIRCH BARK BERRY BUCKET   Use a copier to enlarge the pattern below. Make copies of the enlarged pattern. Have each child cut out one and use it to trace a bucket pattern onto heavy paper, or even lightweight tan or white posterboard. Have each student use the edge of a ruler or plastic picnic knife to score the dotted lines. Then they each decide on a geometric design or a pattern found in nature and carefully draw this in white crayon on the front and back panels of the bucket.

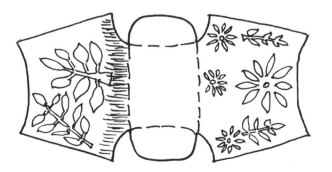

A light brown watercolor wash is next applied to the entire berry bucket. When the paint is dry, have each student cut out the bucket along the solid lines. Next, they fold up the side flaps and front and back panels along the dotted lines.

To give the bucket shape, either use masking tape INSIDE the berry bucket to hold flaps and panels in place, or have the children use large tapestry needles and (linen) carpet thread to sew the basket together.

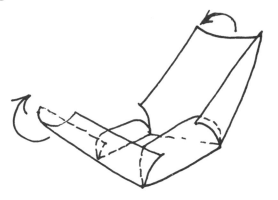

A handle can be added by running heavy black yarn through the holes at the top of the bucket and tying a knot in each end as shown.

yarn Knots
inside bucket

Here are illustrations (to be enlarged) as patterns for other birch bark containers.

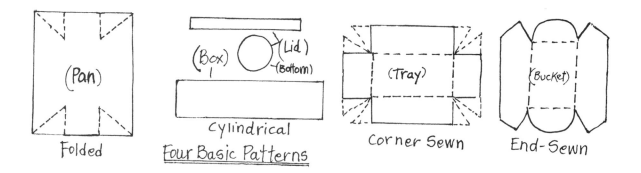

(Pan)

Folded

(Box) (Lid)
(Bottom)

cylindrical

Four Basic Patterns

(Tray)

Corner Sewn

(Bucket)

End-Sewn

Encourage interested students to experiment with the heavy paper in order to create: a round box and lid; dishes made of one rectangular piece of paper with folded-over ends, requiring no cutting—and so on.

NasKapi
Round Box

DREAM SCROLLS (CHIPPEWA)   These 36-inch long pieces of bark had a wooden stick sewn to either end. Pictures recording a dream (or the details of a sacred ceremony) were drawn into the bark and then these lines were rubbed with a red powder. Such scrolls were made and kept by the Grand Medicine Society, the Midewiwin.

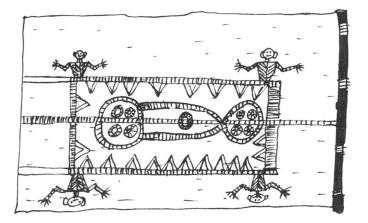

Provide each child with a 7" x 36" long piece of heavy tan butcher paper. Ask each of them to get two 7-inch long sticks (chopsticks work well). Use a (small hole) paper punch to make 11 holes along each 7-inch side of the paper. Children each use red yarn to thread through a hole over the 7-inch stick, around it, and back up through the hole, over the second hole around the stick, and so on. The yarn is neatly tied to the stick at the top and bottom to hold it to the paper.

Ask the children to remember a dream they each have (recently) had and to give the dream four or five very simple drawings to stand for what happened in the dream. These four or five drawings should fill the length of the scroll; wide margins should be left at the top and bottom. Finally, thin brushes and red paint or red markers are used to draw in the "picture writing" itself.

These dream scrolls make an engaging display and invite dream interpretations from all the viewers.

Beading Projects

Using a beading loom is a very rewarding activity for students who already have some weaving experience and want to make such objects as beaded belts and wrist guards.

MAKING AND SETTING UP THE LOOM   Use a two-by-four (board) of appropriate length for a base. Position finishing nails at either end to support the warp. These nails need to be very close together, so they are best staggered in two rows. The number of nails depends on how wide you want the weaving to be. If it is to be six beads wide, for example, you will need a seven-string warp (forming six rows); therefore, seven nails at each end. String the loom with a length of thin cotton string or strong thread.

Tie the string to the first nail on one end of the board and bring it down the length of the board and around behind the first and second nails, at the other end. Now bring the string back up the loom to the second nail, go behind this and the third nail, and back down again around the third and fourth nail, and so on. Continue in this way until the loom is completely strung. Firmly tie off the loom thread at the base of the last nail.

BEADING   Use rather large glass beads and long, thin beading needles. Thread a needle with a 2- to 3-foot strand of strong (nylon) thread. Tie the end of the thread to an outside warp string at one end of the loom. Proceed one row at a time, stringing beads on needle and thread; use as many beads at a time as there are rows between the warp strings. Pass the line of beads under and across the warp strings. In other words, the row of beads is perpendicular to the warp strings, *not* parallel with them. Using a finger, press the beads from below into position between the warp strings, then pass the (now empty) needle and thread back through the beads but, this time, *over* the warp strings. String a second row of beads and repeat the process until you have reached the end. When it is necessary to start a new thread, tie the previous one to the warp.

If a particular pattern is desired, chart it out on graph paper using colored pencils or fine-tip markers; each square represents a bead. Tape this paper directly below the warp strings so it may guide students during the beading process.

A CIGAR BOX LOOM   You can also use a cigar box as a loom. Use an X-acto™ knife to cut slits in the sides of the box for the warp strings. The cover can be closed to protect the weaving while it is in progress, and the beads can be stored inside the box.

Stamp Designs

The Woodland Indians of the Northeast used stamps dipped in dye to print designs on birch bark containers. Some tribes dipped stamps in paint and applied patterns to their skin.

Here is a way to make handmade rubber stamps to decorate "birch bark" containers, greeting cards, student-made books, or scrolls.

RUBBER STAMPS   You will need a used inner tube from a truck tire (they're often free from a tire-repair garage), ballpoint pens, sharp scissors, foam core or corrugated cardboard (squares 3" x 4") hot glue gun and glue, small corks (sold in bulk at hardware stores) or wine corks (each cut into 2 to 3 pieces crosswise), large ink pads (with ink pad refiller applicators) or thick poster paint and big brushes, and household cement (airplane glue).

Once you have the inner tube back home, cut it (along the seams) to make large flat pieces. Use a dishwashing soap to wash off any oils and powders from the rubber's surface. This will assure that the ink or paint will adhere to the rubber stamp's surface—so that the student will obtain clean prints!

The student thinks of a simple shape and, using a ballpoint pen, draws it on a flat unseamed part of the inner tube; this shape should not be larger than 2" x 3".

(The teacher) use(s) sharp scissors to cut out the shape. Next, the student applies a coat of glue to the rubber cutout and then flips it over (glue-side down) and lays it flat on the center of a cardboard square that is a bit bigger than the cutout. Next, this cutout is gently, but firmly, pressed onto the cardboard; it is important that no bumps be allowed to form in the rubber as it's being glued and that the edges all be glued down tight. Finally, the student places the cardboard square under heavy weights for one hour until the glue is completely dry and there are no loose edges.

Now the teacher, or older student, turns over the cardboard and—using a hot glue gun—adheres the cork, for a handle, to the back of the cardboard.

Once the handle is firmly in place, the student presses the stamp down onto an inked stamp pad; several pressings may be necessary to completely ink the rubber cutout.[2] Then he or she transfers the print to a piece of scratch paper. Once the child is satisfied with the image, he or she can use this rubber stamp to make up a story or a comic strip, or the class could work collaboratively, using all their stamps, to illustrate a book or apply designs to birch bark baskets.

CREATIVE WRITING (OR JOURNAL-ENTRY) SUGGESTIONS

The following may be used as themes for oral readings, creative writing self-starters, or jointly written pieces:

1. "Imagine yourself as one of the first Asians who crossed the Bering Strait into North America. Name several things you saw on your walk. What kinds of thoughts did you have? What were you looking forward to? Why would it be a better life for you in this new land?"

2. "Many Native Americans do not believe that their ancestors came to this continent by crossing the Bering Strait. They choose to believe their tribal legends and sacred stories that tell how the first people came up out of the Earth onto the North American continent. Imagine that you were among those first people. Write about what you first saw, smelled, heard, felt. Give good details."

3. *What's in My House?* (This activity may take 2 to 3 sessions to complete.)

    Begin by printing this question on the board or at the top of a large sheet of paper. Give the children 5 to 10 minutes to each make a long list of the many things they can think of that are in their own homes. Then go around the room and have each student contribute a *different* object, person, or animal to the master list that you print on the board (paper) as they say it. Focus briefly on what "categories" these objects or creatures seem to imply: entertainment, eating, sleeping, etc. Next ask them to each make a long list of all the things they might see in a wigwam or a longhouse (or Southeastern townhouse or chickee); encourage them to remember the tools, food preparations, and arts and crafts you have studied.

    Again go around the room to get a different contribution to the group list from each student.

Have some fun finding any comparisons that may be drawn from the two lists; e.g., TV set and birch bark cutout figures (or an elder storyteller)!

Finally ask each student to imagine that he or she is a Woodlands Indian (either sitting or lying) in a wigwam, longhouse, or chickee. Describe in detail what they see as they look around the inside of their house. Include lots of details such as colors, the number of things, any paintings there may be, who sleeps and works in each part of the shelter, and so on. Make the inside of the home come alive to the reader. Students may want to make a fold-out paper longhouse or chickee to illustrate the house." (See the earlier *Shelter Activities* in this section.)

4. "A eulogy is a poem that praises its subject (its beauty, nobility, strength and so on). This kind of poem does not need to rhyme. Write an eulogy for the eagle, the bear, the birch, or cypress tree. Praise many different things about this animal or tree and say why it deserves to have an eulogy written for it."

5. "Rabbit is a creator and a trickster; he is wise and cunning. He makes things happen—sometimes he is too smart for his own good. Make up a rabbit tale to explain how he got his fluffy tail, for example, or how he brought the snow to the Woodlands...or...? *Your* choice. Have fun!"

6. "Imagine yourself to be a young Woodlands Indian child. Think about your favorite toy, for example, a ball and pin game, a doll, tiny bow and arrows, a ball, clay dishes, or birch bark box. Make up a short story that includes a detailed description of your toy; who made it; why you first wanted it; why, in particular, you love it; and how you first learned to use it. Finally, tell what became, or will become, of this special part of your Woodlands Indian childhood."

7. "Brainstorm with your friend (or the class) to create a list of experiences that a birch bark, basswood, elm, or palmetto tree might have. These could include: how it first got planted and took root. What animals use it and how. How a human treats it and why. How weather gives it a big adventure. What its daily life is like."

8. *Going on a Vision Quest.*

You will need 25 to 35 large file cards; on each card glue a small colorful, engaging picture of an Eastern animal, snake, bird, or tree. Explain to the class that a Vision Quest would be taken by young Woodland children in order to find a new name or a personal animal helper.

Bird incised on stone pendant:
red jaspar, 1½"x3½"
N.E. Louisiana c. 1200 B.C.

Place the picture cards face down and have each child pick a card at random. Then each student quietly studies the picture he or she drew. There must be absolute silence for five to ten minutes so that each person's mind may be able to take the child on a quest to a woods or a lake in search of an adventure and a new name! Encourage the children to come up with details about their creature and the time they spent together.

These adventures can be shared orally or put into writing and into personal drawings. Encourage the students to really "see, hear, touch and smell the place they go to" and tell them to "have courage" to go through their quest and return with a new name!

CREATIVE WRITING (STORYTELLING) FOR OLDER STUDENTS

1. "Think of the various tools that were made and used by the early people of woodlands. Make a quick list of such tools, including those used for hunting, fishing, food gathering, making clothing or shelter, and even the tools used to make other tools. Now select 3 or 4 tools and write about:
   - how they might have first been invented
   - what their (daily) lives are like (give details)
   - what you imagine their complaints might be
   - what things make them the happiest"

2. Have the class as a whole dictate a long list of nouns that are connected to their study of the early Woodland peoples, for example, wampum, birch bark, medicine man, hominy, alligator, chickee, and so on. Write this list on the board and then cover it with a pull-down map or a large sheet of paper.

   Next have the class dictate a long list of (provocative sounding) adjectives and write this list to the left of the covered list of nouns. Then have a student quickly draw lines at random, connecting one word from the adjective list to a word from the noun list. This produces two-word descriptions that may be poetic, funny, surreal, or even contradictory.

   Finally, give the class 20 minutes in which to each write about any of the combinations they choose—justifying and explaining exactly how such a word combination could work and be right for the situation.

   Encourage the students to give these explanations in context. Use the two words either as a part of a surrealist's poem, or as a hint to the solution of a murder mystery, or as a clue on a treasure map—the connection making should be as creative as possible!

3. *What Is a Culture?*

   As a group, reach a collective definition of culture. Ask the students to "define (one of) the culture(s) from which you come." This might be based on ethnic, racial, national roots—or others. "Ask yourself what some of the general characteristics of this culture are. Which of these are important to you? What cultural influences have helped to shape this person you have become?" Talk (or write) about this.

Provide each student with a large sheet of newsprint and a marker. Say that they have 15 minutes in which to use these to illustrate Native Peoples. They may do this in any way they like: by drawing pictures or using symbols, words, or phrases to show: what is important to them, what conditions or ideas have helped shape these first North Americans. After 15 minutes each student tapes this piece of newsprint onto the wall of the room. Then everyone takes some time to walk around the room and tries to read these illustrations. Finally, one by one, the students talk about their drawings and the historical, artistic, religious details on these newsprint sheets.

What aspects of cultural background show up on these illustrations?

4. *Riddle-writing:* All early people made up riddles based on parts of the human body. Ask older students to look at the list below* and find natural or man-made objects in the lives of the Woodland peoples (Northeast or Southeast) that could be used to make a body-based riddle. For example: What part of the human body is:

a big birch bark box to hold your valuables? (*the chest*)

two sharp flint knives on the edge of the road? (*the shoulder blades*)

a huge bunch of rabbits? (*hairs [hares...]*)

You get the idea! And once students do, they should have fun writing riddles.

Following such a writing session you may ask each student to pick out his or her three best riddles and share them with the group. This should provide a few laughs or groans!

TIMELINES FOR YOUNGER STUDENTS

Introduce timelines by having each child make a simple timeline of his or her own life, one square for each year he or she has been alive. Next, the children could make a timeline of a usual school day, with each hour or each change of activity being illustrated.

INDIVIDUAL HAND-SIZED STUDENT TIMELINES

Here is an excellent way to reinforce historical information you want your class to remember. This technique also aids sequential thinking and is a very good mnemonic device.

You will need: 5" x 8" file cards (three for each student plus extra for errors), a rubber band for each student, paper cutter, rulers, pencils, 1-inch wide cellophane tape, markers/crayons, glue, scissors, wildlife magazines, and several table knives.

---

* eyelids, knee caps, eardrums, veins, feet, arms, hands, nails, eyelashes, dimples, knuckles, soles, muscles, palms, temples, pupils, insteps, arches, calves, nose, eyes, wrist, elbow, neck, Adam's apple, tongue, teeth, chin, backbone, and so on

Preparing the Blank Timelines

Mark each file card lengthwise at 2-5/8" intervals at top and bottom.

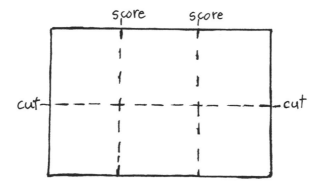

Now use a ruler and the back of the blade of a table knife to connect the first two marks top and bottom; this will score the file card so that it may later be neatly folded. Connect the second set of two marks with a score line also. (This will create two vertical lines and three columns on the card.)

Then, carefully cut each card in half horizontally. (Each card will now be two 2-1/2" x 8" strips, with three sections in each strip, for a total of six sections.)

Using the Blank Timelines

Demonstrate how to neatly tape two strips (six sections) of a timeline together.

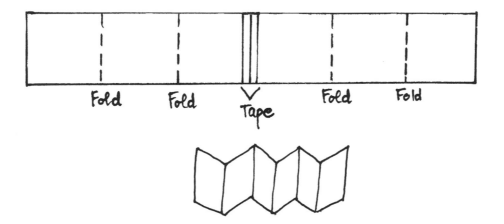

Each student tapes the two strips together to form the beginning of the individual timeline; then he or she designs an appropriate title section (cover) for the timeline using the words and dates: *Native Americans of the Woodlands (23,000 B.C. to A.D. 1800)*. Each prints his or her name neatly in tiny letters somewhere on this first section, and then folds the timeline accordion-like, with the cover showing on top, and secures it closed with a rubber band.

Collect these blank timelines and return them to the students once you have studied: *23,000 to 11,000* B.C. *Siberians cross Bering Strait into North America.** Each will make a drawing (on the empty section next to their title section) to illustrate the Siberians coming over to North America and note the date. Collect the timelines and then return them to the students after you have studied: *c. 1000 B.C. to 200 A.D. The Adena Mound Builders.* Children each make a picture with magazine cutouts and/or drawings to illustrate the Adena Mound Builders. Continue this procedure after the introduction of (each of) the important historical date(s).

You will need to go down the list of dates and, according to the level and interests of your class, select ten dates you will wish to emphasize during this unit of study.

Once your students have illustrated the first five dates, you will need to provide each student with a new index card. Repeat the procedure described above (scoring, cutting, taping) and connect this new part of the timeline to the first part. (Since there are more than eleven sections required to complete this particular timeline, you will have to go through this procedure once more, later, in order to finish this project.)

Before adding (a) new date(s) to the timelines, have the class quickly read through the dates that have already been noted. Repeating the dates, starting with 23,000 B.C. each time a new date is added, will offer good oral review and will help cement the sequential dates in their minds.

Collect the timelines after new addition(s) are made and store them in a specific place. This protects the timelines and keeps the images fresh for the students.

When the timelines covering 23,000 B.C. to 1700 A.D. are completed, neatly display them (in the hallway) at the children's eye-level, using straight pins or double-stick tape on the *back* (not staples, or tape on the front, which would damage the timelines). This will encourage the students to review the dates.

Depending on the time you have, and the emphasis you want to give the 16th to 20th centuries, you may choose to have the children make a large classroom timeline:

Native Americans of the Woodlands A.D. *1200 to...*(your choice).

---

* Some students may also want to show the Native Americans being put on Earth by Old Men, or coming up out of a sacred lake, or down from the sky: Creation-in-place theory.

Dates

The following dates can be used to make a timeline for the Native Americans of the Woodlands:

Creation-in-place (coming [up] out of a natural site): the Native American view of the arrival of the first people to this continent.

c. 23,000 B.C. to c. 11,000 B.C.	The first people come to North America; they use the Bering Strait to cross over to this continent
c. 11,400 B.C.-A.D. 1500	*Woodland cultures in the East,* including:
c. 1000 B.C.-A.D. 200	Adena (Mound Builders) in and around Ohio Valley
c. 300 B.C.-A.D. 700	Hopewell (Mound Builders) of Ohio and Illinois River Valleys and throughout much of the Midwest and East
c. 700-1700	Mississippian (Temple Mound Builders) in Mississippi Basin and Southeast
c.1497-1498	John Cabot (backed by England) explores Eastern coastline of North America
c. 1500	European diseases begin killing North American Indians
1513-1521	Ponce de Leon (backed by Spain) reaches Florida; on second trip (1521) he's wounded by an arrow (Seminole) and dies later in Cuba
1523-1524	Giovanni de Verrazano (backed by France) explores the Atlantic coast, meeting many Indians
1539-1543	Hernando de Soto claims Florida for Spain and explores the Southeast, meeting and making enemies of many tribes; in 1541 he dies and is buried in the Mississippi River; the expedition floats on the river to the Gulf of Mexico
c.1560-1570	The Iroquois League of Five Nations—including the Mohawk, Oneida, Onondaga, Cayuga, and Seneca tribes—is formed by Huron Iroquois prophet Deganawida and his Mohawk helper, Hiawatha
1565	The Spanish, under Pedro de Aviles, found St. Augustine in Florida, first permanent European settlement in North America
1585-1586	First British settlement in North America is founded on Roanoke Island backed by Sir Walter Raleigh; it lasts just one year
1586-1590	Sir Walter Raleigh tries again to settle Roanoke; the settlers disappear
1604	Samuel de Champlain explores from Acadia to New England
1607	Capt. John Smith (English) settles in Jamestown, Virginia
1609-1611	Henry Hudson (Dutch) explores the Hudson River as far as Albany (and Hudson's Bay, Canada)
1615	Squanto, a Wampanoag, is kidnapped and taken to England where, as a servant, he learns English
1616-1620	Smallpox epidemic among New England tribes

1619	Squanto returns to North America where he is able to help save the Plymouth Colony
1620	Pilgrims arrive in Plymouth; Squanto shows them how to plant corn, fertilizing it with fish
1626	Canarsee Indians "sell" Manhattan Island to Peter Minuit, governor of New Netherlands, for 60 guilders worth of trade goods; later the Dutch clear the deal with Manhattan Indians who actually hold that land
1633-1635	Smallpox epidemics among Indians of New England, New Netherland, and New France
1636-1865	The American Indians are embattled, warring against the colonists, the U.S. Government, the various European powers, and among themselves; twenty-one of these major encounters are listed in *The Europeans Come* section
1664	The English get control of New Netherland and become allies with the Iroquois League; New Amsterdam on Manhattan Island becomes New York
1682	Rene de la Salle claims the Mississippi Valley (Louisiana) for France
1738	Smallpox epidemic among Cherokees of Southeast
1775-1783	American Revolution is fought
1776	Declaration of Independence is signed
1799	Handsome Lake, a Seneca chief, founds the Longhouse religion
1803	Louisiana Purchase by the United States from France (which had gained the territory back from Spain two years before) adds a large Indian population to the United States
1809-1821	Sequoyah single-handedly creates a Cherokee syllabic alphabet so that his people's language can be written
1819	Spain cedes Florida to the U.S.
1824	Bureau of Indian Affairs is organized as part of the War Department
1827	Cherokees adopt a constitution patterned after that of the United States, but it is nullified by the Georgia legislature
1828-1835	*Cherokee Phoenix*, a weekly newspaper, is published, using Sequoyah's syllabary
1830	Indian Removal Act passes Congress, calling for relocation of Eastern Indians to an Indian Territory west of the Mississippi River
1832	Cherokees contest the Act in court, and the Supreme Court decides in their favor, but President Andrew Jackson ignores decision
1831-1839	The Five Civilized Tribes of the Southeast are relocated to the Indian Territory

1838-1839	The Cherokee "Trail of Tears" takes place
1861-1865	The Civil War

In 1861, the Confederate government organizes a Bureau of Indian Affairs. Most tribes remain neutral. The South, however, makes promises to Indians concerning the return of their tribal lands to encourage their support. After the war, as punishment for their support of the Confederacy, the Five Civilized Tribes are compelled to accept a treaty relinquishing the western half of the Indian Territory to 20 tribes from Kansas and Nebraska.

1887	Dawes Act passes in which reservation lands are given to individual Indians in parcels; Indians lose millions of acres of land
1912	Jim Thorpe, a Sauk athlete of the Carlisle School, participates in the Olympic Games in Stockholm, Sweden, winning the pentathlon and the decathlon
1913	Thorpe is forced to surrender his medals to the Olympic Committee because he had played one season of semi-professional baseball while he was in school
1914-1918	World War I; many American Indians enlist, fight, and die
1924	With the Citizenship Act, Congress bestows American citizenship on all native-born Indians who have not yet obtained it; thus giving Native Americans the right to vote.[3] This ruling results in part from gratitude for the Indian contribution to the American effort in World War I
1941-1945	World War II; more than 25,000 Indians on active duty and thousands more in war-related industries; Navajo Marines become famous for the use of their language as a battlefield code that the enemy is unable to decipher
1957	Iroquois activism in New York State. Senecas oppose the building of the Kinzua Dam; Tuscaroras fight the New York State Power Authority; Mohawks reoccupy lands taken by white squatters
1958	Miccosukees of Florida resist the Everglades Reclamation Project
1964	Civil Rights Act prohibits discrimination for reason of color, race, religion, or national origin
1968	American Indian Movement (AIM) is founded in Minneapolis to deal with the many problems faced by the urban relocation of Indians; it has since come to be involved in struggles of reservation Indians also
1978	Congress passes the American Indian Freedom of Religion Act which states that Indian religion is protected by the First Amendment
1978	Wampanoags of Massachusetts are denied claims to land because, when their suit was filed in 1976, they did not comprise a legal tribe

1980   Maine Indian Claims Settlement Act is reached in which the
              Passamaquoddy and Penobscot Indians agree to abandon land
              claims in Maine in exchange for a $27-million federal trust fund
              and a $54 million in federal land acquisition fund
1983   Jim Thorpe's awards are reinstated
1984   The "Great Jim Thorpe Longest Run," in which Indian runners
              cross the country, and the "Jim Thorpe Memorial Pow Wow and
              Games" in Los Angeles honor the memory of the Indian athlete
              and Olympian

CULMINATING ACTIVITY: CREATING A MUSEUM OF THE WOODLANDS

When your third- to eighth-grade students have completed their studies of Native Americans, discuss with them how your class might share with others the things you have been doing in the past weeks.

If the idea of constructing a classroom museum appeals to the group, start off by making a class-generated list defining what a museum is, and the many kinds of things you can find there. Next have them list all the things they have made during their studies (tools, food, beading, various crafts, birch bark objects, timelines, and so on). Help them decide how they might best exhibit these.

Next, help them brainstorm how their museum could appeal to all the senses! This could include: *Taste*—dried fruit and vegetables, jerky; *Smell*—leather, smoke, sassafras; *Touch*—Woodland objects, each inside a sock in a shoe box (sock opening stapled to the inside of the shoe box) with the lid taped shut: an identifying label could be in the form of a riddle.

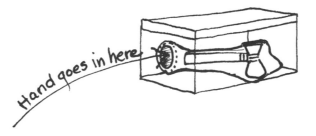

Hear—tape, sound effects, Native American whistle, drum; *Sight*—video, slides, signs, folktale collections; and *Make*—replicas, Sand Clay objects, and so on.

Finally, organize committees to each take responsibility for a specific aspect of your museum. This might involve categories such as: large signs, labels for exhibits, displays of specific objects (shelters or crafts), the large timeline, and so on; let them come up with the specific categories. Then ask for volunteers for each category (committee) and let these children organize themselves, targeting tasks to be done and how best to accomplish them. Each committee should make a list of materials they will need to complete their work. See that these materials are provided.

If at all possible, the students should visit a local museum and keep a list of all the physical elements "a good museum" should have, e.g., well-written labels and signs, intriguing objects, a clear chronology, thought-provoking exhibits, a few unexpected (manipulatives or action-oriented) displays, and so on.

When their museum is completed, invite the public, and open the doors!

OTHER SUGGESTIONS FOR CULMINATING ACTIVITIES

1. A time capsule is a container made to hold and preserve major elements of a historic period or culture. It is filled, and then buried or put into a vault until a much later time (centuries later, perhaps) when it is opened and its contents are studied. Time capsules originated in the 20th century, but if you had lived in the Woodlands in the 18th century and you had a vision that told you to collect things to be placed in a jar for future children to see, what things would you have chosen? Make a list of things that represent the Woodlands Indian culture. Be sure to include examples of food, clothing, tools, children, arts and crafts, religion, war, and so on.

   Make an X-ray picture of the filled jar—as if you were able to see through the sides of the jar and could see all the things in it. Show all the details!

2. **Quick 'n EZ pop-up books**: Pop-up books provide an unusual format for very individual culmination projects. The pictures in each book may be hand drawn, cut from (nature) magazines, or be a combination of the two.

   Each book could illustrate a theme: "A Day in the Life of a Woodland Indian," "My Favorite Facts about Southeastern Native Americans," or "The Mound Builders"—or let each student come up with his or her own title.

   Fold a rectangular piece of heavy (computer printout) paper in half crosswise.

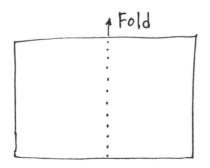

Cut 2 to 5 slits along the fold. Make several slits deeper than others.

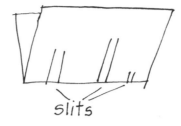

slits

Now fold the tabs made by the slits OUTWARD, so that the tabs stand up.

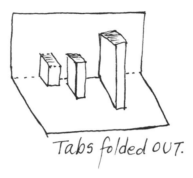

Tabs folded OUT.

These tabs will be the bases for your pop-ups. (The deeper slits will make bases that are closer to the viewer. The shallow slits will make bases that appear to be off in the distance.)

Next either draw and color in the background (sky, hills, trees) on the top half of the folded paper or cut out and glue a magazine picture there.

Then, in magazines, find and carefully cut out 2 to 5 (depending on the number of your tabs) animals, people, or objects you want to use on your pop-up page. Glue each to the front of a fold-out tab. (You can also assemble several magazine images to make one illustration. This kind of surreal assemblage that plays with comparative sizes can be readily made by older students.)

Anything can happen in a POP UP Book!

Use a glue stick to glue the edges of this pop-up page to the edges of a second (or third or fourth...) pop-up page to form a book.

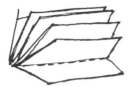

Along the center fold staple the assembled pages to a colored paper cover.

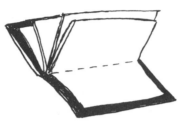

Carefully print the text for each page at the bottom of the pop-ups.

Make your illustrations and story unexpected and funny, too—if you like.

At the end of their Native American studies, have each student list: "Five Things I Didn't Know Before We Studied the Eastern Tribes." (You could also have them make a second list, if you like: "Some Things I Still Don't Know About the Woodland Indians...And Wish I Did...")

As the unit is in progress, you might want to tell your class: "At the end of our Native American studies, I will want each of you to tell me one thing you still don't know concerning the Woodland people, but would like to (have) learn(ed)." This exercise will help you see where their areas of interest lie—and may help you in planning a "Native Americans of the Woodlands" unit for *next* year!

Notes for "Activities for the Classroom":

1. To jerk means to preserve by drying. We got our word "jerky" from the Spanish *charki* (char-kee), a word the conquistadores encountered in Peru, where it means "meat dried in strips."

2. Some children have success using a rather thick poster paint and applying it with a flat 1-inch brush directly to the surface of the stamps. Experiment and see if you prefer the ink pads or the poster paint for your printmaking.

3. A few interesting American Indian voting-related facts: Arizona supreme court declared unconstitutional disenfranchising interpretations of the state constitution and Indians were permitted to vote as in most other states. A 1953 Utah state law stated that persons living on Indian reservations were not residents of the state and could not vote. That law was subsequently repealed. In 1954, Indians in Maine who were not then federally recognized were given the right to vote and, in 1962, New Mexico extended the right to vote to Indians.

   Indians also vote in state and local elections and in the elections of the tribes of which they are members.

THE
WOODLANDS
INDIANS

Ready-to-Use
Reproducible Activities

▼▼▼▼▼▼▼ ▼▼▼▼▼▼▼ ▼▼▼▼▼▼▼

A Note to Teachers about using these Reproducibles

It's really a good idea to quickly work each reproducible before you have your students tackle it. (There are answer keys in the back to facilitate this, but just going through the steps, e.g., of making the Longhouse, will really save you time LATER when your class is constructing it.) You will be familiar with each activity and this is a great help when your students have questions.

Always make clear to your students WHY you are asking them to complete an activity sheet — how it fits in with what you are doing in class.

I hope these few words of introduction will make EACH reproducible all the more valuable — AND FUN-for you and your students to use!

▲▲▲▲▲▲▲▲▲ ▲▲▲▲▲▲▲▲ ▲▲▲▲▲▲▲▲▲▲

HOW THE FIRST PEOPLE CAME HERE

This is a picture of the land we live in: North America.

Long, long ago no people lived here. Ice covered much of the land. The ice made a bridge so people could cross over from Siberia to the land we live in today.

Many scientists believe that the first people came here from Siberia. Many Native Americans do not believe that the first people came here in this way. They believe, instead, the arrival stories of their old songs and myths.

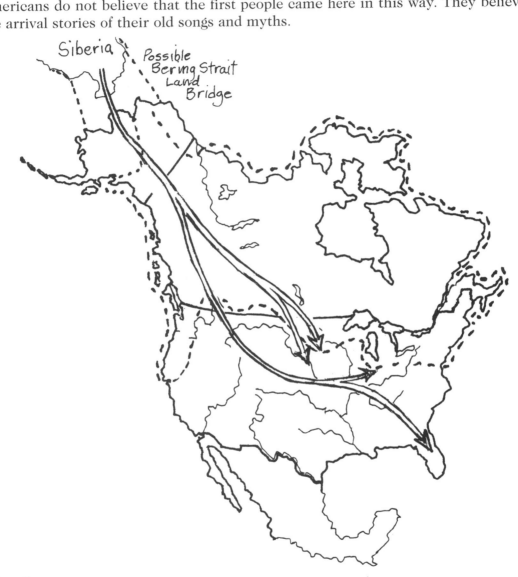

Directions:

1. Use a white crayon to cover all the places the ice covered.
   This is marked by

2. (Ask your teacher to help you) find where you live in North America.
   Mark it with a ☆   there.

3. Use green to outline the Eastern Woodland states that you are studying.

4. Make a long orange arrow to show where scientists think people came from Siberia, through Canada, down to the Northeast and Southeast Woodlands!

CAN YOU FIND THE TWINS?

Draw a line between each pair of twins. Then you can color all the twins.

CAN YOU FIND THE TWINS?

Draw a line between each pair of twins. Then you can color all the twins.

A PICTURE COUNT

Count the things you see and put the number in the circle.

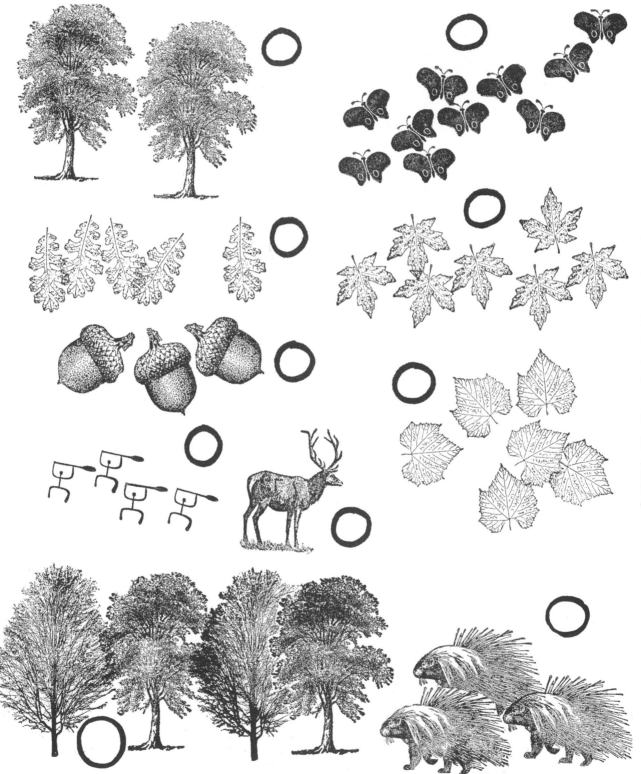

A PICTURE COUNT

Count the things you see and put the number in the circle.

Name _____

WARRIOR HEAD (A.D. 1100–1250)

This design was scratched into a shell cup found at Spiro, Oklahoma.

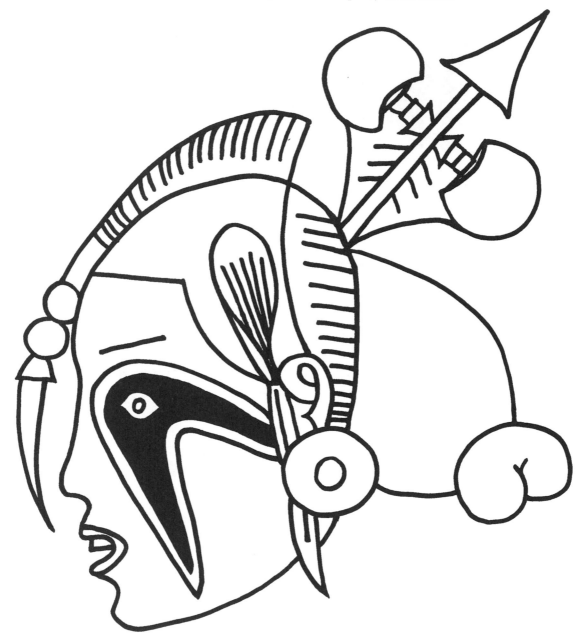

The **warrior** wears his hair in a **bun** and he has two **beads** on the piece of hair on his **fore-head**! He wears two metal **hair ornaments** AND copper **earrings**. His face is painted with "the **weeping eye**" design.

1. Color his hair dark brown.
2. Color his hair ornaments green—and his earring golden yellow.
3. Color the outline of the weeping eye design BLUE and the two beads red. THEN on the back of this sheet, write a story about this warrior using all the **boldfaced** words above. Make it **EXCITING!**

Name _____

THE UNDERWATER PANTHER

A 2000-year-old make-believe creature from the Midwest, he was one of the most important gods of the Ojibwa.*

Look at the creature and find the shapes below. Use crayons (or colored pencils) to give every shape in the panther the right color.

On the back of this paper write a short story as if you were this panther! Tell how you got your name and how you spend your life...Make it scary!

* The Delaware, Sauk, Fox, Menominee, Potawatomi, Peoria, Shawnee, and Winnebago also believed in this creature!

Name _____

A HOPEWELL GORGET

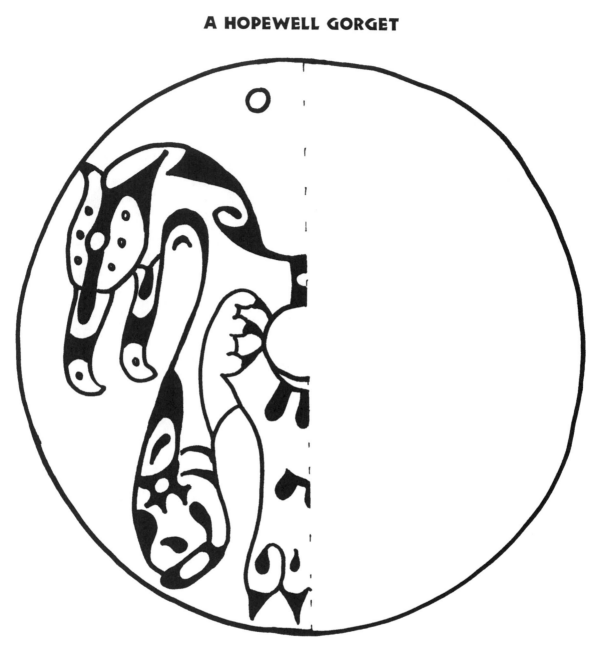

The Hopewell people made jewelry out of copper and mica. They also made gorgets—pendants—like this one out of seashells. This gorget was made about A.D. 200. It was found in Missouri.*

Carefully draw in the other half of this bird design: it should look EXACTLY like a reflection of the bird on the left. Draw your bird looking out to the right! Then carefully color in your Hopewell "thunder" bird!

* How did the Hopewells get SEAshells in MISSOURI??

Name _____

BIRD MAZE*

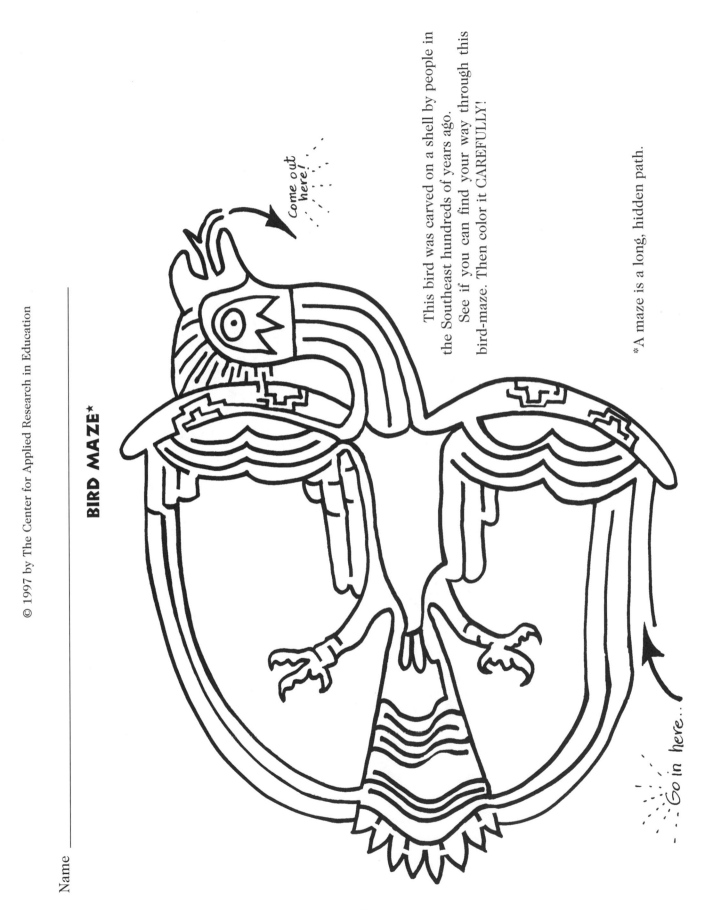

Come out here!

This bird was carved on a shell by people in the Southeast hundreds of years ago.

See if you can find your way through this bird-maze. Then color it CAREFULLY!

*A maze is a long, hidden path.

Go in here...

Name _____

AMAZING MAZE

Which snake will lead you out of this maze?

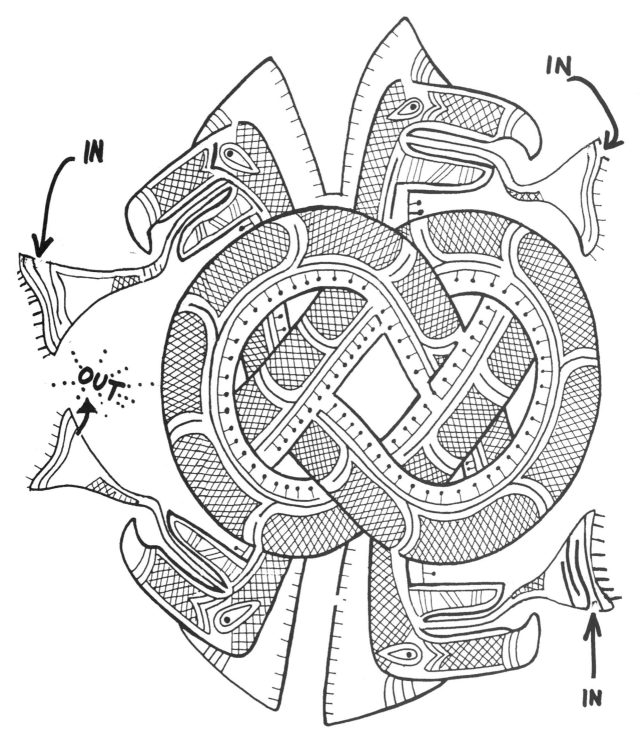

This 4-headed snake was carved on a conch shell in early times and found in the Southeast.

Name _____

ANIMAL MOUND FOLLOW-THE-DOTS

Use your pencil. Start at 1 . . . go to 2 . . . then to 3. Keep going until you get to 31!

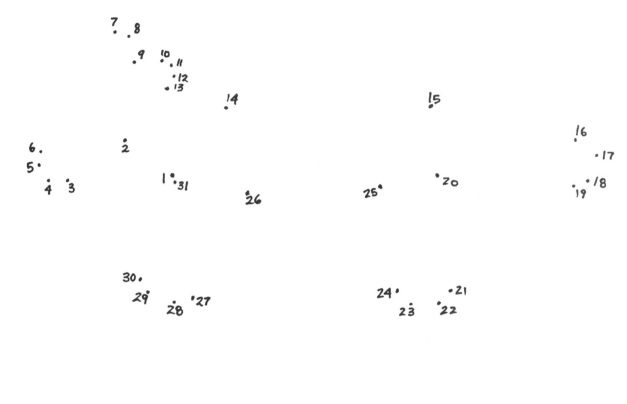

This is an animal mound made by early people in Wisconsin. It was made over a thousand years ago! It is very big. There are three other animals like it nearby. Show green grass and tiny trees alongside this mound.

Draw three other animals like this one on the paper above. Use the back of this paper and write a story to tell WHY those early people made these mounds...for graves?...for maps?...for gifts?...

ABC—ABC FOLLOW-THE-DOTS

Using a pencil, start at A and go to B—go to only the BIG—the capital—letters: **A B C D E F G H I** and so on until you get to **Z**. Next start at **a** and go to **b**—and onto **c d e f g h i** and so on until you get to **z**. GOOD LUCK!!

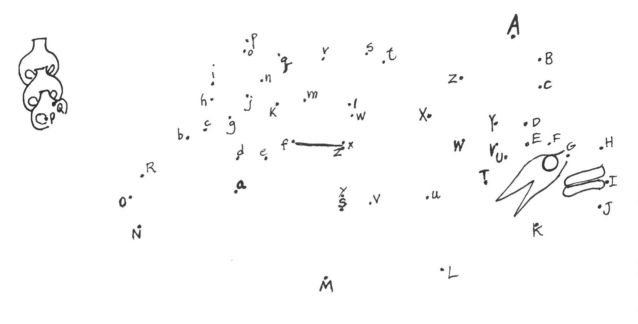

This design—a snake with wings and horns—was used on pottery made by the Mound Builders in Alabama about 1,000 years ago!

Here's how to FINISH your flying snake:
1. Give him a forked tongue! ⟋ or ⟋ or …?
2. Make this ⧙ on: the ends of his wings, a band on his neck, and on the thin part of his tail.
3. Make this ⟅⟆ on the rest of his wings.
4. Do this ⌐⌐ ‖ ⌐⌐ ‖ on his body.
5. AND give him a short beard! Now he looks just right!

Name _____

NORTHEAST INDIAN FOLLOW-THE-DOTS

Use a pencil. Start at 1. Go on to 2 and keep going until you get to 57! Can you tell what you have made?*

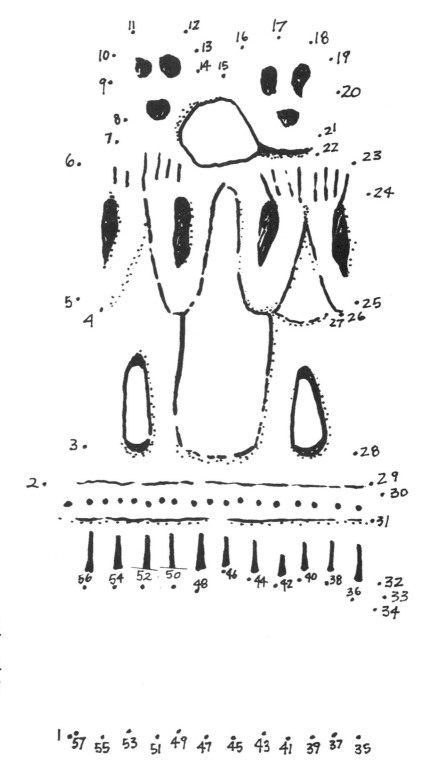

© 1997 by The Center for Applied Research in Education

* Don't read this until you finish the follow-the-dots . . . . It is 400 years old. It is a carved bone comb with twin people on top. This comb was worn in the hair as an ornament.

225

Name _____

THE NORTHEASTERN WOODLAND STATES

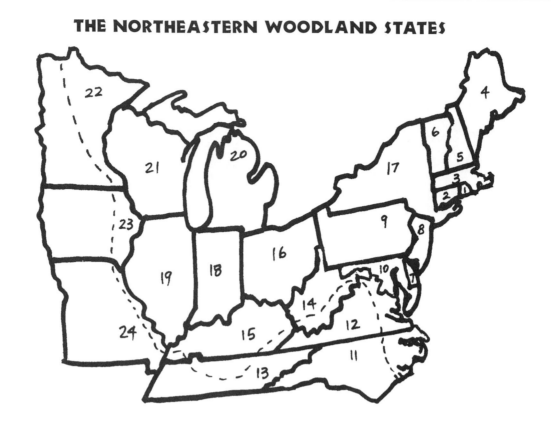

Match the name of each NE state to its number on the map above:

___Connecticut   ___Massachusetts   ___Ohio

___Delaware   ___Michigan   ___Pennsylvania

___Illinois   ___Minnesota   ___Rhode Island

___Indiana   ___Missouri   ___Tennessee

___Iowa   ___New Hampshire   ___West Virginia

___Kentucky   ___New Jersey   ___Wisconsin

___Maine   ___New York   ___Vermont

___Maryland   ___North Carolina   ___Virginia

(Here are a few hints.)

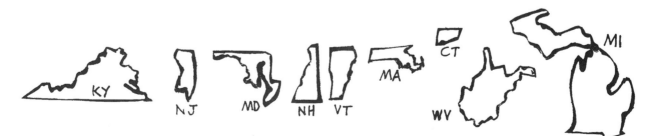

Name _____

THE SOUTHEASTERN STATES

Look at the shapes below. Can you tell what (southeastern) state each shape is? Put the correct number in front of the name of each state.

___Alabama   ___Kentucky   ___South Carolina

___Arkansas   ___Louisiana   ___Tennessee

___Florida   ___Mississippi   ___Texas

___Georgia   ___North Carolina   ___Virginia

    ___Oklahoma   ___West Virginia

Once you have checked your answers to be sure you got them all correct—carefully cut out the 14 southeastern states above and try putting "this puzzle together"!

Maple-sugared Cherries: 20-30 servings

10 (1 lb.) cans of water packed tart pitted cherries

5 cups maple sugar*

hot plate(s)
sauce pan(s)
spoons

Wash your hands.

Put the juice (from 2 cans) of cherries into sauce pan(s). Add (1 cup) maple sugar. Place pan(s) over heat. Bring to a boil. Boil gently for 10 minutes. Stir juice now and then.

Carefully spoon the cherries into the juice and simmer for 5 minutes.

You may eat this treat either warm or cold— just as the northeastern Woodlands people did!

*Sold at health food and specialty food stores.

Roasted Peanuts

2 lbs. blanched green peanuts
¼ lb. butter
salt

cooky sheet
oven
paper towels

Place peanuts and butter
on cooky sheet. Roast in a 300° oven for 2 hours.
Stir often.
Remove from oven; drain on paper towels.
Salt to your taste.

Peanut Soup

4 (10-oz) jars dry roasted peanuts
8 cups milk
8 cups canned chicken broth
4 T. minced parsley

blender
saucepan(s)
spoons
table knives
hot plate(s)

Chop the peanuts fine: in the blender.
Place the nuts and milk and broth
in saucepan(s). Heat, stirring for 15
minutes. Chop parsley fine.
Serve hot. Sprinkle with parsley.
Make the servings small as this S.E. soup is RICH!
Enjoy.

NORTHEASTERN WOODLANDS INDIAN DOLL AND CLOTHING

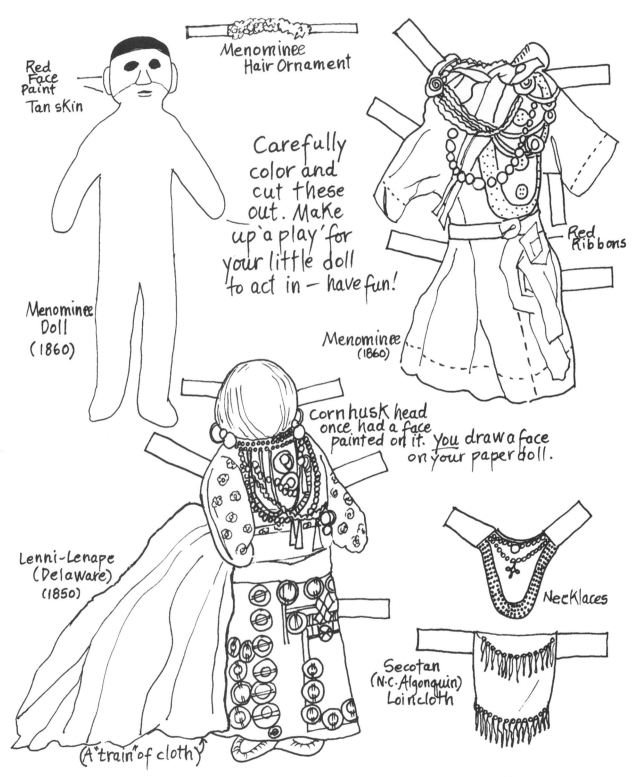

Red Face Paint
Tan skin

Menominee Hair Ornament

Menominee Doll (1860)

Carefully color and cut these out. Make up 'a play' for your little doll to act in — have fun!

Red Ribbons

Menominee (1860)

corn husk head once had a face painted on it. You draw a face on your paper doll.

Lenni-Lenape (Delaware) (1850)

Necklaces

Secotan (N.C. Algonquin) Loincloth

(A "train" of cloth)

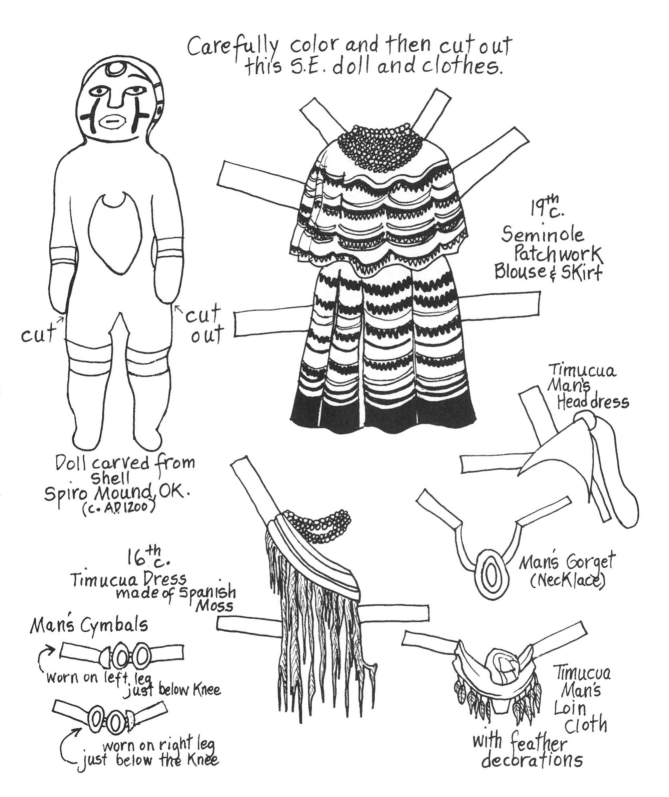

Carefully color and then cut out this S.E. doll and clothes.

cut

cut out

Doll carved from Shell Spiro Mound, OK. (c. A.D. 1200)

19th c. Seminole Patchwork Blouse & Skirt

Timucua Man's Headdress

Man's Gorget (Necklace)

16th c. Timucua Dress made of Spanish Moss

Man's Cymbals
worn on left leg just below Knee

worn on right leg just below the Knee

Timucua Man's Loin Cloth with feather decorations

THE WIGWAM

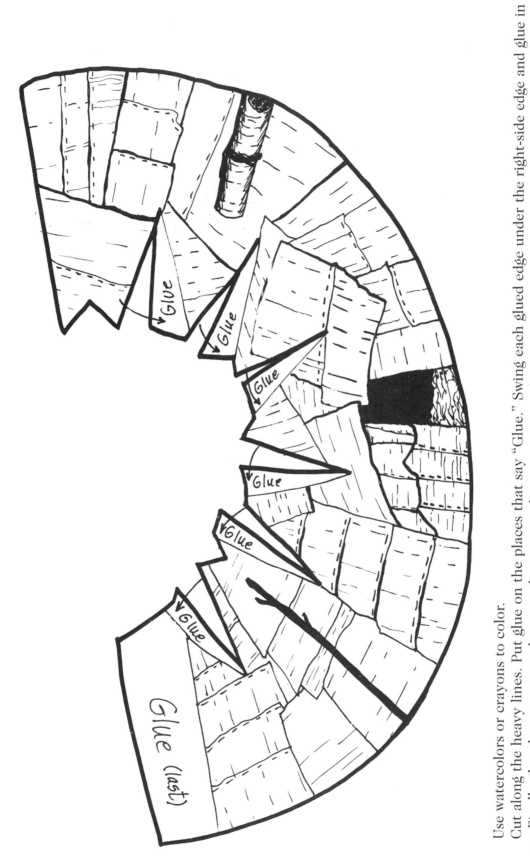

Glue

Glue

Glue

Glue

Glue

Glue

Glue (last)

Use watercolors or crayons to color.

Cut along the heavy lines. Put glue on the places that say "Glue." Swing each glued edge under the right-side edge and glue in place. Finally glue the two open edges together to complete your wigwam!

NORTHEAST WOODLANDS' LONGHOUSE

① Use watercolors or crayons to color the longhouse walls and roof: shades of grey. ② Carefully cut along heavy lines and fold back on - - - - dotted lines.

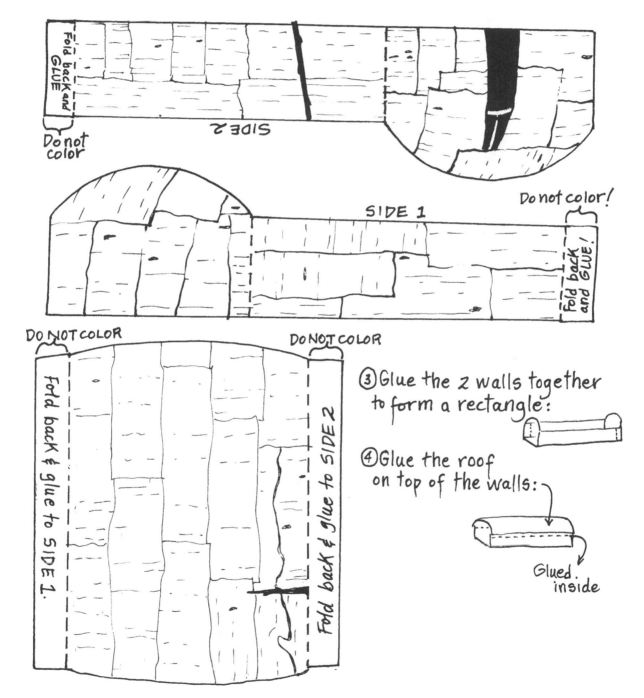

③ Glue the 2 walls together to form a rectangle:

④ Glue the roof on top of the walls:

Glued inside

SOUTHEASTERN THATCHED HOUSE (CHOCTAW)

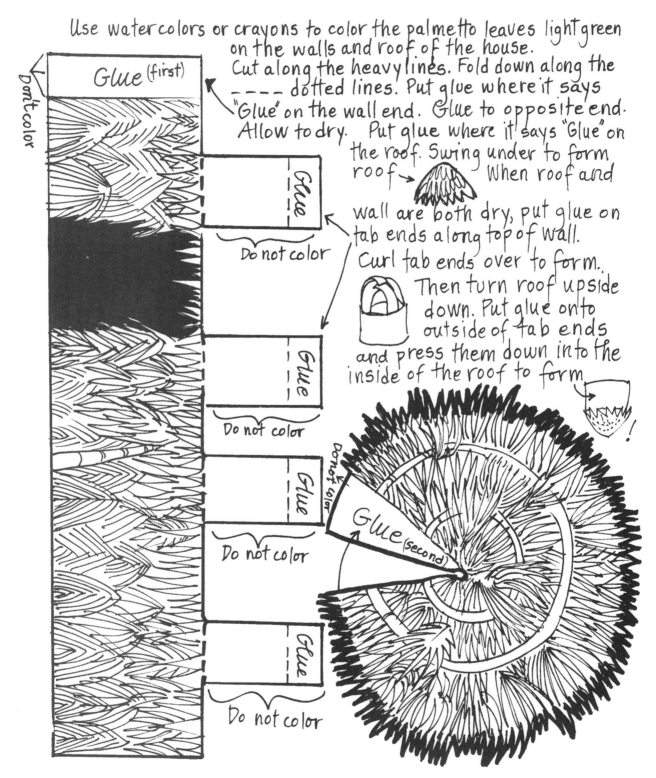

Use watercolors or crayons to color the palmetto leaves light green on the walls and roof of the house.
Cut along the heavy lines. Fold down along the _ _ _ _ dotted lines. Put glue where it says "Glue" on the wall end. Glue to opposite end. Allow to dry. Put glue where it says "Glue" on the roof. Swing under to form roof→ When roof and wall are both dry, put glue on tab ends along top of wall. Curl tab ends over to form. Then turn roof upside down. Put glue onto outside of tab ends and press them down into the inside of the roof to form

Don't color

Glue (first)

Glue

Do not color

Glue

Do not color

Glue

Do not color

Glue

Do not color

Don't color

Glue (second)

234

Name _____

WHERE THE N.E. TRIBES WERE LIVING IN ABOUT 1600!

* Seneca, Cayuga, Onondaga, Oneida, Mohawk, Mahican

Print the names of the tribes that in 1600 were living in each of these states:

Delaware: _____

Illinois: _____

Indiana: _____

Iowa: _____ Kentucky: _____

Maine: _____

Massachusetts: _____

Michigan: _____

Missouri: _____ Rhode Island: _____

New Hampshire: _____

New Jersey AND Pennsylvania: _____

New York: _____

N. Carolina: _____

Virginia: _____ Wisconsin: _____

NOW: Compare this map with the Northeast Reservations map activity. Find 8 tribes that are in about the same area today as they were in 1600. Color their names YELLOW on the map above!

235

Name _____

WHERE THE S.E. TRIBES* WERE LIVING IN ABOUT 1600!

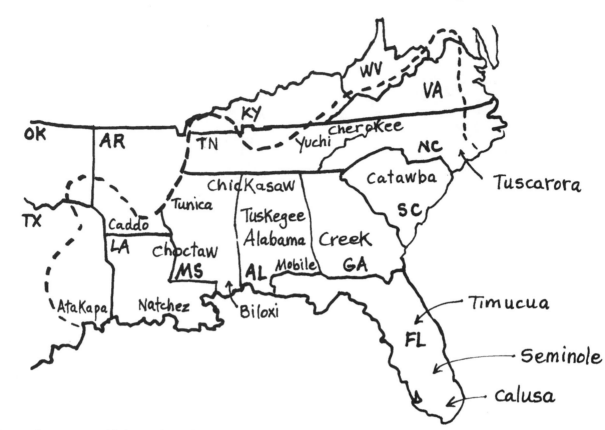

Print the names of the tribes that in 1600 were living in each of these states:

Alabama: _____

Arkansas: _____

Florida: _____

Georgia: _____

Louisiana: _____

Mississippi: _____

N. Carolina: _____

S. Carolina: _____

Tennessee: _____

S.E. Texas: _____

NOW compare this map with the Southeast Reservations map activity. Find 3 tribes that still live where they did in 1600. Color their names RED on the map above!

* We have to remember that the tribes noted on this map are just a FEW of the many, many groups of native people who were living in the southeast in 1600!

Name _____

Here is what TREES gave the early N.E. people!

See how *many* objects you can list that the Northeast Indians made from bark or wood. (There are at least 14 different possibilities.*)

BARK was used to make:

WOOD was used for:

TREES themselves gave: (foods)

                                                (shelters)

                                                (protection)

* Think of objects they made that have to do with: food, tools, play, clothing, houses, children, hunting, religion, war, travel, villages!

Name _____

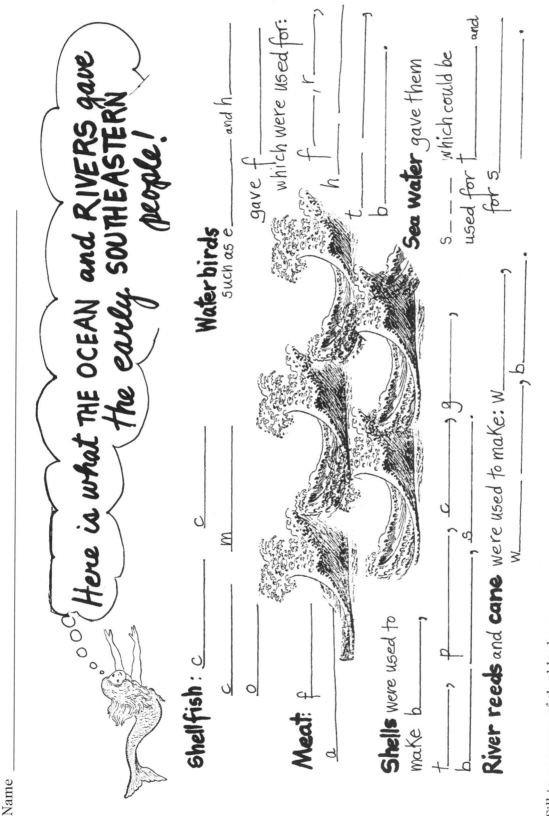

Here is what THE OCEAN and RIVERS gave the early SOUTHEASTERN people!

Shellfish: c _____ c _____ m _____ o _____

Waterbirds such as e _____ and h _____ gave f _____ r _____ which were used for:
f _____
h _____
t _____
b _____ .

Meat: f _____
a _____

Sea water gave them s _____ which could be used for t _____ and for s _____ .

Shells were used to make b _____ , t _____ , p _____ , c _____ , g _____ , b _____ , s _____ .

River reeds and **cane** were used to make: w _____ , w _____ , b _____ .

Fill in as *many* of the blanks as you can.

Here are a few hints: **Kinds of sea and river life**: alligator, clams, crabs, crayfish, egrets, fish, heron, mussels, oysters.

How these were used: beads, trading, whistles, spoons, cups, tools, blowguns, blankets, gorgets, fans, pendants, robes, woven baskets, hair ornaments, seasoning, food, turban, decoration, burial masks.

Name _____

YOUR VISION QUEST IN THE EASTERN WOODLANDS

You have been out in the mountains for 4 days and nights without food—or water—or sleep. Then you have a great dream! Draw here what you see. Be sure to show what animal comes to you. Show LOTS OF DETAILS.

When you finish with your drawing, write about "your experience" and explain how you felt about it.

Name _____

WRITING ABOUT THE N.E. WOODLANDS

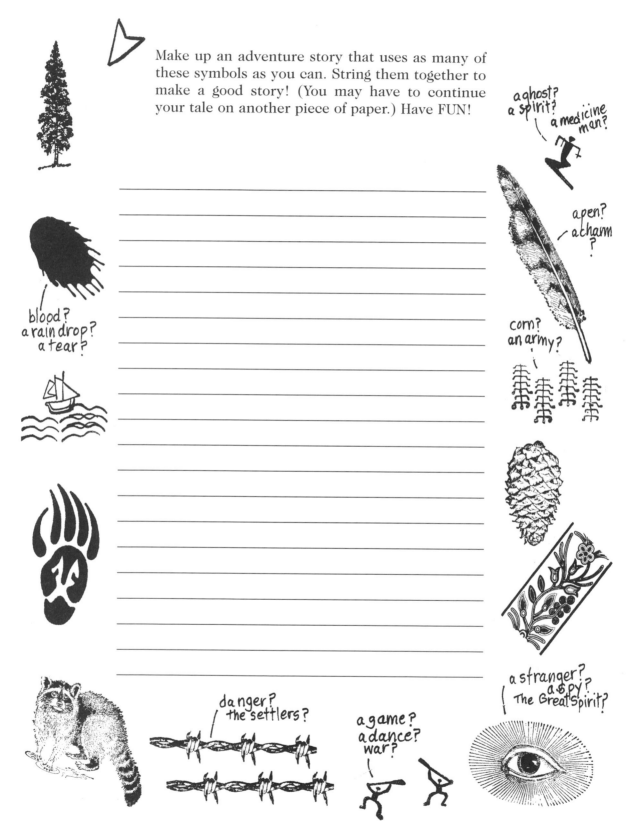

Make up an adventure story that uses as many of these symbols as you can. String them together to make a good story! (You may have to continue your tale on another piece of paper.) Have FUN!

a ghost?
a spirit?
a medicine man?

a pen?
a charm?

corn?
an army?

blood?
a raindrop?
a tear?

a stranger?
a spy?
The Great Spirit?

danger?
the settlers?

a game?
a dance?
war?

WRITING ABOUT THE S.E. WOODLANDS

Make up an adventure story that uses as many of these symbols as you can. String them together to make a good story! (You may have to continue your tale on another piece of paper.) Have FUN!

Tears — or Blood? or Rain drops? or Sweat?

oo DANGER ?

Food?

A storm? Death? a fishing trip?

a pet? a swimmer?

storm? a dream?

RIBBON APPLIQUÉ*

The early European traders brought silk ribbons to the native peoples—who used them to make appliquéd strips to decorate their leggings, shirts, and dresses.

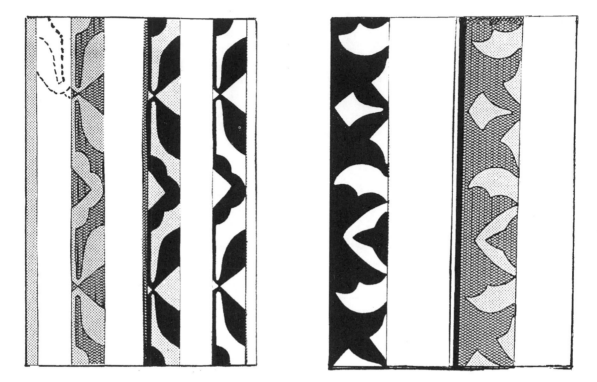

Use a pencil and draw in "the other half" of each design: see example at top left. Then carefully color in each design AND each background. As many as five different colors might be used in one appliqué.

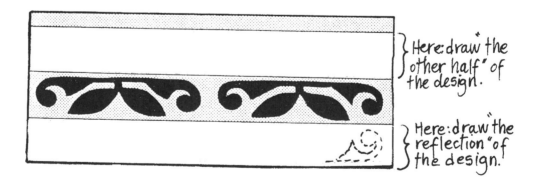

Here: draw the "other half" of the design.

Here: draw the reflection "of the design."

* Appliqué: when one piece of cloth is "applied" by sewing it to another piece.

Name _____

During the 1800s the Oklahoma Territory became the final destination for over 60 American Indian tribes.

This map shows just the major *eastern* tribes that were forced to relocate in Oklahoma. Fill in the names of the tribes on the map.

OTTAWA	FOX	SEMINOLE	CREEK
CHEROKEE	MIAMI	SENECA	CAYUGA
CADDO	PEORIA	SAUK	KICKAPOO
IOWA	SHAWNEE	MISSOURI	
DELAWARE	POTAWATOMI	CHOCTAW	
CHICKASAW			

THE TRAIL OF TEARS

A map showing the Trail of Tears route with states labeled: OKLAHOMA, MISSOURI, ARKANSAS, ILLINOIS, IN. (Indiana), KENTUCKY, TENNESSEE, MS., AL., GA., NORTH CAROLINA.

Towns labeled along the route: TAHLEQUAH, PRAIRIE GROVE, FAYETTEVILLE, SPRINGDALE, ROGERS, MONETT, AURORA, SPRINGFIELD, LEBANON, ROLLA, POTOSI, FARMINGTON, FREDERICKTOWN, JACKSON, CAPE GIRARDEAU, ANNA, GOLCONDA, MARION, PRINCETON, HOPKINSVILLE, CLARKSVILLE, NASHVILLE, MURFREESBORO, McMINNVILLE, ATHENS, CHATTANOOGA, MURPHY, CHEROKEE.

(after D.L.D.)

In 1838-1839 the U.S. Government made many E. Indians leave their homes and move to Indian Territory (present-day Oklahoma). The Cherokees were rounded up, put in stockades and then they were marched 800 miles. They suffered so. It was freezing out. There weren't enough blankets or food or horses. Disease killed many. The U.S. soldiers who were herding them west would not even let them bury their dead. In the end 4000 Cherokees died in the stockades or on the forced march west!

Look at the map above: How many states did the Trail of Tears pass through? _____ How many towns did the Cherokees go through in Tennessee? _____ How many in Kentucky? _____ In Illinois? _____ In Missouri? _____ In Arkansas? _____ Count the number of towns the Cherokees walked through—from Cherokee, N.C. to Tahlequah, O.K. _____ The Trail of Tears covered _____ miles. The Cherokees left N.C. in November and reached Oklahoma in March, about 4 months later. About how many weeks were they forced to march? _____ About how many days were they on the Trail? _____ About how many Cherokees—men, children, women—died every day? _____

© 1997 by The Center for Applied Research in Education

NORTHEAST WOODLANDS TRIBES WORD SEARCH

Look in the puzzle below and try to find the names of 23 Indian tribes.* Circle each name as you find it. The names may be written across or down (or backwards or on more than one line). GOOD LUCK!!

D	E	E	D	A	C	H	I	W	K	I	C	K	E
H	A	N	T	P	X	O	P	P	E	W	A	A	Y
O	T	A	J	L	K	M	E	N	O	B	F	P	Z
P	E	W	E	W	A	S	K	U	A	S	C	O	T
W	R	B	L	I	M	F	O	X	J	G	F	O	J
E	I	I	L	N	C	B	Q	C	T	N	P	Z	I
L	E	J	G	N	I	H	U	C	A	M	C	I	M
L	M	O	N	E	M	T	I	T	I	X	G	H	I
R	I	N	O	B	F	W	A	D	K	M	L	K	J
O	N	E	R	A	F	H	N	E	A	L	G	O	N
Q	I	I	U	G	W	O	Q	L	N	P	H	T	Q
U	B	D	H	O	Z	X	U	A	B	K	L	A	U
O	C	A	P	D	T	T	A	W	A	R	E	W	I
I	S	E	N	E	C	A	Y	U	G	A	O	A	N

Here are the 23 tribes* to look for:

1. Abnaki	6. Delaware	11. Iroquios	16. Ojibwa	21. Sauk
2. Adena	7. Erie	12. Kickapoo	17. Oneida	22. Seneca
3. Algonquin	8. Fox	13. Menominee	18. Ottawa	23. Winnebago
4. Cayuga	9. Hopewell	14. Micmac	19. Penobscot	
5. Chippewa	10. Huron	15. Nanticoke	20. Powhatan	

* or groups

SOUTHEASTERN TRIBES WORD SEARCH

Look in the puzzle below and try to find the names of these 20 southeastern tribes. Circle each name as you find it. The names may be written across or down (or even backwards). GOOD LUCK!!

M	L	O	X	I	Y	K	E	G	A	P	A	L	A
V	I	N	L	U	C	S	O	E	I	A	K	Z	C
E	B	X	H	P	R	U	Q	E	R	V	T	I	H
L	M	C	R	V	E	T	W	O	Z	W	U	M	E
I	I	J	S	L	E	X	R	G	H	D	S	Y	E
B	A	K	O	U	K	A	F	E	P	S	K	T	A
O	M	N	Y	Q	C	A	T	A	W	B	O	A	K
C	I	D	E	S	B	N	O	Z	S	A	G	P	A
M	A	Q	U	A	P	A	W	A	Y	K	E	A	E
E	D	T	A	R	V	T	L	P	K	C	E	L	E
S	O	F	C	H	O	C	T	A	W	I	A	Q	K
W	E	E	N	W	A	H	S	F	B	H	X	U	O
Z	B	U	L	P	A	E	X	R	A	C	H	E	R
T	I	M	U	C	U	Z	O	N	M	A	X	J	S

Here are the 20 tribes to look for:

1. Alabama
2. Apalachee
3. Atakapa
4. Biloxi
5. Catawba
6. Cherokee
7. Chickasaw
8. Choctaw
9. Creek
10. Miami
11. Mobile
12. Muskogee
13. Natchez
14. Quapaw
15. Seminole
16. Shawnee
17. Timucua
18. Tuscarora
19. Tuskegee
20. Yuchi

Cut along the dotted lines on the date slips below.

Arrange the slips in order from the earliest date (top of list) to the most recent date (bottom of list). Then glue them in order along the left side of page 2. Make a small drawing or cartoon to the right of each date to go with (to illustrate) that date.

1675-76	King Philip's War between New England colonies & Nipmucs, Narragansets, Wampanoags. Matacom (King Philip) is killed.
1830	Indian Removal Act passes Congress, calling for relocation of Eastern Indians to an Indian Territory west of the Mississippi River.
1619	Squanto returns to North America where he is able to help save the Plymouth Colony.
1827	Winnebago Uprising in Wisconsin.
1887	Dawes Act passes in which reservation lands are given to individual Indians in parcels. Indians lose millions of acres of land.
1616-1620	Smallpox epidemic among New England tribes.
c. 23,000 B.C. to c. 11,000 B.C.	The first people come to North America.
1799	Handsome Lake, a Seneca chief, found the Longhouse religion.
1809-11	Tecumseh's Rebellion: This Shawnee chief tries to unite the tribes of the NE, SE & Mississippi Valley against the U.S. His brother brings about Tecumseh's defeat.
1664	The English get control of New Netherlands, become allies with the Iroquois League. New Amsterdam on Manhattan Island becomes New York.
1615	Squanto, a Wampanoag, is kidnapped and taken to England where, as a servant, he learns English.
c. 1000 B.C. to A.D. 200	Adena (Mound Builders) in and around Ohio Valley.
1626	Canarsee Indians "sell" Manhattan Island to Peter Miniut, governor of New Netherlands, for 60 guilders' worth of trade goods.

Carefully CUT.... these strips apart.

In each frame draw a cartoon to illustrate one of the date strips. Keep them in the correct order.

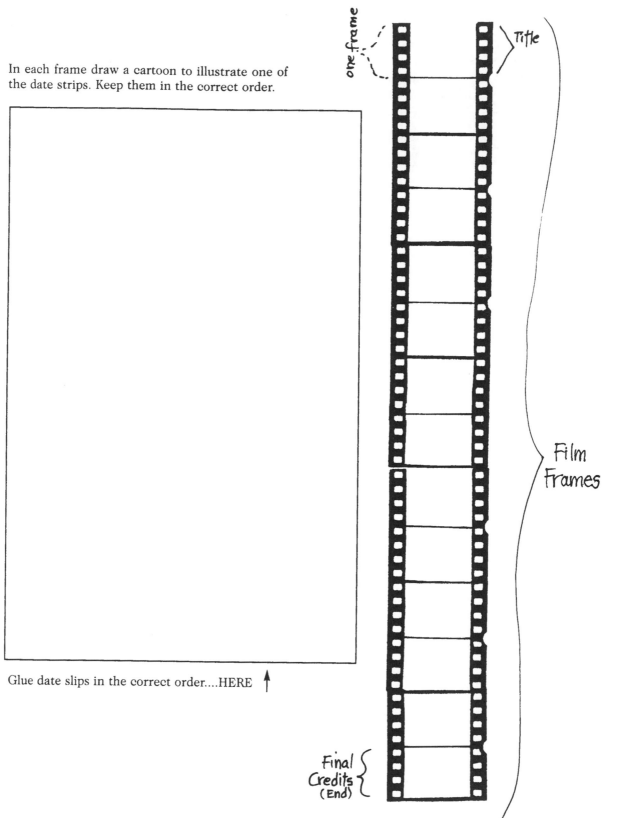

Glue date slips in the correct order....HERE ↑

1830	*Indian Removal Act* passes Congress, calling for relocation of Eastern Indians to an Indian Territory west of the Mississippi River.
1831-39	The Five Civilized tribes of the Southeast are relocated to the Indian Territory.
1513-1521	Ponce de Leon (backed by Spain) reaches Florida. On second trip (1521) he's wounded by an arrow (Seminole) and dies later in Cuba.
1838-39	The Cherokee "Trail of Tears" takes place.
1832	Cherokees fight their removal in courts, the Supreme Court agrees; President Andrew Jackson ignores court's decision.
1738	Smallpox epidemic among Cherokees of Southeast.
c. 500 B.C.	Copper bracelets, weapons, and amulets are made and used.
c. 700-1700	Temple Mound Builders in Mississippi Basin and Southeast.
1803	Louisiana Purchase by the United States from France adds a large Indian population to the United States.
1809-21	Sequoyah single-handedly creates a Cherokee syllabic alphabet so that his peoples' language can be written.
c. 23,000 B.C. to c. 11,000 B.C.	The first people come to North America.
1861-65 Civil War	After the war, as punishment for their support of the Confederacy, the Five Civilized Tribes are compelled to accept a treaty relinquishing the western half of the Indian Territory to 20 tribes from Kansas and Nebraska.

Carefully CUT.... these strips apart.

Cut along the dotted lines on the date slips above. Cut out the date strips.

Arrange the slips in order from the earliest date (top of list) to the most recent date (bottom of list). Then glue them in order along the left side of page 2. Make a small drawing or cartoon to the right of each date (in the film frame) to go with (to illustrate) that date.

Draw a cartoon in each frame to illustrate each date. Keep them in the correct order.

Glue date slips in the correct order....HERE ↑

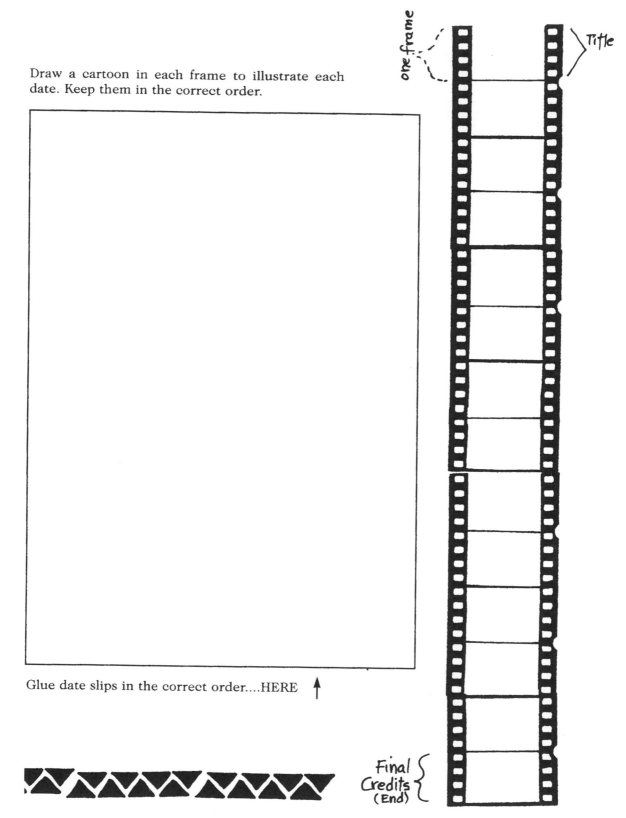

THE NORTHEAST RESERVATIONS

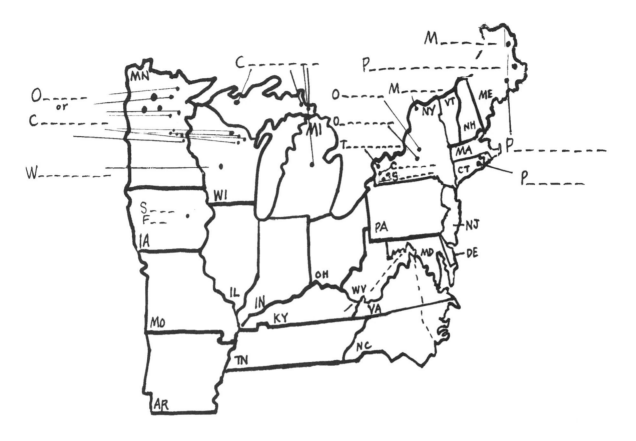

Sixteen of the 24 Northeastern states have *no* federal (U.S.) Reservations. Carefully color in these 16 states: Delaware, Illinois, Indiana, Kentucky, Maryland, Massachusetts, Missouri, New Hampshire, New Jersey, Ohio, Pennsylvania, Rhode Island, Tennessee, Vermont, Virginia, and West Virginia.

Seven* of the Northeastern states *have* federal Reservations: some of these are shown on the map with dots •. Carefully print in the name of each tribe where it belongs on the map above:

Actually, N.C. HAS a federal reservation but it's in the SOUTHeast part of the state.

CT:	Pequot
IA:	Sauk-Fox
ME:	Micmac, Passamaquoddy, Penobscot
MI:	Chippewa
MN:	Ojibwa (Chippewa)
NY:	Mohawk, Cayuga, Onondaga, Oneida, Seneca, Tuscarora
WI:	Winnebago

Name _____

THE SOUTHEAST RESERVATIONS

A reservation is a land set aside by the U.S. Government for use by the American Indians.

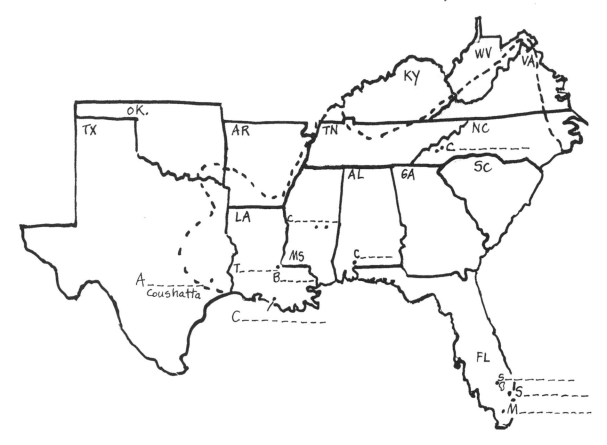

Seven* of the 14 Southeastern states have *no* federal (U.S.) Reservations. Carefully color in these 7 states: Arkansas, Georgia, Kentucky, S. Carolina, Tennessee, Virginia, and West Virginia.

Six of the Southeastern states have federal Reservations: some of these are shown on this map with dots •. Carefully print in the name of each tribe—showing where its reservation is on the map above:

Alabama: Creek
Florida: Miccosukee, Seminole
Louisiana: Chitimacha, Tunica-Biloxi
Mississippi: Choctaw
North Carolina: Cherokee
Texas: Alabama

* Actually OK. has lands reserved for Indians but NOT in the SE part of the state....

WILL ROGERS

Will Rogers, who had Cherokee blood, was a writer, actor, and a peacemaker. During his life he said many memorable things. Here are just a few of his remarks:

1. "My ancestors didn't come over on the Mayflower, but they met the boat."

2. "They may call me a rube and a hick, but I'd a lot rather be the man who bought the Brooklyn Bridge than the man who sold it."

3. "Everybody is ignorant. Only on different subjects."

4. "Even if you're on the right track, you'll get run over if you just sit there."

5. "I don't care how little your country is, you got a right to run it like you want to. When the big nations quit meddling, then the world will have peace."

6. "People talk peace. But men give their life's work to war. It won't stop 'til there is as much brains and scientific study put to aid peace as there is to promote war."

7. "No nation ever had two better friends that we have. You know who they are? The Atlantic and Pacific oceans."

8. "We will never have true civilization until we have learned to recognize the rights of others."

9. "Diplomats are just as essential to starting a war as soldiers are for finishing it."

10. "America is a land of opportunity and don't ever forget it."

11. "Nowadays it is about as big a crime to be dumb as it is to be dishonest."

After you have read these quotations, think about what they "say" about Will Rogers: What did he love?... What made him mad?...What did he believe in?...

THEN turn this paper over and on the back write at least four things you "know about Will" after reading his "notable quotes."

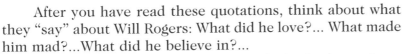

Will Rogers

ANSWERS TO NORTHEAST WOODLANDS TRIBES WORD SEARCH

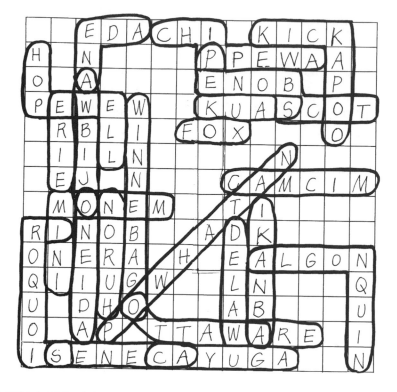

ANSWERS TO SOUTHEASTERN TRIBES WORD SEARCH

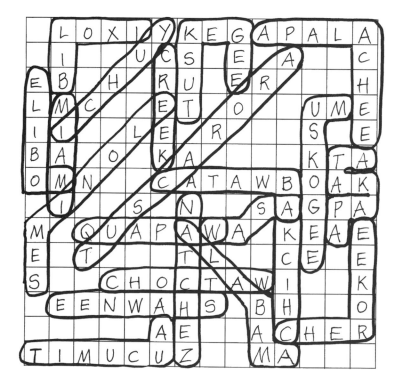

POSSIBLE ANSWERS TO WILL ROGERS

1. He was American Indian.
2. He'd rather have been wrong and even seen as ignorant rather than have been "smart" and purposely hurt an innocent person.
3. Everyone has some things he or she knows—and no one knows it all.
4. You must ask (be active) if you want to get things done.
5. Small nations shouldn't be bothered by countries because they are bigger/stronger.
6. We need to make as big an effort to have peace as we have made to be armed and powerful.
7. We should pay attention to AMERICA and not stick our (political) nose into the business of other countries.
8. We, as a nation, must learn to respect and be tolerant of others.
9. It is the officials in Washington, D.C. who get us into war and then have young people go fight the war.
10. The U.S.A. offers each person a chance to succeed.
11. Everyone should try to get as well educated as he or she can.

THE
WOODLANDS
INDIANS
Teacher's Resource Guide

GENERAL BOOKS

Pictorial Books

The Native Americans—The Indigenous People of North America is richly illustrated with materials from the Smithsonian Institution and The American Museum of Natural History. The U.S. publisher is Smithmark of New York.

America's Facinating Indian Heritage is easy to read and has excellent illustrations. It is published by The Reader's Digest Association, Inc., Pleasantville, NY.

The World of the American Indian, another very accessible reference book with many colorful photographs, is published by The National Geographic Society, Washington, D.C.

Reference and History

Atlas of the North American Indian is a scholarly work loaded with maps and charts. It is by Carl Waldman and published by Facts on File Publications, New York.

In *American Indian Digest—Facts About Today's American Indian*, George Russell, a Saginaw Chippewa, publishes contemporary census information on American Indians and a bibliography of reference sources. He also produces classroom maps for American Indian studies. For more information, contact:

Thunderbird Enterprises
8821 N. 1st Street
Phoenix, AZ 85020-2801
1-800-835-7220

Native American Architecture by Peter Nabokov and Robert Easton is the definitive resource book on this subject. It is published by Oxford University Press, New York.

The Portable North American Indian Reader, edited by Fredrick Turner, is a scholarly work that includes myths, tales, poetry, and oratory. It is suggested for use with older students. The book is published by Penguin Books, New York.

Native American Testimony—A Chronicle of Indian–White Relations from Prophecy to the Present, 1492-1992, edited by Peter Nabokov, with a foreword by Vine Deloria, Jr. It shows five hundred years of contact between Native Americans and Europeans as seen through Indian eyes. The book is for use with older students. It is available from Penguin Books, New York.

Brave Are My People—Indian Heroes Not Forgotten by Frank Waters, author of *Book of the Hopi*, contains twenty short biographies of Native American heroes. ("Brave are my people" is a quote from Tecumseh.) The book is available from Clear Light Publishers of Sante Fe, NM.

Healers on the Mountain—Traditional Native American Stories for Cleansing, Healing, Testing, and Preserving the Old Ways, as retold by Teresa Pijoan is published by August House Publishers, Inc.

Arts and Crafts

The American Indian Craft Book, written by Marz and Nono Minor and published by University of Nebraska Press, contains materials from the collections of the Kansas City Museum of History and Science.

North American Indian Arts is a Golden Guide written by Andrew Hunter Whiteford. The editor is Herbert Zim. A tiny book with a wealth of information and illustrations, it is published by Western Publishing Company of Racine, WI.

American Indian Design and Decoration by Le Roy H. Appleton is part of the Pictorial Archives publications by Dover Press. Other books in this series are *Authentic Indian Designs* (illustrations selected by Maria Naylor from the Annual Reports of the Bureau of American Ethnology for the years 1881-1928) and *North American Indian Designs for Artists and Craftspeople* by Eva Wilson.

Dover republishes many older books relating to Native American subjects, among them *The Handbook of American Indian Games* by Allan and Paulette Macfarlan.

Dover Publications, Inc.
31 East 2nd Street
Mineola, NY 11501

WOODLANDS BOOKS

Tribes of the Southern Woodlands is part of the Time-Life series "The American Indians," which also includes the title *Realm of the Iroquois*.

For information about these titles and other in the series, contact:

Reader Information
Time-Life Customer Service
P.O. Box C-32068
Richmond, VA 23261-2068

Remember Native America by Richard Balthazar is a picture album of ancient earthworks located in the eastern states. It was published by Five Flower Press of Santa Fe, NM.

The Great Tree and the Longhouse—The Culture of the Iroquois by Hazel Hertzberg (published by Macmillan of New York) is part of a series of anthropological books for classroom use.

Teachings from the Longhouse by Chief Jacob Thomas outlines the Code of Handsome Lake—the precepts of a Native American religion that had its origin in the 18th century and is still practiced today among the Iroquois.

Stoddard Publishing Co., Ltd.
34 Lesmill Road
Toronto, Canada M3B 2T6

We Have Not Vanished—Eastern Indians of the United States, written by Alfred Tamarin, offers a view of everyday life among Eastern Indians in 1974. It is published by Follett Publishing Co., Chicago.

Paths of the People—The Ojibwe in the Chippewa Valley is an award-winning book that traces the history of American Indian people living in the Chippewa River Valley (Wisconsin) to present times. It is published by the Chippewa Valley Museum of Eau Claire, WI, and is distributed outside Wisconsin by:

University of Washington Press
P.O. Box 50096
Seattle, WA 98145-5096

Art of the Great Lakes Indians, published in 1972, catalogs the exhibition of that name put on at the Flint (Michigan) Institute of Arts. It documents the decorative arts of the region and gives historical background for the pieces illustrated.

Indians in North Carolina is a pamphlet published by the North Carolina Department of Cultural Resources. It summarizes what is known about the various native peoples who have lived in that state during the last 10,000 years.

Finger Weaving: Indian Braiding is an instructional booklet written by Alta Turner and published by Cherokee Publications, an enterprise of the Cherokee Indian Reservation. For a free catalog of teaching and reference materials, contact:

Cherokee Publications
P.O. Box 430
Cherokee, NC 28719
1-704-488-8856

Sun Circles and Human Hands; The Southeastern Indians—Art and Industry, edited by E.L. Fundaburk and M. Douglass Foreman, illustrates and analyzes hundreds of artifacts found in southeastern United States.

Southeastern Publications
P.O. Box 750
Fairhope, AL 36533

(This book may be out of print, but it's worth requesting through your local inter-library loan program.)

CULTURE AND BIAS

In *Partial Recall,* Native American writers and artists reflect on photographs of American Indians, both old and recent. In many cases, they point out how the medium was used to "mythify" the American Indian for the convenience of the white man. (This is provocative material, and is suitable for mature students only.) It is edited by Lucy Lippard and published by The New Press, New York.

Through Indian Eyes—The Native Experience in Books for Children, edited by Beverly Slapin and Doris Seale, contains reviews of children's literature with American Indian subject matter.

New Society Press
4527 Springfield Avenue
Philadelphia, PA 19143

This book was originally published by Oyate, a nonprofit Native American organization dealing with issues of cultural and historical bias. For a list of Oyate's materials, write to:

Oyate
2702 Mathews Street
Berkeley, CA 94702

VIDEO

The Cahokia Mounds—Ancient Metropolis is a co-production of Camera One and Cahokia Mounds Museum Society. You can write (requesting current price) to:

Cahokia Mounds Museum Society
P.O. Box 382
Collinsville, IL 62234

CYBERSPACE

Many Eastern tribes maintain their own sites on the World Wide Web. Furthermore, there is a vast amount of other American Indian Studies material on the Internet; the problem is working one's way through the maze of links to get to the information you want. Here are some starting points.

The Institute of Learning Technologies (Columbia University) has a well-organized digital education program for grades K-12. One entryway to its massive Native American Study Project is at:

Native American Navigator
http://www.ilt.columbia.edu/k12/naha/nanav.html

Another useful site with classroom-oriented materials and links to tribes is:

Maps of Native American Nations, History, Info
http://indy4.fdl.cc.mn.us/~isk/maps/mapmenu.html

Lee Sulzman is writing compact but thorough histories of 240 American Indian tribes. All northeastern tribal histories are now complete and posted at:

Compact Histories of the First Nations
http://www.dickshovel.com/Compacts.html

Subjects of interest to Native Americans and educational materials compiled for their own education programs can be found at the following two sites (among others):

Native American Home Pages
http://earth.library.pitt.edu/~lmitten/indians.html

Native Web Home Page
http://www.maxwell.syr.edu/nativeweb/

As is often the case on the Internet, many of these sites cross-link with one another, so you can sometimes find yourself going around in circles. Also, although the addresses listed above are current as of this writing, they are, obviously, subject to change without notice.

NOTES